Contemporary perspectives on early childhood education

Contemporary perspectives on early childhood education

Edited by Nicola Yelland

 Open University Press

Open University Press
McGraw-Hill Education
McGraw-Hill House
Shoppenhangers Road
Maidenhead
Berkshire
England
SL6 2QL

email: enquiries@openup.co.uk
world wide web: www.openup.co.uk

and Two Penn Plaza, New York, NY 10121-2289, USA

First published 2010

A catalogue record of this book is available from the British Library

ISBN-13 978–0–33–523787–6 (pb)   978–0–33–523786–9 (hb)
ISBN-10 0335237878 (pb)   033523786X (hb)

Library of Congress Cataloging-in-Publication Data
CIP data applied for

Typeset by RefineCatch Limited, Bungay, Suffolk
Printed in the UK by Bell and Bain Ltd, Glasgow

Fictitious names of companies, products, people, characters and/or data that may be used herein (in case studies or in examples) are not intended to represent any real individual, company, product or event.

The **McGraw·Hill** Companies

Mixed Sources
Product group from well-managed
forests and other controlled sources
www.fsc.org Cert no. TT-COC-002769
© 1996 Forest Stewardship Council
FSC

For Sophia May (9 May 2009). The first of a new generation.

Imagination is more important than knowledge . . .

Albert Einstein (1879–1955)

Contents

Figures

Contributors

Marina Umaschi Bers is an Associate Professor at the Eliot-Pearson Department of Child Development and an adjunct professor in the Computer Science Department at Tufts University, Massachusetts, USA. She is also a scientific research associate at Boston Children's Hospital. Her research involves the design and study of innovative learning technologies to promote children's positive development. At Tufts she directs the Developmental Technologies interdisciplinary research group. Professor Bers received the 2005 Presidential Early Career Award for Scientists and Engineers, the highest honour given by the US government to outstanding investigators at the early stages of their careers. She also received a National Science Foundation's Young Investigator's Career Award, a five-year grant to support her work on virtual communities of learning and care. In 2005, she was awarded the American Educational Research Association's Jan Hawkins Award, which is given for Early Career Contributions to Humanistic Research and Scholarship in Learning Technologies. Her book *Blocks to Robots: Learning with Technology in the Early Childhood Classroom* was published by Teachers College Press in 2008.

Erica Burman is Professor of Psychology and Women's Studies at Manchester Metropolitan University, UK, where she co-directs the Discourse Unit and Manchester Feminist Theory Network. Her most recent books are *Deconstructing Developmental Psychology* (Routledge, 2nd edition, 2008) and *Developments: Child, Image, Nation* (Routledge, 2008). Her current projects address consequences of connections between national and international asylum, immigration and domestic violence policies, and the child–woman relationship. She is also a group analyst.

Judith Duncan is an Associate Professor in Education at the University of Canterbury College of Education, Christchurch, New Zealand. Judith came to the College from the Children's Issues Centre, at Otago University. Her research and teaching interests include early childhood education, children's voices, gender and education, and education policy and practice. Since her doctoral studies, which examined teachers' perspectives of education reforms in the kindergarten sector, she has been involved in a range of projects that examine early childhood from multiple and interdisciplinary perspectives, placing central to each research project the perspectives of children and their families. Judith has been involved in a range of collaborative research projects with other national and international researchers and education practitioners, and most recently with health professionals in the early years. She is a member of a range of national and international advisory and editorial boards.

Anne Haas Dyson is a former teacher of young children and, currently, a Professor of Education at the University of Illinois at Urbana-Champaign, USA. Previously she was on the faculty of the University of Georgia, Michigan State University, and the University of California, Berkeley, where she was a recipient of the campus Distinguished Teaching Award. She studies the childhood cultures and literacy learning of young schoolchildren. Among her publications are *Social Worlds of Children Learning to Write in an Urban Primary School* (1993), which received the David Russell Award for Distinguished Research from the National Council of Teachers of English, *Writing Superheroes: Contemporary Childhood, Popular Culture, and Classroom Literacy* (1997) and *The Brothers and Sisters Learn to Write: Popular Literacies in Childhood and School Cultures* (2003). She recently co-authored *Children, Language, and Literacy: Diverse Learners in Diverse Times* with Celia Genishi (2009).

Karen Gallas has been an early childhood and elementary teacher for more than thirty years in urban, suburban and rural public schools. She received her doctorate in Education in 1981, was a member of the Faculty of Education at the University of Maine, USA, and an adjunct faculty member in Education with Lesley University Graduate School and Wheelock College Graduate School in Boston. Karen's work as a teacher researcher is recognized nationally and internationally. She has written many articles and four books about the role of literacy learning across all disciplines, the arts as a vehicle for learning, the process of conducting teacher research, and regarding the role of imagination in literacy learning. Karen consults with public school systems, government agencies and research foundations in the areas of science, multiple literacies, imagination and literacy, early childhood education and teacher research. She also works with children as a psychotherapist in community mental health and school settings and collaborates with schools around issues of managing symptoms of post-traumatic stress disorder in the classroom.

Rachel Holmes works in the Educational and Social Research Institute at Manchester Metropolitan University, UK. She is a Senior Lecturer and researcher within the Centre for Cultural Studies of Children and Childhood. Her research interests are among the interstices of applied educational research, social science research and arts-based research within the field of childhood. She also has interests in notions of childhood territories such as ways that childhood becomes imag(in)ed through fictional, documentary and ethnographic film; children's child(self)hood, identities and objects; and ways to (left)field childhood via opening up off-centre research methodologies.

Liz Jones is Professor of Early Years and Childhood Education in the Education and Social Research Institute at Manchester Metropolitan University, UK. Her research interests span post-structuralism, feminism and postcolonialism. Much of her work is located within mainstream UK early years settings. A key concern centres on children's identities. Here the task is to reinvigorate existing canons of thought so as to break with systems that are increasingly incapable of grasping the complexities of young people and the cultures which they create.

Michele Leiminer is a Lecturer in the School of Education at the Southern Cross University in Australia. Her research interests are focused on making visible the interactional competences of marginalized children, and understanding the intersection of stage of life, gender and class positions in early childhood contexts. Leiminer uses feminist sociological perspectives in qualitative research and in crossing theoretical borders.

Hillevi Lenz Taguchi is an Associate Professor of Education in the Department of Education at Stockholm University, Sweden. Lenz Taguchi has mainly published books in Swedish on her experiences with reflexive, deconstructionist and collaborative work with preschool teachers and teachers using pedagogical documentation as a methodological tool for learning and change. Her books include *Why Pedagogical Documentation?* (1997) and *Pedagogy of Listening* (2004), both of which have been translated into Danish and Norwegian. She has also written on feminist post-structural theory and educational practices in *Down to Bare Bone: An Introduction to Poststructural Feminism* (2004). Forthcoming in English is *Going Beyond the Theory/Practice Binary in Early Childhood Education: Introducing an Intra-active Pedagogy* (2010). This book summarizes her collaborative research with preschool teachers, teachers and teacher educators in preschools, teacher education and in-service training programmes. Her current research project concerns preschool children's gendered constructions of subjectivity, as well as methods and strategies of academic and interdisciplinary writing.

Maggie MacLure is Professor of Education in the Education and Social Research Institute at Manchester Metropolitan University, UK. Her research interests include qualitative methodology, especially discourse analysis, deconstruction and post-structuralist approaches. She is the author of *Discourse in Educational and Social Research* (Open University Press, 2003). See http://www.ioe.mmu.ac.uk/research/res-ppl/m-maclure.shtml

Joanna McPake is Reader in the Faculty of Education at the University of Strathclyde, UK. Her research career has focused on issues of equity in education and on languages and literacies at all educational stages. From 2004 to 2007 she directed, with Lydia Plowman and Christine Stephen, the Economic and Social Research Council project 'Entering e-Society: Young Children's Development of e-Literacy'.

Christina MacRae has sixteen years' experience as an early years practitioner and more recently as a researcher into early years practice. Her PhD offered a critique of normative ways of interpreting children's representations in the early years classroom where it examined the practice of child observation and how it serves to frame what we see when we look at young children. Additionally, Christina has been involved in research into children's learning in museums and art galleries. Alongside her research interests Christina is an artist whose practice is interested in the connections that peoples make with the objects that they collect.

Veronica Pacini-Ketchabaw is Associate Professor and Coordinator of the Early Years Specialization in the School of Child and Youth Care at the University of Victoria, Canada, and the co-director of the Investigating Quality project and the British Columbia Early Learning Implementation Framework project. She has worked professionally in the field of early childhood education for over fifteen years and taught at different levels in a variety of educational settings in Argentina and Canada. She teaches and conducts research on issues related to post-structural, feminist and postcolonial theory-practice in early childhood education.

Alan Pence is UNESCO Chair for Early Childhood Education, Care and Development, and Professor, School of Child and Youth Care, University of Victoria, Canada. He has worked in the field of early childhood care and development (ECCD) since 1971, with a primary focus on cross-cultural and international early childhood care and development since the late 1980s. In 1989 he established the First Nations Partnerships Program (FNPP), a community-based indigenous early childhood undergraduate education programme, and in 2000 he commenced development of the Early Childhood Development Virtual University (ECDVU) a multifaceted leadership and capacity-building programme active in Africa and the Middle East. Dr Pence has authored over 110 journal articles, chapters and monographs and edited or authored 12 books on a variety of child care and development topics.

Helen Penn is Professor of Early Childhood in the Cass School of Education, University of East London, UK, and co-director of the International Centre for the Study of Mixed Economies of Childcare (ICMEC). She has undertaken policy work on early childhood education and care (ECEC) at national and international levels for transnational organizations such as the OECD and European Union. She publishes in a range of journals, including economic journals. She has also worked in the global south, in particular in Southern Africa, and has recently published two booklets about this work: *ECEC in Southern Africa: A Think-Piece* for the CfBT Educational Trust Perspectives series (2008), and, with Trisha Maynard, *Siyabonana – We all see each other: Early Education and Care in South Africa* in the Children in Scotland Building Better Childhoods series (2009).

Lydia Plowman is Professor and Director of Research in the Stirling Institute of Education, UK. She has particular interests in digital technologies and children's learning in a range of formal and informal settings and, with Joanna McPake and Christine Stephen, currently directs a project funded by the Economic and Social Research Council (ESRC) entitled 'Young Children Learning with Toys and Technology at Home'. She has previously directed an ESRC-funded project on play, learning and technology in preschool, and co-directed a project on young children, technology and digital literacies, also funded by ESRC. Before moving to Stirling, Lydia Plowman was Research Programme Manager at the Scottish Council for Research in Education, and Senior Research Fellow in the School of Cognitive and Computing Sciences at the University of Sussex. She was also a teacher in Norfolk secondary schools for nine years.

Valerie Polakow is a Professor of Educational Psychology and Early Childhood Studies at Eastern Michigan University, Ypsilanti, Michigan, USA. She has been active in local, state and national advocacy organizations that support welfare rights, post-secondary educational access, and child care for low-income women. She has written extensively about women and children in poverty, homelessness, welfare and child care policies in national and international contexts. She was a Fulbright scholar in Denmark and in 2002 was awarded the distinguished scholar award at Eastern Michigan University. She is the author/editor of seven books: *The Erosion of Childhood, Lives on the Edge: Single Mothers and their Children in the Other America* (1992; this won the Kappa Delta Pi book of the year award in 1994), *The Public Assault on America's Children: Poverty, Violence and Juvenile Injustice, Diminished Rights* (with T. Halskov and P.S. Jørgensen, 2001), *International Perspectives on Homelessness* (with C. Guillean, 2001), *Shut Out: Low-Income Mothers and Higher Education in Post-welfare America* (with S. Butler, L. Deprez and P. Kahn, 2004). Her latest book, *Who Cares for Our Children: The Child Care Crisis in the Other America* (2007), focuses on poverty, human rights and the crisis of child care in the United States.

Christine Stephen is a Research Fellow in the Stirling Institute of Education, UK. Her research focuses on early years provision, young children's learning and articulating the perspectives of children, parents and practitioners. She has co-directed a series of Economic and Social Research Council funded studies of young children learning with technology at home and in preschool with Lydia Plowman and Joanna McPake. She is currently researching the pedagogical approaches that children experience in preschool and early primary school.

Nicola Yelland is a Professor at the Hong Kong Institute of Education. Over the past decade her research has been related to the use of information and communications technology (ICT) in school and community contexts. This has involved projects that have investigated the innovative learning of children as well as a broader consideration of the ways in which new technologies can impact on the pedagogies that teachers use and the curriculum in schools. Her multidisciplinary research focus has enabled her to work with early childhood, primary and middle school teachers to enhance the ways in which ICT can be incorporated into learning contexts to make them more interesting and motivating for students, so that educational outcomes are improved. Her latest publications are *Rethinking Learning in Early Childhood Education* (Open University Press, 2008) and *Rethinking Education with ICT: New Directions for Effective Practices* (Sense Publishers, 2008). She is the author of *Shift to the Future: Rethinking Learning with New Technologies in Education* (Routledge, 2007). She is also the author of *Early Mathematical Explorations* with Carmel Diezmann and Deborah Butler (Pearson Publishing Solutions, 1999) and has edited four books: *Gender in Early Childhood* (Routledge, 1998), *Innovations in Practice* (NAEYC, 2000), *Ghosts in the Machine: Women's voices in Research with Technology* (Peter Lang, 2002) and *Critical Issues in Early Childhood* (Open University Press, 2005). Nicola has worked in Australia, the United States, the UK and Hong Kong.

Gail Yuen is an Assistant Professor in the Department of Early Childhood Education at the Hong Kong Institute of Education. Her research interests include early childhood policy, advocacy and teacher development.

PART 1
Contemporary perspectives on global and policy issues

1 Extending possibilities and practices in early childhood education

Nicola Yelland

Mediocrity thrives on standardisation

– Bumper stickers 13 (2006)

Introduction

As we approach the new decade of this second millennium it is increasingly apparent that we continue to live in a complex world and it is essential that we take the opportunity to critically reflect on the salient aspects of teaching and learning inherent to our profession, as well as to consider the additional elements that make up the lives of the children who attend our early childhood centres and classrooms. These are not simple tasks to complete in an atmosphere where accountability and outcomes dominate educational conversations and time is not to be wasted on idle matters that cannot be measured, at least in the short term; yet the issues may have considerable long-term impacts in terms of the health and well-being of citizens worldwide.

In the past two years we have had significant changes in governments that ultimately control education systems and policy making in the United States, Europe and Australia, and in the election process education was frequently touted as being the essential element that makes a difference to societies. In Australia, there was one side of the political spectrum calling for an 'education revolution' while on the other there was a conservative coalition with the slogan of 'Australia rising', saying that Australia would not be able to assume a role on the world stage without a 'world-class' education system. In presenting their cases both sides highlighted the importance of the early years in providing the foundation for later (successful) educational experiences and talked about the necessity of ensuring that standards should be rigorous and that teachers should be accountable for the outcomes of education in schools, which were always observable and measurable. However, discussions about what characterized the 'educational revolution' mainly occurred in the conservative media where those who argued for a 'back to the basics' approach, focused on the teaching of phonics and spelling lists, the necessity to know the names of the prime ministers of Australia and supported the memorization of multiplication tables and basic facts, exerted the most influence on policy and practice. Those with alternative views were labelled 'left-wing idealogues' who indulged in promoting 'educational fads' which were transitory, and since the election of the Labour government, they have been generally excluded from government decision-making processes. The call for a National Curriculum in Australia is one manifestation of the desire for standardization, based on the flimsy excuse that it will support those in transition from state to state, who in fact represent only a minute part of the total school population. It is increasingly evident that what characterizes our students across the world is their *diversity*, and in this way the call for standardization is even more problematic since it suggests a 'one size fits all' approach in which children are viewed as all needing the same type and form of education.

The desire for standardized curricula is not of course just an Australian phenomenon. In the United States it has been a fact of life for nearly twenty years. It is part of a growing movement to regulate, and goes hand in hand with policy statements that purport to have children's best interests in mind. Such policies are written in language that is crafted with political skill. They dare you to disagree with them, and if you do, accuse you of not wanting the *best* for *all* children. Take 'No Child Left Behind' (US Department of Education, 2001) as an example. In the spirit of 'You are either with us or against us!', if you oppose it, are you *wanting* children to be left behind?

In the UK the language of the early years documents have a similar flavour. For example: The statutory framework for the early years foundation stage (EYFS) has on its cover the words, 'Setting the standards for learning, development and care for children from birth to five'. This is accompanied by photographs of six children, representing boys and girls with a variety of different hair and skin colour. Under them are the words, 'Every child matters' and 'Change for children'.

Implicit in this is the assumption that this particular framework is aimed at making the lives of *all* children change with new regulated statutory goals to improve what currently exists for all young children in the UK. The words are of course repeated as you open the document so as to ensure that you know they mean what they say.

The opening words behind the purposes and aims of the EYFS are: 'Every child deserves the best possible start in life and support to fufil their potential', and continues with:

> The overarching aim of the EYFS is to help young children achieve the five Every Child Matters outcomes of staying safe, being healthy,

enjoying and achieving, making a positive contribution, and achieving economic well being by [another five points here!]:

- setting the standards for the learning, development and care
  young children should experience . . . ensuring every child
  matters and that *no child gets left behind*;
- providing for equality of opportunity and anti-discriminatory
  practice and ensuring that every child is included and not
  disadvantaged because of ethnicity, culture or religion, home
  language, family background, learning difficulties or disabilities, gender or ability;
- creating the framework for partnership working between
  parents and professionals, and between all the settings the
  child attends;
- improving quality and consistency . . .;
- laying a secure foundation for future learning through learning and development that is planned around the needs and
  interests of the child and informed by the use of ongoing
  observational assessment.

(DCSF, 2008: para. 1.2, emphasis added)

The document assumes that those involved in the care and education of
young children have shared understandings about the meanings of all these
terms and phrases, and that they are readily attainable in a principled
approach that guides the work of *all* practitioners in four distinct but complementary themes:

- A unique child
- Positive relationships
- Enabling environments
- Learning and development

And further there are EYFS principles into practice cards to explain how practitioners can use these in their day-to-day work. They aim to 'set standards to
enable early years providers to reflect the rich and personalised experience
[note the singular] that many parents give their children at home' (para. 1.13).

The bullet points of individual behavioural items that make up the rest of
the document entice teachers to consider them all and tick them off as they
occur as part of an ongoing assessment arrangement. It is required that this
should be formalized in the final year (prior to the final term of the school
year and no later than 30 June) of the EYFS by a practitioner who must use the
thirteen scales and have regard to the scale points as set out in their appendix.

This document *also* describes in bullet points and short paragraphs, what many of the key terms refer to. For example at a basic level, high quality early years provision can be defined as provision which:

- improves all children's outcomes (which can be measured by children's progression and achievement in the EYFS profile);
- provides increased support for children at risk of exclusion or poor outcomes;
- builds the foundations of future attainment in key stage 1.

So what you have is policy by bullet points and short-paragraph definitions which have been generated by government department personnel in explicit ways – so that within a specific time frame, usually three to five years, they can show that they have added value to the lives of young children in very definite, specific and narrow ways. Teachers and carers are expected to assume and absorb the general definitions and observable behaviours as representative with little or no discussion about what constitutes 'quality', the most effective, or best (for example) taking place.

The messages seem to be the same globally, from both conservative and more liberal governments. They are in government for three to five years and want to show their impact in overt ways that can be measured both nationally and internationally. They need and want to keep education quantifiable and accountable. This avoids complex discussions and consideration of the long-term goals for an education system that exists in new times that are radically different from those many politicians have experienced.

In reviewing what is, this quest for standardization, regulation and reporting, is there a space for critical and essential discussions about our work and also for considering opportunities about how to reshape it based on our professional experiences? Is there time to link this with the research literature, our experiences in both formal and informal contexts as well as for listening to parents and communities about what they want and need?

After all, if we can learn from commercial experiences of standardization what we find out is that even though they have branded a product and boast that it will be the same no matter where in the world you find it, we also know that local communities and contexts appropriate ideas, products and concepts and tweak them to fit their local circumstances. In fact, the *greatest* branding of fast-food (McDonald's) was founded on the notion of standardization. No matter where you went – firstly across America then across the UK and the rest of the world – the goal was that your Big Mac would taste the same and your fries would be just perfect. The logo became the most recognizable in the world. It remains the last thing you see as you move from the first world (United States) over the border to Mexico. However, as the symbol became more ubiquitous, things began to change. An early scene in the film *Pulp Fiction* (dir. Tarantino, 1994) advises us that in Paris the Quarter Pounder is called a

'Royale'. We know from our travels that in China you can get chicken wings in McDonald's. In Greece you have the choice of a bun or a wrap (souvlaki) that links to the country's traditional food. In Thailand you can buy a sticky rice roast pork burger, in Japan a Samurai pork burger, a Kosher burger is available in Israel, and in South American countries they have a McHuevo (burger and fried egg). The Finns have even customized their McDonald's street advertisements to make them more stylish, as befits a people known for their design flair. They have appropriated McDonald's and made it fit their lifestyle, which calls for more curves and softer lines to seats that were designed with hard lines to move customers through quickly. The Finns like to linger over their food! Is it possible that even within standardized systems there is scope to move. Can we achieve the same outcome in the educational arena?

This move to standardize education and practices is just one of the issues that has become pervasive over the past few years and is already entrenched as practice and policy in so many locations. Yet there are many others, as well as some that warrant critical reflection, that don't seem to make it onto government agendas.

Overview of the book

This book is concerned with contemporary (critical) issues in the field of early childhood studies which are wide-ranging and significant. So many more issues could have been included, which serves to illustrate how we need to be aware and critical of the myriad of aspects that make up education and the schooling processes that we have devised for children. Here, we have grouped the issues and present them in two parts that constitute the book:

Part 1 Contemporary perspectives on global and policy issues. The first part of the book is concerned with the broader big picture of early childhood in terms of the ways in which we conceptualize and rethink our views of children and childhood, the nature of 'provision' for young children in homes, centres and schools, find out about how systems work in the global context and reflect on that elusive component – quality.

Part 2 Critical views in practice. Here we move to specific perspectives and examples of practice that are related to the lives of young children and curriculum contexts. These are pedagogues who are thinking differently about the ways that they work with young children and their families, both in school and out, and are challenging the traditional views and reactions to everyday activities and ideas of what is regarded as normal. In these illuminating scenarios the authors share with us rich narratives about various aspects of teaching and learning with young children in a variety of contexts and environments. All too often schooling is reduced to the minutiae, and outcomes in literacy and numeracy assume primacy over all else. Perhaps they are the building blocks for later successes, but one thing we do know is that literacy and numeracy are more than a set of definable skills; they are a way of life, and create discourses for interacting with others that require more than simple skill acquisition and application. They need to be *lived* as an integral part of our lives in school and out.

In Chapter 2 Hillevi Lenz Taguchi asks us to move away from a one-dimensional view of early education where standardization, attaining benchmarks of performance, goal-oriented structures and a 'one size fits all' curriculum reign supreme. Lenz Taguchi calls for a non-hierarchical, multidimensional system that incorporates inventive and creative pedagogies. She points out the paradoxes that go unchallenged in our education systems whereby we strive for simple solutions that are rarely possible in a complex world. Her chapter highlights the increasing diversity that we are experiencing in our classrooms in new times; diversity which is not being catered for with enforced strategies designed to reduce complexity and attain superficial and short-term solutions. Lenz Taguchi poses an interesting question at the beginning of her chapter: Why is it that although we delve deeper into understanding human cognition, thinking that we can produce a scientifically grounded neutral and truly individualized pedagogy that works irrespective of gender, race, ethnicity, class and disabilities, that we end up with curricula and practices that normalize and produce exclusions and deviances in similar ways to the former collective forms of socialization practices? Her work follows the lead of Biesta who suggested that we need to *transform* contexts rather than keep adding to them. Lenz Taguchi postulates a rhizomatic approach characterized by an ontology of immanence which enables us to shift our focus to the *intra*-active processes that emerge between discourse/language and organisms in learning environments. She illustrates how this might work in a learning story located in a preschool setting where a new approach to dealing with pervasive issues has a very different outcome from that which results when traditional approaches are taken.

Erica Burman (Chapter 3) interrogates the notion of children being *between* diverse 'instabilities'. These are between human and child development, between children and (inter)national development, between national and international developments, between past and present, and between 'debt' and 'death'. Her consideration of the economic circumstances and actions that impact on so many children globally is timely in an era when so much policy making is taking place across the world in the name of the child. Burman's work requires us to think carefully about the positioning of the child in these situations, from a variety of perspectives, as she explores the contested relations between the (symbolic) debts that have been generated around the world under the guise of providing for their education and well-being. Burman's questioning of the gap between the symbolic actions and the material outcomes on a global scale, uncovers ideas for overcoming the overwhelming global disparities that young children experience that go beyond simplistic solutions of provision and materials and the training of personnel in the image of western practices.

This idea is taken up by Helen Penn in Chapter 4, as she explores the ways in which human capital arguments are being misused in the global south, and in Southern Africa in particular. She examines the rhetoric of aid for education in these countries which is justified on the basis of improving economic outcomes in the long term. She criticizes the approaches taken for their unwillingness to carefully analyse local conditions and for taking inequality as unproblematic as well as for ignoring the adverse impact of their macroeconomic policies on children and their families. Penn recognizes that western views of early education form the basis of the corpus that informs practice, but criticizes those who then think it offers universal solutions to a multitude of contexts. Her examples of the misapplication of policies and practices from the northern hemisphere to Southern Africa serve to illustrate the ways in which narrow and simplistic views are transposed to complex contexts to create scenarios that are highly problematic.

A concern for children in poverty is the subject of Valerie Polakow's chapter. She discusses global poverty and its impact on women and children and presents a critique of the dominant discourses in early childhood that ignore the fact that so many exist in extremes of poverty. Polakow problematizes interventions characterized by policy discourses that are largely instrumentalist. She uses the United States as an example to discuss the salient issues in this discussion.

In Chapter 6 Gail Yuen describes how early childhood education has been displaced to the margins in the colonial and postcolonial eras in Hong Kong. Her careful analysis of what has occurred highlights how a recent initiative, a voucher system, for parents whose children attend kindergarten (ages 3 to 6 years) has disadvantaged access for low-income families as not only have these families had their financial subsidies reduced but also the kindergartens that their children attend have had to reconsider the nature and timing of the care that they offer so as not to suffer adverse financial effects.

The final two chapters in this first part of the book explore the contested conceptualizations of the child and quality in early childhood education. Judith Duncan begins with a discussion of the images of childhood in society and then she uses New Zealand as the context to examine the link between early childhood policy and the discursive constructions of childhood. Alan Pence and Veronica Pacini-Ketchabaw share the findings from a large-scale study that took place in Canada in which they worked with early childhood stakeholders to interrogate the sector. The 'Investigating Quality in Early Childhood Education' project was seen as an opportunity to engage with new critical ideas on a large scale with practical benefits for changing practice in Canadian early childhood contexts. The linking of theory and practice enabled the participants to reflect on a variety of contemporary issues in depth and make changes to their own educational contexts. However, what they did not want was the replacement of one set of universal practices with another. Their story of the navigation is revealed in their chapter.

Part 2 begins with Karen Gallas's reflections on teaching in a Navajo community located in New Mexico. With over thirty years of teaching experience, Karen beautifully describes the evolution of her new teaching practices as she lives diversity in this 'challenging setting'. She shares with us her journey of love with the children and how their hearts and minds met in this well appointed but remote classroom. Her narrative enables us to view literacy as a continuous apprenticeship grounded in authentic activities and a respectful relationship between adults and children.

Anne Haas Dyson's chapter continues with literacy, as she describes the rich contexts in which young children articulate stories and write texts. Her rich learning scenarios of children engaging with language show us that despite being under pressure from state regulations that detail behaviours in literacy to the minutiae, the children in Mrs Kay's and Mrs Bee's classrooms deviate from 'normal' practices and create contexts for communication and creativity that go beyond 'the basics'. They are learning about discourses and linguistic practices that give them a sense of 'meditational agency' – a consciousness of the ways in which symbolic media assist them to engage with others in effective and dynamic ways.

In Chapter 11 Liz Jones, Rachel Holmes, Christina MacRae and Maggie MacLure explore the fascinating topic of children who are deemed to have behaved inappropriately in school. The authors present various scenarios where inappropriate behaviour – these are actions that are considered not to be 'normal' – has occurred and interrogate how they are dealt with. The problematizing of these situations encourages us to think about how we react to various situations and how alternative explanations and strategies might be deployed to reinterpret and act upon them.

Behaviour that is different from 'normal' is also the subject of Chapter 12. Michele Leiminer considers how one particular teacher reacts in a conversation with a girl and her mother. It reveals how the girl has been positioned by the teacher as deviant in that she does not usually behave in the way that girls do, and illustrates how this girl and her mother competently navigate their way through the discourse that forms the conversation.

The next two chapters are concerned with new technologies and the ways in which the attitudes of adults might impact on how young children can use them effectively. Joanna McPake and Lydia Plowman report on two studies that reveal that unequal access to digital technologies might not be solely due to economic disadvantage, but rather that parental attitudes are more influential. Marina Bers describes two examples of ways in which teachers and parents can work with young children on innovative science/engineering projects that incorporate ideas and concepts from the social sciences and arts. Her work with groups and robots highlights the creative processes inherent to the designs that they created and the shared adult–child learning opportunities that were rich in conversations and discovery. The project illustrates the ways in which, in collaborative contexts, children and adults can work together to support each other on high-level conceptual ideas with sophisticated equipment that enabled them to create objects and integrate ideas in new and dynamic ways.

The book ends with a comprehensive analysis by Christine Stephen of how we can link research, policy and practice in early childhood in order to ensure that not only do we have an empirical research base but also that what we are researching is relevant. Her summary of what has been achieved in the field reveals where we are at the current time and highlights the need for practitioner researchers to work with those in academe in order to build a substantial corpus of research that is both relevant and meaningful.

What now? Where next?

The chapters in this book require us to reflect on the nature of our work and interactions with young children and their families, what types of places we want our early childhood centres and classrooms to be, as well as to think about our role as teachers, pedagogues or knowledge workers in these contexts. They link to specific questions that were raised at an early childhood conference held at Manchester Metropolitan University[1] a few years ago:

- What kinds of lives do young children deserve/want in these times?
- What kind of professional/worker will work with these young children and their families?
- What is the purpose of our pedagogical work with young children and their teachers?
- How do we relate our work in early childhood education to the world beyond education and the lives of the young children?

The issues raised here do not have simple right or wrong answers. Many exist as paradoxes or as dilemmas that we respond to in the best way we can at that moment and may change the next time it occurs. This reflects the nature of our lives in the twenty-first century. So many issues are complex and need varying responses while others require problem solving that takes a brave person to initiate. But we need to engage with those issues and to realize the huge impact we have on children's lives and how they view the world.

It might seem as if we raise more questions than we have answered. In thinking about each of the chapters to come, the following immediately spring to mind:

- Are schools concerned only with the mechanics of education? Are they places in which curriculum is about 'knowing stuff' (usually old stuff) rather than creating new ideas?
- How do we reconcile and negotiate education systems that will support young children to realize their potential in multiple cultural contexts?
- Can education solve the problems associated with poverty, families and inequity, or should it respond to them in fluid ways?
- In what practical ways can educators support children's rights and embed the principles in our school systems?
- Is parental choice an integral part of our goals for the education of all children?
- How can popular images of children distort our desire to create equitable learning opportunities for young children?
- How can we address the complex issues of quality provision for young children?
- What pedagogical practices support teachers to become responsive to diverse learning contexts?
- How can we make spaces for extended literacy discourses that go beyond the basic utilitarian approaches of skills-based literacy programmes?
- When we are confronted by behaviour that disrupts our traditional discourses of adult–child or child–child interactions, how can we navigate through them?
- In what ways can we engage with young children so that they become confident in articulating and expressing their own ideas and views on issues through a variety of media?
- What strategies can be deployed to encourage parents to become flexible in their thinking about new learning experiences for their children that are different from those they lived in the previous generation?
- Can we extend learning opportunities for parents and teachers to become more confident and fluent with working with scientific knowledge in practical ways that impact on our lives?
- How can we identify research areas that are of relevance to educators' daily lives and encourage them to incorporate research as an integral part of their everyday practices?

Note

1. 'The 3 Rs: Reviewing, Renegotiating and Reframing Early Childhood', Manchester Metropolitan University. 20 June 2007.

References

DCSF (Department for Children, Schools and Families) (2008) *Statutory Framework for the Early Years*. http://nationalstrategies.standards.dcsf.gov.uk/node/ 151379 (accessed 12 July 2009).
US Department of Education (2001) *No Child Left Behind. Executive Summary*. http:// www.ed.gov/nclb/overview/intro/execsumm.html (accessed 12 July 2009).

2 Rethinking pedagogical practices in early childhood education: a multidimensional approach to learning and inclusion

Hillevi Lenz Taguchi

Introduction

Education today is characterized by a paradox of two competing movements: one of complexity and diversity increase and one of complexity and diversity reduction. On the one hand, increased complexity, multiplicity and diversity push for increased inclusion of children and families with diverse ethnic, racial, religious, cultural, social and economic backgrounds into early childhood provisions. On the other hand, these circumstances seem to enforce strategies of *complexity reduction* in the realization, accomplishment and evaluation of early childhood education (ECE). It appears to be against our better judgement, but the more we seem to know about the complexity of learning, children's diverse strategies and multiple theories of knowledge, the more we seek to impose learning strategies and curriculum goals that reduce the complexities and diversities of this learning and knowing. Policy makers and practitioners look for general structures and one-dimensional standards for practices. These are based on contemporary and updated developmentally appropriate practices (DAP) with the aim to enforce a socially just and equitable practice for all (Bredekamp and Copple, 1997; Gestwicki, 2006). The goal would seem to be to provide consistent and equal quality for everyone by treating and evaluating them with regard to the same universal, comparable and centralized standards (Dahlberg and Moss, 2005; Osberg and Biesta, 2008). In fact, the more complex things become the more we seem to desire processes of reduction and thus increase control, but such reduction strategies simultaneously make us risk shutting out the inclusion and social justice we say that we want to achieve.

In this context, I want to pose the central questions of: What are the basic theoretical assumptions that these dominant educational discourses rely on? And, are there alternative assumptions that can be used to inform pedagogical practices? Contemporary education is, as I will discuss, underpinned by ideas about predetermined universal learning-goals and values. In such an approach, the processes of learning and becoming a learning subject (a learner) are understood to be basically separated from each other. Learning is achieved by picking up and understanding concepts and their definitions in language. These concepts are understood to mirror or represent the world 'outside' of and separate from the learner. Osberg and Biesta (2009) have suggested that in complex and diverse societies it is problematic to rely on such a representational theory of knowledge and learning because doing so produces a linear and one-dimensional curriculum, which cannot be inclusive of diversity and complexity.

In this chapter I will argue that there is an alternative approach, which is inclusive of and *makes use* of diversities and complexities. In such an approach, learning and becoming are not seen as separated from each other, but understood as immanent to each other; that is, they are interdependent processes. Thus, to learn to know is a process that is intertwined with becoming a human subject and learner. Learning can take many different routes in this approach; it is *rhizomatic* (Deleuze and Guattari, 1987, 1994) and resembles a complex web of interconnections. The alternative approach presented in this chapter also involves our interrelations and *intra*-activities with material artefacts, things, teaching materials and furniture in the educational contexts, following the science theorist and physicist Karen Barad's *agential realism* (1998, 1999, 2007, 2008).

In what follows, I will start by outlining the dominant one-dimensional approach, before presenting the alternative multidimensional approach to learning and inclusion for ECE practices. A commonplace example with 2-year-olds playing with sticks in the preschool yard is then provided in order to discuss and explore the different ways in which the two different approaches produce different ways of understanding and producing learning and inclusion.

Education in the context of liberal humanism

Today's educational thinking has moved into the ideological realm of liberal humanism. It is concerned with an idea of the learner as a unique and self-actualizing agent. S/he is to make autonomous decisions, in order to release their inherent potential and become 'who s/he is', while performing being a responsible citizen (Rose, 1999; Burman, 2007; Osberg and Biesta, 2009). Rose (1999) writes that the notion of *freedom* becomes a formula of power which perhaps has more power over our everyday lives today than anything else. A liberal humanist education paradoxically combines attending to each individual child with treating and assessing everyone in relation to the same universal standards (Dahlberg and Moss, 2005). This becomes obvious in the child-centred pedagogies that have emerged. Developmental psychological and constructivist learning theories outline increasingly refined stages of cognitive development in a growing range of cognitive knowledge constructs and abilities that are seemingly neutral and applicable to everyone. By developing methodologies with which we can guide individual students to predetermined learning outcomes, we think we have moved away from the constraints of the general and collective, where every one was supposed to do and learn everything in the exact same manner. 'Lesson-studies' from Japan and China are copied and adapted into 'learning-studies' in Europe, even for children aged 1–5 years (Marton and Booth, 1997; Marton and Tsui, 2004; Pramling Samuelsson and Pramling, 2008). Yet perhaps we have missed the point? Maybe the dominant constructivist, cognitive and developmentally appropriate learning practices that we conceive as uniquely 'child-centred' and 'inclusive' are just as one-dimensional as the ones that they sought to replace? Education in the liberal humanism frame is built on underpinning assumptions that produce specific kinds of subjectivities in just as powerful ways as any previous education policy. The former socialization of the masses is replaced with what Osberg and Biesta (2008: 315) call a 'planned enculturation' aimed at each individual child.

It is relevant to pose the question here: Why is it that although we delve deeper into understanding human cognition, thinking that we can produce a scientifically grounded neutral and truly individualized pedagogy that works irrespective of gender, race, ethnicity, class and disabilities, that we end up with curricula and practices that normalize and produce exclusions and devi-ances in similar ways to the former collective forms of socialization practices? One of the major problems seems to be that scientifically based constructivist and cognitive learning theories deny the fact that neutral, value-free and culturally independent theories cannot exist. This denial correlates with for-mulating preset goals and taking universal values as well as normalized practices for granted. We need to consider if this is the case.

In line with Osberg and Biesta (2008, 2009), I think the present develop-ment is due to the fact that education is based on a logic that always begins with formulating preset goals and universal values for our educational prac-tices. *We start with the end* – what is to be achieved and assessed. Advocates for constructivist learning studies deem it necessary to define the 'capability' that is to be developed and to determine exactly '*what* it is that should be learned in each case' (Marton et al., 2004: 3, italics in original). Built into such thinking is a clear *direction* of the relationships in teaching and learning. Marton and Booth (1997) write in the preface of a book on learning studies for preschool children: 'This book contains a number of studies where adults (pedagogues, teachers) *help* children to learn something *pre-decided* that the adults consider good and important for children to learn' (Marton in Pramling Samuelsson and Pramling, 2008: 1, my translation and emphasis). This direction is vertical and hierarchical, with 'the one who already knows' in a position over and above 'the one who does not already know' and is to be educated. Correspondingly, learning, in constructivist learning studies is thought of as a process that progresses in a linear fashion from a stage of a lower degree of cognitive complexity and abstraction in the individual child's language construction, to an increasingly more advanced conceptual stage (Marton and Booth, 1997; Bredekamp et al., 2000; Marton and Tsui, 2004; Gestwicki, 2006, Pramling Samuelsson and Pramling, 2008). By observing and identifying an individual child's level of conceptual comprehension, it is implied that inclusion of children of diverse gender, cultural, social and ethnic backgrounds is practised in the process. However, these practices reduce educational curricula to 'one-size-fits-all curricula' (Osberg and Biesta, 2009). They assert that: 'Such an understanding implies that people can only be included into a set of norms defined in advance by those who are already "on the inside" and have decided what it is that is "normal" ' (2009: 2). In this way our thinking is reduced to a one-dimensional linear reductive thinking that *excludes and closes off* all other ways of thinking and doing (Osberg and Biesta, 2009).

A dominant representational theory of knowledge and learning

The theory of knowledge and learning that basically underpins contemporary educational and ECE practices is, as noted above, that of a *representational epistemology*, formulated by cognitive and constructivist learning theories. Knowledge is understood as cognitive constructs in language. These language constructs are believed to represent pre-existing things and phenomena in reality (Barad, 2007; Osberg and Biesta, 2007; Hekman, 2008). *Representational epistemology* builds on the belief that a learning subject's knowledge is constituted on a different (superior) level from the material experience it is based on. Knowledge becomes a rational and intellectual representation of 'inferior' material environments, objects and matter found in lived reality. Knowledge constructs are more or less fixed conceptual and meaning-bearing units that are presented by the teacher to the student for her/him to pick up and integrate with previous knowledge constructs.

Ontology is an understanding of 'what is' – of *being*. This includes how we understand what a learning subject is as a living being or organism. In an ontology of *transcendence*, which the *representational epistemology* relies upon, it is assumed that the learning subject is a *being* that is independent and separate from other subjects as well as from the material environment, matters and artefacts in the world around them. S/he acts upon their world in order to discover the 'laws of nature' and uncover its hidden truths. These universal laws stand above and transcend humans. This is why this ontology is called an *ontology of transcendence* (May, 2005). As an intentional and rational subject with a free will, the learner is responsible for her own learning and her/his ability to accept or comply with the help and support offered by the child-centred teacher. This is a teacher who is ultimately flexible in their own ability to be 'response-able' as well as 'response-ready' in relation to each individual child, the group and the surrounding world (Fendler, 2001). The material world is itself a passive and a fixed stage, upon which we perform our learning endeavours. When we understand learning in this way, we see ourselves as 'beings-*in*-the-world' (Barad, 2007: 160), who discover and learn about it, as we inhabit it as independent and free subjects and make use of it for our own benefit. Humans have, in line with this thinking, always sought a position of mastery over nature *in* the material world. There are distinct boarders and hierarchical and value-laden differences between subjects, objects, matter and artefacts that keep them separated, in line with these assumptions.

Problematizing the dominating assumptions of learning and becoming a learner

The truths, values and ideas of an *ontology of transcendence* are not only separated from us but are also considered to be true for everyone and thus universal as well as neutral (May, 2005). For example, ideas and values of 'pure justice', 'real democracy' and 'truthful knowledge' are essential to the way we understand our being *in* the world. Being the imperfect humans we are, we can, however, only *strive* for such ideas and values, since they are virtually impossible to fully achieve. Following from this, our *being* is, in a sense, always defined in terms of lack and negation (Smith, 2003). In line with this thinking, it is our personal failures and lack that prevent us from achieving these goals. We are, in a sense, doomed to fail in taking an absolute responsibility for the other, or fully satisfy the infinite call to justice and inclusion of this other, in line with these assumptions (Smith, 2003: 62). In educational practices these assumptions are materialized as pedagogical practices by formulating preset goals and learning outcomes to reach, and performing endless observations, tests and assessments of children's and students' development and learning progress in order to identify deviance from what is defined as the normal (Burman, 2007 and this volume). In relation to these dominating assumptions of learning and becoming a learner, Osberg and Biesta conclude that in any of today's dominant curricula '*everyone* is led to conform to *someone's* idea of the "good" society' (2009: 4, italics in original). The unavoidable question arises of *who* is to decide what, or *whose* culture, knowledge or understanding of an appropriate development should be promoted through education, in today's complex, global and multicultural world (Osberg and Biesta, 2008: 315).

Problematizing inclusion and introducing an alternative thinking

It seems as if these dominant assumptions render inclusion into the democratic community as something that is 'done *to* people rather than *by* them', writes Biesta (2007: 20). He contests an 'inside/center' position that seeks to extend democracy and justice by forcing those positioned on the 'outside/ margin' to escape their minority position, to be integrated into and be emancipated inside the centre of democracy (2007: 27). In Biesta's analysis, social inclusion can only be achieved when the opposition of 'inside/center' versus 'outside/margin' is overcome by a *mutual transformation of subjectivities*. Democratic inclusion is thus to be understood *not* in terms of adding more people to the existing order, but rather as a process that necessarily involves the *transformation of that order* (Biesta, 2007: 27–28).

A perspective of *mutual* transformation means a *negotiation* of the values and goals of the 'inside/center', which means a reformulation of the dominant values. It requires work in open, living and changing systems that can identify, include and *make use of difference, diversities and complexities* (Lenz Taguchi, 2007, 2009). Osberg and Biesta (2009) maintain that these systems thrive on the *recursivity* and feedback loops that emerge because of their complexities, and that the processes are centrifugal rather than linear. In the field of education, a centrifugal logic means not to submit to pre-formulated goals and values, but to begin *in the middle of things*. This means, beginning in the middle of the processes that take place *in-between* human learners, and *in-between* learners and material artefacts and things in the educational context – processes that simultaneously widen and deepen, rather than following linear preset paths. A centrifugal (or *rhizomatic* logic) is about constantly renegotiating and reinventing the goals of learning in the specific local context of learners and teachers. Such logic forces us to be in a state of affirmation and positivity in the creation and renegotiation of goals and values, relevant to the local context, rather than in a state of negation about unreachable universal goals and values (Smith, 2003). The learning processes that ensue – processes based on listening, curiosity, openness and of willingness to change – concern adults as much as children in participative and negotiating contexts (Åberg and Lenz Taguchi, 2005). Such thinking is based on assumptions about us being in a mutual state of *coexistence* and *interdependence*, both in relation to other human beings as well as in relation to the material world around us. A centrifugal and rhizomatic logic of learning to become a learner hence reminds us, in Barad's (2007) terms, of our role as 'beings-*of*-the-world', instead of isolated and separated 'beings-in-the-world'. We are in a state of coexistence and immanence with everything else. Barad writes:

> We are not outside observers of the world. Neither are we simply located at particular places *in* the world; rather we are *part of* the world in its ongoing intra-activity.
>
> (Barad, 2007: 184, emphasis added)

An alternative approach to learning and becoming – an ontology of immanence

As an alternative approach, I turn to this understanding of *being*, an inter-dependent part of the world – an *ontology of immanence*. Such an understanding offers us assumptions that make it possible for us to shift from a vertical, hierarchical and reductive one-dimensional, goal-oriented, 'one size fits all curriculum'; to a horizontal, 'flattened-out', non-hierarchical, multidimensional, inventive and creative pedagogy. The latter focuses on a collaborative process of meaning making that emerges *in-between* learners, and learners and matter in the learning context. Instead of focusing on the inner cognitive development and the *intra-personal* processes of learning as inner speech and meta-cognition in each separate individual, a pedagogy that relies on this alternative approach shifts our attention to the relational *intra-active* processes that emerge *in-between* discourse/language and organisms or matter in the environment of learning. Thus, in*tra*-activity is different from in*ter*-activity. Whereas the latter refers to *interpersonal* relationships (Hartley, 1999) between at least two persons such as the teacher and the student, in*tra*-activity relates to physicist terminology and to relationships between any organism and matter (human or non-human). The inclusion of the material in this approach to learning and becoming has made me call this pedagogical approach an *intra-active pedagogy* in my previous writings (Lenz Taguchi, 2010).

   Important to this thinking is Barad's theory that suggests that it is not only humans that have agency in processes of knowing. Rather, all material things have agency: they are also considered to be 'performative agents' in their intra-action with other material things, living organisms or with humans (Barad, 2007). This is a relationship in which all performative agents (including humans) will mutually change and alter in our ongoing intra-actions with each other. So, how can a chair or a pen be thought upon as an actor or an agent? Bruno Latour, one of the central theorists of what has been called the 'material turn' (Alaimo and Hekman, 2008) in the social sciences, writes: '*any thing* that does modify a state of affairs by making a difference is an actor' (Latour, 2005: 71). Things, such as a chair or a pen are more than just symbols for some ideas or cultural values; they 'perform actions, produce effects, and alter situations' (Bennett, 2004: 355). No actor can ever be said to act on its own. The agency or power is to be thought upon as generated relationally. Thus, we need to trouble the concept of the social, since there can be no such thing as a pure social relationship involving only humans (Hultman, 2009).

The critical issues here are that there are no inherent and clear borders between the learner and what is learned, being and knowing, and between matter and discourse (language). This makes knowing just as much a matter of the body and the material as it is a matter of understanding and thinking through language and discourse, which of course has vast consequences for teaching and learning (Barad, 1999, 2007; Alaimo and Hekman, 2008). There is no border between what the child *is* right now and what s/he continuously *becomes*. The child becomes, in a specific sense, what it learns, in a steadily ongoing flow of *material-discursive* events of intra-activities. Hence, what philosophers call ontology (theories of being) and epistemology (theories of knowledge and knowing) cannot be separated in the way they have been. Hence, Barad talks about an *onto-epistemology*, defining it as 'the study of practices of knowing *in* being' (2007: 185, emphasis added). She writes that it is impossible to isolate knowing from being since they are mutually implicated. Barad's onto-epistemology and agential realist theory constitutes what can be called a *posthumanist* understanding of the 'human' where the ontological and epistemological cannot be separated but merge (Barad, 2007, 2008). Individuals, just as non-humans and things, *emerge* through, and as an effect of, their entangled intra-actions with everything else. Therefore we do not even pre-exist our interactions with the world. We are nothing until we connect to something else (Latour, 2005; Hultman, 2009), even if it is simply the intra-activity with oxygen in our breathing. Every organism connects with at least one other organism or matter, in order to live, as a condition of its existence. This is why we cannot consider ourselves as a separate entity *in* the world, but rather as a consequence *of* the world in a state of mutual interdependence with everything else. We are in processes of *becoming-with*, as Haraway contends (2008: 4). This means that practices of knowing cannot, as Barad stated,

> fully be claimed as human practices, not simply because we use non-human elements in our practices but because knowing is a matter of *part of the world making itself intelligible to another part*.
>
> (Barad, 2007: 185, emphasis added)

All active performative agents are busy learning to know each other – making each other intelligible to one another – and thus transform and change each other (in one way or another) in the process (Barad, 2007). Learning events are taking place frequently and simultaneously between my hands manipulating material things as well as with my thinking body/mind, handling concepts, notions and emotions (Lenz Taguchi, 2010). In such an understanding we go beyond the taken-for-granted ways of thinking of the binary divides of *subject/object, theory/practice, intellect/body* and *discourse/matter*, in order to make *matter* matter in learning and knowing (Barad, 1999, 2007, 2008; Alaimo and Hekman, 2008; Hekman, 2008).

A multidimensional and rhizomatic curriculum of invention and creation

Learning processes that are inclusive of complexity, diversity and multiplicities cannot have a fixed origin, end point or linear trajectory, as Osberg and Biesta (2009: 6) state. Instead of being linear, the process can start at multiple points and moves rhizomatically (Albrecht-Crane and Slack, 2007). If we connect this to Barad's terminology – rooted in physics – we can say that the process of learning follows the flows of waves of diffractions (as in water or sound-waves in the air) that emerge when different organisms and material things intra-act with each other and with discursive meaning making. Waves of diffractions thus are caused by obstacles or interferences that alter and transform meaning in unpredictable ways as the result of the intra-actions at work. Such interferences, create new interconnections or interrelations and might cause what Deleuze and Guattari (1987) have called 'a line of flight'. A line of flight can be understood as the event of unthought possibilities that leap away from immobile fixed and structured (stratified) spaces regulated by taken-for-granted habits of mind and body. The line of flight is a state of *in-betweeness* that works like a positive force or energy and creates new spaces of thought. It also 'extrac[ts] an event from things and beings, to set up a new event' (Deleuze and Guattari, 1994: 33). In other words, rhizomatic learning processes allow for new interrelations to take place and are inclusive of new connections, intensities of affects and desires in the learning process. Learning deepens, widens and expands, and takes irregular paths, rather than follows a linear progression. This is because it always aspires to formulate new problems and be creative and inventive of new ways of thinking and doing things. The rhizomatic process takes us beyond the fixed, predefined, structured and taken-for-granted in its movements and experimentations (Olsson, 2009). Hence, the 'line of flight' constitutes what Colebrook refers to as 'a form of experience itself' (2002: 113). Deleuze and Guattari noted:

> To think is to experiment, but experimentation is always that which is in the process of coming about – *the new, remarkable, and interesting* that replace the appearance of truth and are more demanding than it is.
> (Deleuze and Guattari, 1994: 111, emphasis added)

I emphasize the last part of the quote because what we experience, as we move away from habits of thinking and doing on a 'line of flight', demands us to think and live – do our practices – in new ways. As teachers we should try to be attentive to and make use of the 'new, remarkable, and interesting that replaces the appearance of truth' (Deleuze and Guattari, 1994: 111) as we go on preparing for new learning events with children or students. In the multi-dimensional and rhizomatic flow of learning, there is no other direction than the opening up of closures, the unpicking of fixed destinations, the occasional leaps of thought, or taking off on a 'line of flight', from the ongoing move-ment of simultaneous deepening and widening of our meaning making in intra-activity with our bodies and the material world. Learning and knowing, in this approach, is firstly most about an affirmative openness to what *might* become, and the yet unthought *potentialities* of learning and in all of us, as learners (Colebrook, 2002; Smith, 2003; May, 2005).

Again, in this approach, inclusion is viewed as a process that transgresses the idea of the subject being included into the centre of universal values, ideas and normative destinations. Inclusion is instead about an undefined rhizo-matic process of interdependence, mutual transformation and an ongoing emergence of subjectiveity, where the *singular* is allowed to emerge. As Osberg and Biesta (2008) have stated, we must be inclusive of the singularity of each learner whose subjectivity emerges in the processes of learning:

> [I]t is no longer possible to understand 'educational responsibility' as being to bring about the successful transit of an object (a student) from point A to point B, or assisting students in reaching a pre-determined destination. With the logic of emergence it becomes possible to understand educational responsibility as continuously complicating the scene, thereby making it possible for those being educated to continue to emerge as *singular* beings. Educational res-ponsibility is about continuously re-opening subjectivity, unsettling closures, and unpicking 'destinations'.
> (Osberg and Biesta, 2008: 326, emphasis added)

Thus, inclusion becomes a process of affirmation of singular beings – in all of their diversities and complexities – in a state of interdependence and intra-activity in their ongoing processes of learning and becoming.

Reading an example from a one-dimensional and a multidimensional perspective on learning and inclusion

The example: Two- and three-year-olds playing with sticks

During her vocational training, an undergraduate student in early childhood education, Kristine Rende presented a sequence of documentation from a small project she had conducted with children aged between 1½ and 3 years. I use different ontological and epistemological assumptions to analyse this documentation in an attempt to illustrate the theoretical reflections just presented.

The students had been asked to document processes that they were observing among the children they were working with in preschool, for example a particular form of play. Kristine documented 2- and 3-year-old boys using wooden sticks as guns or pistols when playing outside in the afternoons. The boys used the sticks to shoot at each other, hunting each other around the yard. According to Kristine, the efforts by staff members to restrain the boys in their aggressive play were in vain. Either they ended in sheer frustration, or the staff reverted to authoritarian methods, ordering the boys inside for a lecture on the preschool's norms and values, which did not incorporate the use of guns and aggression. One day Kristine overheard one boy – here called Andy – saying: 'My gun is alive and it wants to kill you!' while pointing a stick at his 1½-year-old friend. She then queried the boy: 'If your gun is alive, it must have a name, right? What's the name of your gun?' When the boy seemed startled, she continued: 'Does it live with you? Or does it live here in the preschool yard?' After some time of contemplation, the boy answered: 'His name is Erik and he lives with his mum under that tree,' pointing to where he had found the stick. When the boy ran off, Kristine took a note of the conversation in her process diary.

The next morning, Kristine asked the boys if she could talk to them. They agreed and Kristine went with them to sit on the floor. She said that she had talked to Andy the previous day and then asked whether it was OK to share their conversation with the group, which he agreed to. All the boys instantly claimed that their sticks had names and homes too. Kristine asked them to each tell their story, one at a time. The boys' stories became increasingly elaborate and imaginative as they progressed. They ascribed their sticks certain characters, specific traits and invented whole social contexts of families and friends. Kristine finally suggested that they should 'get your sticks and paint and decorate them so we can identify each one'.

Without further pursuing the story in detail, it became apparent that Kristine was able to shift the boys' interest from using sticks as guns to turning them into friends. This was achieved by basically transforming them into a doll to play with and decorate, and by providing a social environment for playing with them. To use them for shooting had become entirely impossible in this context. The new approach to the random sticks found in the yard also made those children interested in them who had previously had no interest in using them as guns. Eventually, all children developed an interest in the 'history' of the sticks, which trees they had been a part of, how they were integrated into the natural environment, how they were dependent on rain, sun, soil, etc. What now emerged were further investigations of the sticks and of leaves from the trees. The children learned to know the life cycle of the tree and leaves by drawing, moulding sticks in clay while thinking, talking and imagining.

Reading the event from a dominant representational epistemology

Kristine's story began with the initial reactions from her colleagues at the preschool to boys creating guns from sticks. Relating this to the universal values of non-violence and peace they tried to get the boys to understand that pretending the sticks were guns and using them to shoot each other was wrong and was a game that should be stopped. The issue at stake was how adults, as the ones 'who know' what is right in accordance with universal values, are able to *get* or *help* children to take up these values as their own. This involves a consideration of how the adults enculturate children into the value system of a democratic society without themselves taking on an authoritarian role. When Kristine asked Andy about the name of his stick, she found a non-authoritarian way to divert the boy's interest from the stick as a weapon to 'humanize' it instead. She used her documentation to understand the level of the children's cognitive development to challenge them into thinking about the stick in a more abstract way, as a 'humanized' doll to play with and care for. By engaging Andy in an intimate conversation of interpersonal relationship he was able to understand the stick differently. She also managed to convince the rest of the group to think differently about the sticks in another conversation of interpersonal communication that took place the next morning. On the level of cognition, Kristine managed to shift the boys' thinking to go to what can be regarded as a more advanced level and to take up the values of non-violence, love and care. As the children later began to ask questions about sticks, life and death, trees and leaves, what would a teacher relying on an epistemology of representation have done next? The teacher would probably have formulated specific and desirable learning goals for the upcoming work. For example, understanding the life cycle in nature in relation to different seasons and weather. This way the children could develop specific concepts and learning contents on a more advanced cognitive level in relation to this area of knowledge (Marton and Booth, 1997; Marton and Tsui, 2004; Pramling Samuelsson and Pramling, 2008).

Reading from an alternative multidimensional approach

Informed by assumptions from an immanent ontology there is no true or privileged position from which to understand the event or what values are the right ones. We must start *in the middle of things* to understand what is going on. This way we can be inclusive of many different ways of unfolding what the boys were doing running around the yard with their sticks. Maybe we would understand that the boys were simply bored and not seriously challenged to play in any other way? Maybe they were busy positioning themselves in the group of boys playing like boys do? Maybe they were imitating other boys they had seen playing like this, or imitating something they had seen on TV? Or, might it be that these boys had just got the strong message in our culture about what a boy should be doing to perform masculinity in expected ways – being forceful and questioning authorities? Perhaps they enjoyed the turmoil that their play aroused among the other children, and all the attention they got from the teachers? Or maybe, even, they enjoyed experimenting with the stick as an extension of their arms and hands, which also made them understand the limits and possibilities of their own bodies? Or, could it be that they simply answered the sticks calling on them from the ground, and thereby engaged in a material-discursive intra-action where all the above mentioned possibilities intersected in complex ways? In this event, all of the above reasons are viable.

Kristine chose to disrupt the play with a question without having any specific ideas or agendas. Posing her question, a new wave of diffraction started which produced new waves of thinking and caused different things to happen. We can think of this in terms of the fact that Kristine simply took a *chance*, and in doing so caused a *turning point* in the passage of events – from one way of understanding the play to another. This turning point activated boys' fantasies, affects and bodies in intra-action with the question and the materials they used when decorating their sticks (Lenz Taguchi, 2010). The questions posed and enacted in the pedagogical space can, with inspiration from Deleuze and Guattari, be understood in terms of evoking an inventive 'line of flight' (Deleuze and Guattari, 1987). It is made possible as the boy made a leap of fantasy from how the play has, up to this moment, been structured according to specific rules negotiated among the boys during several days of outdoor play. The question produces a shift in the space of the event, from being a structured space with rules of gun-play, to an unpredictable space where new understandings of the stick emerges. Kristine actualizes this event in her documentation, so it becomes possible for her to *revisit* the event the next day (Lenz Taguchi, 2010).

What happened when the sticks were given names was not simply about a heightened cognitive awareness of meaning making or of transmitting proper values among the boys, as we might think when relying on a thinking in line with a representational epistemology. Rather, what happened was a much more complex process of intra-activities taking place that transgress the binary divides of *cognition/body*, *discourse/matter* and *knowledge/imagination*. Hence, the material and the body of the learner are just as important in these processes of learning and transformation – imagination and creation – as are the conceptual meaning making and cognitive thinking (Palmer, 2009). We need to displace our thinking from understanding the child only as an intentional subject who uses passive materials to transform the stick (Hultman, 2009). If we change our gaze to be inclusive of the performative agency of matters and artefacts, we can identify the important force and intensity which aroused in the *discursive-material* intra-active processes taking place *in-between* the materials, the children's meaning-making fantasies and their affects at work. It becomes possible to see how the shiny glittering papers evoke desires in the child to transform the stick in ways previously unimaginable. It becomes possible to listen to the rustle or swish of the wafer-thin see-through papers swirling around in the air from the top of the stick. The rustle intra-acts with affect and creative imagination, and the stick transforms again, becoming a horse galloping in a circus ring (Lenz Taguchi, 2010). In the way Barad thinks about *materialization* it is not just a matter of how discourse and meaning comes to matter, but how matter comes to matter in its own agency (Barad, 1998: 108).

Our perspective as theorists and teachers shifts from the interpersonal and hierarchical interactions between Kristine and the boys, to a much wider, expanded gaze, where we read the event just as much from the point of view of the swirl and rustle of the paper and its intra-action with the discursive understandings, as we read it from the words and affects that emerge in the play. There is no clear direction to follow and no end point of learning outcome to reach: there are just intersections and turning points and passages, where bodily affects matter just as much as words, and thinking just as much as dancing, running and gluing. So, when the children start to discuss life and death in relation to the sticks, the adults do *not* decide to *help* the children get to know the basics of the life cycle of nature, relating to the discussion of life and death. Instead they rely on being attentive to what emerges in the inter-activities taking place in each *singular* event, and making visible each *singular* child's strategies and different ways of understanding (Lenz Taguchi, 2010).

Hence, we will not follow predetermined paths of learning stages, preplanned experiments and building knowledge with pre-decided learning units and conceptual stages of development. There is no predetermined direction for learning – it is rhizomatic (Deleuze and Guattari, 1987). It can begin anywhere and go any place, although we are circulating, *as in a centrifugal movement, around a specific problem and theme of investigation*, which is simultaneously deepened and widened. Teachers thus rely on listening and picking up on what the children bring with them into the event, with all of their differences. They rely on trying to identify what it is that emerges from these differences, and to challenge the learning processes of the children in relation to the problem or theme of investigation negotiated with them, and look out for new problems that arise in the process. This might either slow down or speed up the movement in the learning event. When the movement is deliberatively slowed down, getting the children to reflect upon what happened before, this is about putting in motion a 'circular movement' of counteractualizations (Lenz Taguchi, 2010). This entails questioning what happened and identifying multiple ways of doing and thinking to understand what they did differently. However, presenting the children with an actualization of a previous event in the documentation of photographs or transcribed dialogue might bring about a speeding up of the movement, or cause a leap of thought into a new direction – a 'line of flight'. In this 'horizontal movement' previous structures of thinking are challenged and transgressed to make new imaginative creations possible (Lenz Taguchi, 2010).

The direction of learning is negotiated and continuously renegotiated with the participants of the process as it goes along. But it can also involve, as we saw above, chance and imagination, causing a turning point. By shifting our attention to be inclusive of affect, body, matter, environment, time, space and other material aspects of learning, what will emerge among the children as learners is *engagement, mutual acknowledgement and ratification of singular events of collaborative learning*. It is in this way that we can say that an intra-active pedagogy starts in the middle of things, rather than at the end of the learning outcome to be achieved. Osberg and Biesta (2009) challenge our taken-for-granted ways of thinking about the direction of learning in relation to judgement, or, rather, assessment and evaluation, which resonates with the notion that we can only start in the middle of things. They write:

> We should not try to judge [value or assess] what emerges before it has taken place or specify what should arrive before it arrives. We should let it arrive first, and then engage in judgement so as not to foreclose the possibilities of anything worthwhile to emerge that could not have been foreseen.
>
> (Osberg and Biesta, 2009: 21)

The consequences of this thinking is that the teacher needs to make herself aware of how the room, space, time and things are organized and structured, and consider what kinds of intra-action between different people and materials might be possible. S/he needs to be ready for the kinds of learning that emerge in the rhizomatic movement. In this kind of inter- and intra-active learning process we can challenge our own potentialities and what we thought of as our limits of knowing or the limits of what can be known. It is because *we don't know what might be possible for a child or student to learn, to know or become*, that this potential and transformation of the learner become the most important element for the teacher both to affirm and to create a pedagogical space for where it can be actualized (Lenz Taguchi, 2010).

Summarizing the shift from a dominant to an alternative approach

The aim of this chapter has been to outline the dominant approach as well as an alternative approach to education and ECE practices in our contemporary complex, diverse, global and fast changing societies. I argue that the dominant and alternative approaches rely on very different assumptions of what knowledge, learning and becoming a learner mean. Thereby very different practices of learning and becoming a learning subject are produced based on these assumptions. Moreover, inclusion of diversity and difference is understood in very different ways, depending on the underpinning assumptions that are adopted. I have used an actual example so that we can think around the shifts that an alternative approach to learning and inclusion can produce for educational practices. These shifts can be summarized as follows:

On how to understand learning:

- from end-point goals and values *to* learning 'in the middle of things' in collaborative processes of negotiation and renegotiation;
- from vertical and hierarchical relationship between human organisms and material reality *to* a horizontal and non-hierarchical 'flattened-out' relationship in which we cannot separate the learner from what is learned;
- a shift in direction from linear *to* rhizomatic learning processes;
- a shift from a notion of an independent responsible learning subject *to* interdependence, collaboration and a mutual responsibility in learning;
- from the individual learner and its cognitive development *to* collaborative processes of meaning making in material-discursive intra-actions;
- from the notion that there is only human agency *to* understanding both human and non-human organisms and matter as performative agents;
- from representations of the world in language *to* invention and creation of new concepts, ideas, problems of investigation and strategies of doing;
- from identifying lack and deviation *to* affirmation of difference, diversity and new inventions.

On how to understand inclusion:

- from regarding inclusion as incorporating the margin into the centre *to* inclusion as mutual transformation and an ongoing negotiation of values and goals;
- from 'one-size-fits-all' measures of inclusion *to* identification and affirmation of singular subjects and the singularity of learning events;
- from inclusion into best practice and liberal humanist subjects *to* inclusion of unthought potentialities of the learning subject and practices;

- from inclusion only of other human subjects *to* inclusion also of the material.

Shifting from a linear and one-dimensional approach to a multidimensional and rhizomatic approach to learning and inclusion in education requires us to rethink the nature of our being in the world. This might sound like an unthinkable or difficult thing to do, but when you think about what an ontology of immanence means, it isn't that strange. It is, as Barad writes, simply about acknowledging, understanding and making use of *entanglements*: because learning, *as existence*, is not and can never be an individual, isolated or independent affair (2007: ix). Hence, learning cannot be defined or pre-exist its emergence through interactions between meaning/language/discourse, bodies/minds, and matter/objects/materials involved in the spaces and processes of learning. We are beings in a state of interdependence and entanglement with the rest of the world for our learning and being, in this thinking.

If we accept this logic and believe that the child, when learning, engages in intra-actions and interconnectedness with the rest of the world, then it becomes impossible to adhere exclusively to pre-formulated stages of maturity or stages of understanding and learning-specific contents, that characterize constructivist theories of learning and developmentally appropriate practices (DAPs). In other words, our focus as teachers should *not* be with what we think is the right or correct thing to do in relation to such norms or truths, and being fixated with learning goals and outcomes. Instead, we should learn to look for the differences in and emergence of strategies and thinking in the investigation of a negotiated problem. We should learn to look for ways in which materials are productive of what children do and say, and how the intra-activities between the material conditions and the actions of the children alter their understandings and strategies. We should try to make ourselves aware of what happens now and what *might* be possible, what emerges, and what *can* become. This way of addressing the child and our pedagogical practice constitutes, in my understanding, a fundamental shift when we think of ethics and justice in education.

References

Åberg, A. and Lenz Taguchi, H. (2005) *Lyssnandets pedagogik. Demokrati och etik i förskolans lärande* [Pedagogy of listening. Democracy and ethics in preschool learning practice]. Stockholm: Liber.

Alaimo, S. and Hekman, S. (eds) (2008) *Material Feminisms*. Bloomington, IN: Indiana University Press.

Albrecht-Crane, C. and Slack, J.D. (2007) Toward a pedagogy of affect. In A. Hickey-

Moody and P. Malins (eds), *Deleuzian Encounters: Studies in Contemporary Social Issues*. New York: Palgrave Macmillan.

Barad, K. (1998) Getting real: technoscientific practices and the materialization of reality, *Differences: A Journal of Feminist Cultural Studies*, 10(2): 87–128.

Barad, K. (1999) Agential realism: feminist interventions in understanding scientific practices. In M. Biagioli (ed.), *Science Studies Reader*. New York: Routledge.

Barad, K. (2007) *Meeting the Universe Halfway: Quantum Physics and the Entanglement of Matter and Meaning*. Durham, NC: Duke University Press.

Barad, K. (2008) Posthumanist performativity: toward an understanding of how matter comes to matter. In S. Alaimo and S. Hekman (eds), *Material Feminisms* (pp. 120–154). Bloomington, IN: Indiana University Press.

Bennett, J. (2004) The force of things: steps toward an ecology of matter, *Political Theory*, 32(3): 347–372.

Biesta, G. (2007) 'Don't count me in': democracy, education and the question of inclusion, *Nordisk Pedagogik*, 27(1): 18–31.

Bredekamp, S. and Copple, C. (eds) (1997) *Developmentally Appropriate Practice in Early Childhood Programs*, NAEYC Series, no. 234, revised edition. Washington, DC: National Association for the Education of Young Children.

Bredekamp, S., Copple, C. and Neuman, S.B. (2000) *Learning to Read and Write: Developmentally Appropriate Practices for Young Children*, NAEYC Series no. 161. Washington, DC: National Association for the Education of Young Children.

Burman, E. (2007) *Deconstructing Developmental Psychology*. London: Routledge.

Colebrook, C. (2002) *Gilles Deleuze*. London: Routledge.

Dahlberg, G. and Moss, P. (2005) *Ethics and Politics in Early Childhood Education*. London: Routledge.

Deleuze, G. and Guattari, F. (1987) *A Thousand Plateaus: Capitalism and Schizophrenia*, trans. Brian Massumi. Minneapolis: University of Minnesota Press.

Deleuze, G. and Guattari, F. (1994) *What is Philosophy?*, trans. Graham Burchell and Hugh Tomlinson. London: Verso.

Fendler, L. (2001) Educating flexible souls. In K. Hultqvist and G. Dahlberg (eds), *Governing the Child in the New Millennium*. London: RoutledgeFalmer.

Gestwicki, C.L. (2006) *Developmentally Appropriate Practice: Curriculum and Development in Early Education*, 3rd revised edition. Florence, KY: Delmar Learning.

Haraway, D.J. (2008) *When Species Meet*. Minneapolis: University of Minnesota Press.

Hartley, P. (1999) *Interpersonal Communication*. London: Taylor & Francis.

Hekman, S. (2008) Construction the ballast: an ontology for feminism. In S. Alaimo and S. Hekman (eds), *Material Feminisms* (pp. 85–119). Bloomington, IN: Indiana University Press.

Hultman, K. (2009) Making matter *matter* as a constitutive force in children's gendered subjectivities, *Subjectivity* (submitted).

Latour, B. (2005) *Reassembling the Social: An Introduction to Actor-Network-Theory*. Oxford: Oxford University Press.

Lenz Taguchi, H. (2007) Deconstructing and transgressing the theory–practice dichotomy in Swedish early childhood education, *Educational Philosophy and Theory*, 39(3): 275–290.

Lenz Taguchi, H. (2008) An 'ethics of resistance' challenges taken-for-granted ideas in early childhood education, *International Journal of Educational Research*, 47(5): 270–282.

Lenz Taguchi, H. (2010) *Going Beyond the Theory/Practice Divide in Early Childhood: Introducing an Intra-active Pedagogy*. London: Routledge.

Marton, F. and Booth, S. (1997) *Learning and Awareness*. Mahwah, NJ: Lawrence Erlbaum Associates.

Marton, F. and Tsui, A.B.M. (eds) (2004) *Classroom Discourse and the Space of Learning*. Mahwah, NJ: Lawrence Erlbaum Associates.

Marton, F., Runesson, U. and Tsui, A.B.M. (2004) The space of learning. In F. Marton and A.B.M. Tsui (eds), *Classroom Discourse and the Space of Learning*. Mahwah, NJ: Lawrence Erlbaum Associates.

May, T. (2005) *Gilles Deleuze: An Introduction*. Cambridge: Cambridge University Press.

Olsson, L.M. (2009) *Movement and Experimentation in Young Children's Learning: Deleuze and a Virtual Child*. London: Routledge.

Osberg, D.C. and Biesta, G.J.J. (2007) Beyond presence: epistemological and peda- gogical implications of 'strong' emergence, *Interchange*, 38(1): 31–51.

Osberg, D.C. and Biesta, G.J.J. (2008) The emergent curriculum: navigating a com- plex course between unguided learning and planned enculturation, *Journal of Curriculum Studies*, 40(3): 313–328.

Osberg, D.C. and Biesta, G.J.J. (2009) The end/s of school: complexity and the conundrum of the inclusive educational curriculum, *International Journal of Inclusive Education* (forthcoming).

Palmer, A. (2009) 'Let's dance': theorising alternative mathematical practices in early childhood teacher education, *Contemporary Issues in Early Childhood Education* (submitted).

Pramling Samuelsson, I. and Pramling, N. (eds) (2008) *Didaktiska studier från förskola och skola* [Studies in didactics from preschools and schools]. Malmö: Gleerups.

Rose, N. (1999) *Powers of Freedom. Reframing Political Thoughts*. Cambridge: Cambridge University Press.

Smith, D.W. (2003) Deleuze and Derrida, Immanence and Transcendence: Two Directions in Recent French Thought. In P. Patton and J. Protevi (eds), *Between Deleuze and Derrida*. London: Continuum.

3 Between two debts: child and (inter)national development

Erica Burman

Introduction

The title of this chapter alludes to Lacan's portrayal of the subject as positioned 'between two deaths'. At the risk (and I recognize this rhetorical move is risky in a number of ways) of instituting yet another rhetorical abstraction to reify children and childhoods, I want to (mis)apply this Lacanian motif to inform, and so to disrupt, prevailing models of the relationships between children and development – in particular between models of child development and models of national and international development. Hence while Lacan discusses the subject as 'between two *deaths*', I am going to wilfully misread or misrecognize this trope as 'between two *debts*'. Thus in the chapter I will attempt to explore the contested relations between the symbolic debts both incurred by and demanded of children, in relation to societal (national and international) investments in them and distributed across different countries, to reassert the need to attend to the physical materiality of children's lives over their symbolic status. This analysis arises from a more extensive study of the conditions for and functions of models of children and childhoods (Burman, 2008a). I suggest that rather than eliding models of child, national and international development (as usually happens in policy and practice contexts), such analysis may help us to distinguish between the rhetorical load, or symbolic debt, carried by children from the physical and material challenges they both face and pose.

Between two deaths: Antigone

The classical story (from Sophocles) tells of the daughter of Oedipus, Antigone, who witnesses the enmity and rivalry of her brothers, one of whom, Polyneices, incites rebellion against Creon, king of Thebes, and for this he is killed. Creon decrees that Polyneices' body should be denied burial, as a final gesture extinguishing his symbolic as well as physical being (a second death). But

Antigone defies Creon's law by performing burial rituals over her dead brother, and consequently she is condemned to being buried alive; confined to a living grave, isolated, banished from society.

Lacan (1992) discusses the fate of Antigone as being between two deaths: physical and symbolic. Her punishment reverses the usual relations understood as holding between physical and symbolic death: for while typically our symbolic lives and their trace outlive our physical beings, in the case of Antigone, her fate is to be symbolically erased although not (yet) physically dead. That is, the ethical choice she makes condemns her to exile and expulsion. She is alive but not living; physically existing but prevented from asserting her symbolic life; therefore neither alive nor dead, but (so it is said) in a zone 'between two deaths'.

From Hegel to Butler (2000), Antigone's 'choice' has inspired much philosophical and political (including feminist and psychoanalytic) discussion as a forum in which to pose questions of ethics (Copjec, 2004; Neill, 2005; De Kesel, 2009). It is the sense of being caught up in forces not of, or only partially of, one's making – yet with fateful consequences – that I mobilize here in relation to children and transpose 'debt' for 'death'. And while these analyses make great play of Antigone's gender, they seem to say little about her youth (despite the fact it has been suggested that she – or her character – was supposed to be only around 14 years old; Wilson, 2002). It is this omission/occlusion of the multiple and intersectional positioning around the motifs of the child-subject that I want to attend to here (while elsewhere (Burman, 2008a: chapter 12), I take this further to engage with Lacan's formulation of 'between two *deaths*').

Here I consider the condition of children in relation to forces of economic development, and the ways in which the latter structure the forms of life available to live and develop within, as *'between two debts'*. These debts are macroeconomic, national and familial, and with multidirectional effects – since children are positioned between the (financial and affective) debts to and of their parents, but also between national and international development because of their rhetorical status as supposed investments for the future.

The 'debt' is, correspondingly, both physical and material and symbolic, and functioning (as does the political and representational economy of children and childhoods) at national and international as well as individual levels. It is this double sense of the mutual shaping and significance of individual actions within larger and apparently implacable forces that I am concerned with here. Importantly, I do so not to reduce one to the other but, rather, to trace unstable and uneasy connections amid the shifting, uncertain but intertwined, trajectories of individual lives and social conditions.

The paradigmatics of 'between'

First, it is necessary to explicate the economic and political subtleties of the relations implied by children's positioning 'between' (two debts), as well as how this structures *what* it is between. This relation is best described in terms that are neither entirely *experiential*, as this would run the risk of precisely invoking the idealist trope of personification that has characterized modernist models (Steedman, 1995), nor *spatial* – as the trope that links one space or place to another – as this would take the form of a comparative approach across sites or fieldwork arenas – the approach of anthropology or of cross-cultural psychology. These disciplines implicitly, if not explicitly, presume hierarchy to allow normative assumptions to structure research questions and instruments, and so cannot quite shed their colonialist heritages (see Burman, 2007). Moreover they threaten to overlook the temporal dimension, the processes of historical change that drive such processes to produce these diverse effects across different contexts. Rather, what is needed perhaps resembles what Katz (2004) calls a 'countertopological' approach.

Thus, in this chapter I will focus on different readings of 'between' as a key analytic strategy to unravel the idealist trope of 'the child'. I will consider it in material terms; working (in the sense of putting to work, and also working with and against) five diverse instabilities of 'between' in order to disrupt the normalized assumptions and foreclosed political possibilities. These five 'betweens' are: between human and child development; between child and (inter)national development; between international and national developments; between past and present; and between 'debt' and 'death'. I end with some speculations about whether it is possible to go beyond or otherwise displace this 'between' paradigm.

1. Between human and child development

Most significant are the range of conceptually produced 'betweens' that mobilize children and childhood, but where nevertheless children still disappear into the gaps and cracks. The interrelations between child and human development have formed a substantive focus of critique (see Kessen, 1979; Henriques et al., 1984; Morss, 1996; Burman, 2008a,b), and critiques trace the slippages between models of developmental psychology and human development, and how this conflation has then been transposed onto the story of child development. They show how this story confuses, or at best presumes, units of analysis (from an organ, or organism, or species to an individual) and ties development to a historical chronology of the body (from womb to tomb), that has rightly attracted criticism for its devaluation of positive learning and transformative processes in adulthood and especially ageing.

This also commits the evolutionist error of reading off the story of general-typical development from that of an individual embodied child, so foreclosing analysis of contingencies of time and place in favour of the rampant individualism and voluntarism that characterize modernity and its even more exploitative successors.

This pressure towards measuring (and so better governing) produces a fictional 'child' that is abstracted from gender, class, racialized and other social axes and divisions (Viruru, 2006). It also creates the occlusion of the cultural and national frame of individual human development. The subscription to a prototypical subject avoids analysis of the evaluation of different childhoods in different circumstances and the ways in which the political boundaries of national belonging, or exclusion, delimit what kind of childhood is available to be lived. It is worth attending to this point since most policy documents from around the globe stress diversity and social inclusions, while understating the complexities associated with multicultural societies and especially with mobile populations (see also Kumar and Burman, 2009, in relation to the ways this problematic underlies the United Nations Millennium Development Goals).

2. Between child and (inter)national development

It is where models of child development connect to international development policy that the problem really bites. As illustrations, I will take four contemporary examples, one addressing the hidden privileging of national agendas, and the others focusing on the complex negotiations between national and international understandings, or national renderings of international models – or rather the problems generated by the failure to acknowledge such complexity.

First, let us take the problem of the meanings accorded with age. Not only does this matter legally – in terms of age thresholds determining access to, and prohibition from, for example, alcohol, sex or armed combat – but there also is considerable variation in national legislative definitions regarding at what age particular activities can be conducted legally. In some cases this arises from significant political events. Park's (2006) discussion of government attempts to reintegrate and rehabilitate child soldiers active in the Sierra Leone civil war is instructive; recognition of the dangers of radicalized and militarized young people is giving rise to attempts to involve them in a meaningful way in post-war reconstruction and representation as political agents.

This account still leaves intact the criterion of age, a marker whose inadequacy is well known in manifold ways (as an indicator of mental, emotional, physical qualities, for example) – where, even outside discussions of so-called learning disability,[1] the set of equivalences elaborated between age, maturity, responsibility and autonomy can be questioned.

Another example can be found in the assumption guiding current British policy discussions of strategies to counter 'forced' marriage. The assumption is that raising the age threshold for state recognition of marriage will maximize young women's capacities to resist the pressure to comply and to assert their free will. Here we might note in passing the conceptual limits structured around notions of 'choice' that are intensified in the context of discussions of children, and which conflate competence with confidence or status, alongside the cultural tendency to ignore how the typology of 'forced' versus 'free choice' or 'love' marriages presumes not only prevailing discourses of compulsory heterosexuality but also conditions of economic and interpersonal constraint.

A further key issue illustrated by this example is the assumption that greater age produces some ineffable sense of empowerment, authority, agency or other kind of capacity to control or direct key features of one's life course. Indeed, it seems likely that in this case greater age may be a disadvantage; in the sense that an older woman is likely to be subject to greater pressure to marry and be perceived to be too old to be 'choosy' about whom she marries (Hester et al., 2007). But beyond this, and without disrupting the key human (and sometimes child) rights issues involved, this debate – as it is currently formulated – focuses on presumed minority ethnic cultural practices at the expense of majority practices, ignoring how many pregnant women could be described as pressured, if not 'forced', into marriage. Even more significant is how this apparently child-sensitive and even pro-feminist agenda is deployed to cover for national agendas on immigration. For what is at issue is not the proscribing of certain marriage practices but rather the introduction of differential state recognition of marriage for the purposes of sponsoring a spouse to enter the country.[2] Not only is age a gender-related matter, then, but age criteria are deemed to matter legally only arbitrarily and opportunistically for other reasons.

This also opens up the question of national interests in the determination of chronological age, for legal purposes. A third significant example, in terms of legal interpretations of what constitutes childhood, is the question of parental obligation to support young people in higher education, as in Canada where the current debate focuses on parental responsibilities to children which effectively define childhood as a state of (financial) dependence that has no temporal end point. Of course what is absent from this discourse – as Cradock (forthcoming) points out – is how this contest over definitions of child–parent rights overlooks the responsibilities of the state to resource higher education (see also Cradock, 2006, 2007). So we see how, even within the same geographical and political context, discourses of the active, 'smart' child and future citizen-worker can coexist with those of protection and provision in the service of the neoliberal state (Ailwood, 2008).

So while every child may matter according to British government policy (cf. DfES, 2003), a fourth example illustrates how some children clearly matter more than others (see Williams, 2004, for a critique of the British policy of this name, while Mayes-Elma, 2007, notes that the US programme 'No Child Left Behind' might better be described as 'Every Child Left Behind'; see also Bloch et al., 2006). Since the definition of a child under international legislation is a person under 18 years of age, then refugees under 18 are entitled to specific (financial, health and social) provision *as* children. Interestingly, given the acknowledged limitations of physical indicators of age, and the fact that some young refugees do not know or are not willing to disclose their age, the British government has made recourse to psychological (rather than, say, medical) tests to determine age in order to structure eligibility to services, and social workers are obliged to conduct so-called Merton assessments (named after the case determining legal precedent) for this purpose.

How these psychological measures can be any more reliable than physical ones is a matter of debate, yet we should not miss the historical repetition – from the turn of the twentieth to the twenty-first century – of psychology once again rushing to fill in for the authority of medicine in claiming this testing expertise (cf. Rose, 1985).[3] The arbitrariness and injustice of such measures gives rise to horrific and tragic responses, as in the case of a detained asylum seeker who committed suicide indicating in his final note that he was doing this so as to ensure that at least his son, now an unaccompanied minor, would not be deported and would be able to access the services he had so far been denied (Athmal, 2006). It is worth noting, too, that suicide rates among detained asylum seekers are astronomically high. It is a significant indicator of the political allegiances made by the dominant psychological institutions, that the American Psychological Association (APA) effectively supported President George W. Bush's policy on torture (and only after major protests reversed this position; see http://www.ethicalapa.com; Burton and Kagan, 2007).[4]

3. Between international and national developments

As well as illustrating further 'betweens' that link 'the child' and other axes of social structures and relations – including 'race', class and sexuality (see Burman, 2008a) – the above discussion brings us to the relationships between international and national developments. It is now nearly two decades since discussions of globalized childhoods entered the social sciences. These discussions largely addressed concerns about the ways that northern models of psychological development were coming to structure both international development policy and national models of child development (cf. Boyden, 1990; Woodhead, 1990). At that point the purpose of the intervention was to highlight the limitations of the models in use, in terms of its inadequate representation of the range of childhoods lived in the countries from which the models were drawn, and their even greater inappropriateness or irrelevance to the lives of children and households in other countries. My earlier contributions to this debate distinguished between local, global and globalized models, where I addressed how the homology between, or similarity of structure of, individual and economic models of development worked to warrant each a spurious, but circular, legitimacy (Burman, 1996).

In particular, the spectacular uptake and near universal (with the USA a notable exception) international subscription to the United Nations Convention on the Rights of the Child marks 'child rights' as a privileged discourse around which international relations take place. Some of this concern around childhood has other effects, and possibly other motivations, as with the Harkin Bill put forward to abolish the import to the United States of goods manufactured using child labour (which effectively bolsters national market agendas and undermines southern hemisphere export programmes to the North). But, more than this, the discourse of child rights has come to mediate relations between international and national child-focused agencies such that it can also obscure recognition and evaluation of good as well as bad practice. Moreover, as Duffield (2001) has argued, national and international relations are now mediated by the increasing power wielded by international non-governmental (INGO) (as well as governmental) (IGO) agencies – which include child-focused INGOs such as the UN and highlight the waning power of the nation-state.

Burr's (2006) analysis of child programmes in Vietnam offers an important set of case studies that illustrate the contested and interactive character of national and international policy. Development studies analysts (for example Crewe and Harrison, 1998; Laurie and Bondi, 2005) have emphasized the gaps between policy and practice, and the scope for local partners and stakeholders to transform a (perhaps inappropriately formulated) proposal into something more adapted for the context (or perhaps too adapted, in the sense of failing to generate the changes intended). Similarly, Burr shows how the complex relations between NGOs and INGOS, in a context of vigilant and rigid government surveillance, can undermine effective change: 'Different agencies remain unaware of each other's activities, so the children who are meant to be the ultimate beneficiaries of the aid programs are supported in a fragmented and often inappropriate manner that often ignores their real interests' (Burr, 2006: 84). Burr is especially critical of INGO workers, whose efforts to introduce and implement child rights become meaningless or even counterproductive when they depart so far from local customs and understandings. She gives the graphic example of an INGO visiting a reform school set up by the Vietnamese government and to which it has only grudgingly allowed involvement from a local non-governmental agency:

> The next day, when Jack and I arrived, we discovered boys in his classroom tearing pages from the UNCRC [UN Convention on the Rights of the Child] pamphlets and rolling cigarettes from them. We were surprised, and as we tried to work out how they had gotten hold of the UNCRC, boys crowded around Jack and chanted laughingly,

'Freedom, we want our freedom now!' followed by 'We have the right to freedom'. The more astute children in the class, such as Thang and Diep, asked, 'OK, Mr Jack you give us some money and then we will have our freedom.' In other words, they knew, as did we, that the only way they could be released early was if they bribed their way out of the school.

(Burr, 2006: 149)

This was not (only) a matter of limits of children's or national agencies' awareness of the Convention, but rather of the lack of national political infrastructure and service provision to be able to meaningfully implement change.

Burr (2006) emphasizes the neglect within INGO practice of Vietnam's own national law on children, which specifies children's responsibilities as well as their rights, which was introduced to coincide with recognition of the Convention. While discourses of culture are often mobilized to account for resistance to change around women and children's status (see also Burman et al., 2004), this explanation fails to acknowledge the cultural form and content of the international instruments and their agencies. Once rendered invisible, culture-blaming comes into play in the portrayal of obstacles to programming: 'International planners often attribute failures to the fact that cultural influences can lead people to reject programs. Yet, the bureaucrats have their culture too; one that may obstruct their views of other cultures, resulting in programs that are destined to fail' (Justice, 1989: 151).

Burr's analyses dramatically show how initiatives formulated with the intention of empowering children and improving their lives can be counter-productive if they fail to take account of the local context and cultures of their application. Further, they will be resisted as imperialist or colonialist initiatives on such grounds. In this sense, international instruments such as the UNCRC can be regarded as an instrument potentially, and sometimes actually, imposing a globalized model of childhood, and that features as part and parcel of a neocolonial, neoliberal world scene and the new global governance (Duffield, 2001; Droz, 2006). Similarly, Bornstein's (2001) discussion of child sponsorship illustrates how international humanitarian agencies can have unintended effects, so that the transnational exchanges and relationships elaborated through aid can produce new kinds of felt deficits as well as riches.

4. Between past and present

There is also a temporal 'between'; the 'between' that lies across, that both bridges and separates 'before' and 'after', between then and now, past and present. Children are positioned in multiple senses in this; with their 'now time' taken to exemplify the existential challenge to live in the present. Once again, the child becomes the token of something else, of everyone else: she is not herself. The problem of developmentalism's focus on children as 'becoming adults', rather than focusing on the current lives lived by children, has been extensively addressed by the new sociology of childhood (for example James et al., 1998). Yet incipient idealisms need to be warded off from both directions: the futurity privileged in dominant models of development (via the unproblematic status until recently accorded 'progress') should not be matched by an equivalent sentimentalization of past.

Problems of cross-cultural comparison are matched by those of history. Along with descriptions of contemporaneous childhood and child-rearing practices in different parts of the world, histories of childhood are mobilized to destabilize the presumptions of the present tense; to intimate that children and childhoods are, and have been, 'other' than the ways they are lived now. There are of course risks in juxtaposing historical examples of child labour under industrialization with twentieth- and twenty-first-century accounts of advanced capitalism penetrating southern contexts. This is not only to do with the problematic of 'underdevelopment' that, along with polarized subject positions between 'us' and 'them', invites a discourse of backwardness and inferiority in comparing 'their' current history with 'what we did back then'. For it also ignores how global capitalism has different effects both locally and globally, and, in elaborating the relations between these, that mark it as a distinct economic form. It is too simplistic to map power differentials as geographical distributions (as well as to fail to acknowledge these, and indeed both threaten to institutionalize certain normalizing homogeneities); so, too, are naïve 'radical' historical narratives in danger of normalizing the very 'conservative' historical narratives they seek to put in question.

Foucault's (1980) notion of the 'history of the present' changed all that, along with Benjamin's (1955/70) challenge to *triumphalist* notions of progress. All claims to history are motivated by demands of the present; while what counts as history is often only the story of the winners, leaving subjugated stories and unrealized possibilities untold. Both such lenses transform traditional modes of viewing children and childhoods, just as constructionist approaches to memory have impacted on therapeutic practices (see Burman, 1996/97, 2002, 2009). Instead of recovering unknown pasts, we generate accounts to answer the questions we pose, whose narrative form offers the only record of what we cannot know.

Hence, the ambivalence that surrounds children – interpersonally, and especially within social policy. It is an impossible task for children to personify both past and future, whether ours or theirs. As Elias (2000) shows, the task of shaping a future society has long been linked with practices of child-rearing, while Foucault (2006) was similarly preoccupied with the role of state regulation of child–family relations as constitutive of specific modern disciplinary practices such as psychiatry.

5. Between 'debt' and 'death'

> Every day this Government has been in power, every day in Africa, children have lived who otherwise would have died because this country led the way in cancelling debt and global poverty.
>
> – Tony Blair, final address to Labour Party Conference, Manchester, 26 September 2006

Despite their over-narrativized forms, more than alliteration and typographical substitution connect 'death' and 'debt', as they articulate the complex relations between children and development. There are of course overdetermined connections between 'debt' and 'death' structured into the inequalities of relationship between richer and poorer countries under regimes imposed by the International Monetary Fund (IMF) for aid that increasingly has become redefined as debt. These policies, as also the prototypical form of global capitalism, increasingly pressurize and transform local economies and ecologies with their focus on cash crops and international export markets, have destabilized fragile governments, and have produced the detrimental conditions, including famines, that have continued to claim so many children's lives (de Rivero, 2001; Penn, 2005). As Blair's claim illustrates, children also figure rhetorically as metaphors of economic dependence and as tokens of the salvationary impact of economic support. In this sense children are positioned between two debts both literally and rhetorically.

In the context of rigid Structural Adjustment Policies imposed by the IMF, policies have been introduced that contravene the articles of the UNCRC by privatizing education and health services in poor countries, and so illustrate how discretionary and dispensable the discourse of child rights really is. Hence it is clear that poor children and families bear a disproportionate burden of the national debt, and suffer accordingly. As Burr (2006), Nieuwenhuys (2001) and many other child researchers have pointed out, to stigmatize working children in such contexts is to blame poor people for their poverty. Indeed, Burr points out how, contrary to INGO expectations, many children working on the streets do have families with whom they retain contact and to whom they may even send money. In some cases they support siblings back home to pursue their education. She comments:

> Perhaps we want to think of street children as abandoned because to do otherwise potentially casts the blame for their difficulties outside their immediate world. If parents actually love and care for these children, why are they having to work?
>
> (Burr, 2006: 121)

Similarly, Burr notes how children in orphanages may have at least one living parent (as highlighted by the fracas over Madonna's adoption of a Malawian child in 2006, and the scandal in autumn 2007 over a French agency's alleged attempts to kidnap Chadian children to place them in France as Rwandan orphans). In Burr's study this was especially the case for girls, who, because of the 'two-child policy' in Vietnam, and because of the pressure on widowed or divorced mothers to have male children with new partners, are more likely to be placed in an orphanage. Once again this question of gender preference and gender ratios can be seen to arise from a fateful conjunction of familial, cultural, national and poverty issues.

It is important to recall that UNICEF first focused on preventing child malnutrition and reducing rates of infant mortality. It was only comparatively recently that the organization acknowledged the complex intersections between physical and psychological thriving and, along with a shift to also address older children, espoused the child rights agenda, including participatory rights. This shift posed in new form the question of how to promote and engage with children's agency alongside the even more vexing and contested issue of how to evaluate or arrive at a common view of *what* they are, or should be, participating *in* (so importing the question of the political contexts of lived childhoods).

Beyond 'between'?

In this chapter I have attempted to explore the contested relations between symbolic debts both incurred by and demanded of children in relation to societal (national and international) investments in them, and distributed across different countries, to reassert the need to attend to the physical materiality of children's lives over their symbolic status. Rather than eliding models of child, national and international development, such analysis may help us to distinguish the rhetorical load, or symbolic debt, carried by children from the physical and material challenges they both face and pose. It has been useful to draw upon critics of economic development, post-development theorists such as Sachs (1992), Escobar (1997), Rahnema with Bawtree (1997), Mehmet (1995), as well as counterhegemonic readings of the emergence of development studies (for example Kothari, 2005) since these provide the clearest analyses of the problems with, and effects of, development discourse. But while these accounts describe the changing social conditions that set the contours and limits of children's lives, there is comparatively little literature that actually explores children's lives in these contexts. Canella and Viruru (2004) use postcolonial analysis to inform their postcolonial critique of the position of children – as developmentally immature and therefore 'other' – and Hevener Kaufman and Rizzini (2002) provide an international relations focus on children's changing lives through globalization. Nevertheless, there are comparatively few analyses so far that address the mutual dynamic of children's development in the context of global economic changes, and those that there are typically (and often usefully) focus on one site or country (for example Viruru, 2001; Katz, 2004; Burr, 2006).

Thus we might note how a final link between 'death' and 'debt' lies within the very formulation of the two forms of developmentalism – socio-economic and individual – as their joint and combined conceptual–political impoverishment, and the limits of their mutual implication. I have drawn on the trope of 'between two debts' in an effort to identify intellectual resources necessary to disrupt the economic instrumentalization of children and childhoods, by de-linking models of individual, social and national development and attending to the varying and variable states of childhood rather than state or global conditions. I recognize that this is a project fraught with political and conceptual problems, and of course (as readers may have already surmised), it could be argued that taking a classical Greek myth as a prototype for the position of the child-subject is a case in point.

Clearly, what is needed is the repudiation of both ahistorical nostalgias of fantasized lost childhoods and the orientalisms of 'other' childhoods lived in less segregated and industrialized countries. While both these strategies can offer counterpoints challenging the hegemony of contemporary models, their humanism risks a recentring of the adult western subject. Rather, the task posed here is one of interrogating the gap between the symbolic uses of *rhetorics* of childhood and their material effects in national and international arenas. There are practical and methodological consequences that follow from the analytical perspective I have outlined (see Burman, 2008a, chapter 11; 2008c). At least six such strategies can be discerned from critical debates across the conceptual terrain covered by 'developments'. These are: to go beyond local versus global; beyond work versus play; beyond women versus children; beyond production versus reproduction; beyond identity-politics-driven programming; beyond colonialism versus development and, finally, beyond fact versus fiction. It is a paradox that such conceptual analysis may appear arcane in relation to the blunt and overwhelmingly urgent global disparities that also structure children's lives. I hope that this chapter might provide the groundwork for taking up these issues.

Notes

1. Itself a contested category whose 'age-correlates' themselves contribute to the very structure of normalization they deviate from (Goodley and Lawthom, 2004).
2. Indeed the government agency commissioning this research (the British Home Office) pressed forward with measures to raise the age of a sponsored

spouse to 21 years even before the delivery of the final research report. This example would seem to serve as a precise exemplification not only of political opportunism but also the discretionary relationship between research and policy – in this case even where the policy makers have commissioned the research.

3. Rose (1985) offers documentation indicating that early twentieth-century medicine became wedded to a social environmentalist perspective that was consistent with a focus on investments to improve public health, while the budding psychologists of this time focused on the classification and evaluation of individual differences, as linked to eugenic theories. While Richards (1997) offers a carefully framed historical assessment of the (limited and not exclusive) complicities of the discipline of psychology within scientific racism, Rose highlights the different perspectives adopted by the two disciplines of psychology and medicine, and also how the rivalry between them focused on which could come up with a testing apparatus first. A key claim of Rose's account is that psychology's increasing status relied upon the success of this claim to testing expertise, and it is because of this that psychology has become an administrative discipline focused on technologies of assessment rather than having any clearly formulated or tenable theoretical basis as its core. It is this rather circular relationship between psychological techniques and social policy, alongside the increasing circulation of psychological notions in culture, that gave rise to what both Rose (1985) and Ingleby (1985) termed the 'psy complex' and contributes to subsequent discussions of governmentality (Rose, 1990; Hultkvist and Dahlberg, 2001).

4. At the time of writing, the campaign for psychologists to withhold dues from the APA on the basis of its role within coercive interrogations is in full swing (see http://www.ethicalapa.com).

References

Ailwood, J. (2008) Learning or earning in the 'smart state': changing tactics for governing early childhood, *Childhood*, 15(4): 535–551.

Athmal, H. (2006) *Driven to Desperate Measures*. London: Institute of Race Relations.

Benjamin, W. (1955/70) 'Theses on the Philosophy of History'. In W. Benjamin, *Illuminations*. London: Jonathan Cape.

Bloch, M., Kennedy, D., Lightfoot, T. and Weyenberg, D. (2006) *The Child in the World/The World in the Child: Education and the Configuration of a Universal, Modern and Globalized Childhood*. New York: Palgrave Macmillan.

Bornstein, E. (2001) Child sponsorship, evangelism and belonging in the work of World Vision Zimbabwe, *American Ethnologist*, 28(3): 595–622.

Boyden, J. (1990) Childhood and the policy makers: a comparative perspective on the globalization of childhood. In A. James and A. Prout (eds), *Constructing and*

Reconstructing Childhood: Contemporary Issues in the Sociological Study of Child-hood (pp. 184–215). Basingstoke: Falmer Press.

Burman, E. (1996) Local, global or globalized: child development and international child rights legislation, *Childhood: A Global Journal of Child Research*, 3(1): 45–66.

Burman, E. (1996/97) False memories, true hopes: revenge of the postmodern on therapy, *New Formations*, 30: 122–134.

Burman, E. (2002) Therapy as memorywork: dilemmas of construction and reconstruction, *British Journal of Psychotherapy*, 18(4): 457–469.

Burman, E. (2007) Between orientalism and normalisation: cross-cultural lessons from Japan for a critical history of psychology, *History of Psychology*, 10(2): 179–198.

Burman, E. (2008a) *Developments: Child, Image, Nation*. London: Brunner-Routledge.

Burman, E. (2008b) *Deconstructing Developmental Psychology*, 2nd edition. London: Brunner-Routledge.

Burman, E. (2008c) Beyond 'women vs. children' or 'womenandchildren': engendering childhood and reformulating motherhood, *International Journal of Children's Rights*, 16(2): 177–194.

Burman, E. (2009) Therapy and memorywork: political dilemmas of (re)construction. In J. Haaken and P. Reavey (eds), *Memory Matters*. London: Routledge.

Burman, E., Smailes, S. and Chantler, K. (2004) 'Culture' as a barrier to domestic violence services for minoritised women, *Critical Social Policy*, 24(3): 358–384.

Burr, R. (2006) *Vietnam's Children in a Changing World*. New Brunswick, NJ: Rutgers University Press.

Burton, M. and Kagan, C. (2007) Psychologists and torture: more than a question of interrogation, *The Psychologist*, 20(8): 484–487.

Butler, J. (2000) *Antigone's Claim*. New York: Columbia University Press.

Canella, G. and Viruru, R. (2004) *Childhood and Postcolonization*. New York: RoutledgeFalmer.

Copjec, J. (2004) *Imagine There's No Woman: Ethics and Sublimation*. Cambridge, MA: MIT Press.

Cradock, G. (2006) Distributing children's rights and responsibilities: children and the neoliberal state. Paper presented at the Child and Youth Rights Conference 'Investment and Citizenship: Towards a Transdisciplinary Dialogue on Child and Youth Rights', Brock University, Canada, July.

Cradock, G. (2007) The responsibility dance: learning or earning in the neoliberal state, *Childhood*, 14(2): 153–172.

Cradock, G. (forthcoming) Young adults in the neoliberal era: too many children or too few?, *Canadian Journal of Sociology*.

Crewe, E. and Harrison, E. (1998) *Whose Development? An Ethnography of Aid*. London: Zed Books.

De Kesel, M. (2009) *Eros and Ethics*, trans. S. Jöttkandt. New York: SUNY Press.

De Rivero, O. (2001) *The Myth of Development: The Non-viable Economies of the 21st Century*. London: Zed Books.

DfES (Department for Education and Skills) (2003) *Every Child Matters*, Green Paper, Cm 5860. London: The Stationery Office.

Droz, Y. (2006) Street children and the work ethic: new policy for an old moral, Nairobi (Kenya), *Childhood*, 13(3): 349–363.

Duffield, M. (2001) *Global Governance and the New Wars*. London: Zed Books.

Elias, N. (2000) *The Civilising Process*, revised edition. Oxford: Blackwell.

Escobar, A. (1997) The making and unmaking of the Third World through development. In M. Rahnema with V. Bawtree (eds), *The Post-Development Reader* (pp. 85–93). London: Zed Books.

Foucault, M. (1980) Truth and power. In C. Gordon (ed.), *Michel Foucault: Power/Knowledge. Selected Interviews and Other Writings 1972–1977*. Brighton: Harvester.

Foucault, M. (2006) *Psychiatric Power*. London: Palgrave.

Goodley, D. and Lawthom, R. (eds) (2004) *Psychology and Disability: Critical Introductions and Reflections*. London: Palgrave Macmillan.

Henriques, J., Hollway, W., Urwin, C., Venn, C. and Walkerdine, V. (1984) *Changing the Subject: Psychology, Social Regulation and Subjectivity*. London: Methuen.

Hester, M., Chantler, K., Gangoli, G., Devgon, J., Sharma, S. and Singleton, A. (2007) *Forced Marriage: The risk factors and the effect of raising the minimum age for a sponsor, and of leave to enter the UK as a spouse or fiancé(e)*. London: The Home Office.

Hevener Kaufman, N. and Rizzini, I. (eds) (2002) *Globalization and Childhood: Exploring Potentials for Enhancing Opportunities in the Lives of Children and Youth*. New York: Kluwer Academic/Plenum Publishers.

Hultkvist, K. and Dahlberg, G. (eds) (2001) *Governing the Child in the New Millennium*. London: Brunner-Routledge.

Ingleby, D. (1985) Professionals as socializers: the 'psy-complex', *Research in Law, Deviance and Social Control*, 7: 79–100.

James, A., Jenks, C. and Prout, A. (1998) *Theorizing Childhood*. Cambridge: Polity Press.

Justice, J. (1989) *Policies, Plans and People*. London: Jessica Kingsley.

Katz, C. (2004) *Growing Up Global: Economic Restructuring and Children's Everyday Lives*. Minneapolis: University of Minnesota Press.

Kessen, W. (1979) The American child and other cultural inventions, *American Psychologist*, 34(10): 815–820.

Kothari, U. (2005) Authority and expertise: the professionalisation of international development and the ordering of dissent. In N. Laurie and L. Bondi (eds), *Working the Spaces of Neoliberalism: Activism, Professionalisation and Incorporation* (pp. 32–53). Oxford: Blackwell.

Kumar, M. and Burman, E. (eds) (2009) Critical/Subaltern approaches to the millennium development goals, *Journal of Health Management* (Special Issue), 11(2/3).

Lacan, J. (1992) *The Ethics of Psychoanalysis, 1959–1960. The Seminar of Jacques Lacan Book VII*, trans. D. Porter. London: Routledge.

Laurie, N. and Bondi, L. (eds) (2005) *Working the Spaces of Neoliberalism: Activism, Professionalisation and Incorporation*. Oxford: Blackwell.

Mayes-Elma, R. (2007) Judith Butler. In J. Kincheloe and R. Horn (eds), *The Praegar Handbook of Education and Psychology* (pp. 62–67). Westport, CT: Praeger.

Mehmet, O. (1995) *Westernizing the Third World*. London: Zed Books.

Morss, J. (1996) *Growing Critical: Alternatives to Developmental Psychology*. London: Routledge.

Neill, C. (2005) An idiotic act: on the non-example of Antigone, *The Letter*, 34: 1–28.

Nieuwenhuys, O. (2001) Who profits from child labour? Children, labour and reproduction. Paper for Contested Childhood Seminar Series, Michigan University, 21 October.

Park, A. (2006) Children as Risk or Children at Risk? International Law, Child Soldiers and Citizenship: The Case of Sierra Leone. In S. Bittle and A. Doyle (eds), *Paradoxes of Risk: Inclusions and Exclusions*. Halifax, Nova Scotia: Fernwood.

Penn, H. (2005) *Unequal Childhoods: Children's Lives in Poor Countries*. London: RoutledgeFalmer.

Rahmena, M. with Bawtree, V. (eds) (1997) *The Post-development Reader*. London: Zed Books.

Richards, G. (1997) *'Race', Racism and Psychology*. London: Routledge.

Rose, N. (1985) *The Psychological Complex: Psychology, Politics and Society in England 1869–1939*. London: Routledge.

Rose, N. (1990) *Governing the Soul*. London: Routledge.

Sachs, W. (ed.) (1992) *The Development Dictionary: A Guide to Knowledge as Power*. London: Zed Books.

Steedman, C. (1995) *Strange Dislocations: Childhood and Sense of Human Interiority, 1780–1930*. London: Virago.

Viruru, R. (2001) *Early Childhood Education: Postcolonial Perspectives from India*. New Delhi: Sage.

Viruru, R. (2006) Postcolonial technologies of power: standardised testing and representing diverse young children, *International Journal of Educational Policy, Research and Practice: Reconceptualising Childhood Studies*, 7: 49–70.

Williams, F. (2004) What matters is who works: why every child matters to New Labour. Commentary on the DfES Green Paper 'Every Child Matters', *Critical Social Policy*, 24(3): 406–427.

Wilson, A. (2002) Antigone's age: notes and discussions of Sophocles' tragedy. http://www.users.globalnet.co.uk/~loxias/antigone02.htm (accessed 26 January 2007).

Woodhead, M. (1990) Psychology and the cultural construction of children's needs. In A. James and A. Prout (eds), *Constructing and Reconstructing Childhood: Contemporary Issues in the Sociological Study of Childhood* (pp. 60–77). Basingstoke: Falmer Press.

4   Shaping the future: how human capital arguments about investment in early childhood are being (mis)used in poor countries

Helen Penn

Introduction

This chapter explores how policy on early childhood is being developed in the countries of the global south (also known as developing countries/majority world/poor countries)[1] with particular reference to Southern Africa. Many international agencies – including the World Bank, UNESCO and UNICEF – are currently arguing that investing in early childhood in poor countries will help turn those countries around and enable them to become more competitive in a global market. The World Bank has even sponsored the development of an ECD (early child development) calculator which enables policy makers to compute the likely long-term economic benefits of such investment in their country. These ideas frame current debates about donor interventions in early childhood in poor countries and shape recipient responses. In taking inequality as unproblematic, and individual effort and success as the motor of economic development, such interventions overlook or ignore the adverse impact of macroeconomic policies on families. While laying claims to being culturally sensitive the implementation of such ideas frequently tends to be culturally abrasive.

Conceptualizations of early childhood

In broad terms, there are three main perspectives for considering early childhood:

- An *education* perspective which considers children's cognitive development and readiness for school as paramount. The emphasis here tends to be on providing teacher-led preschooling that is generally attached to schools or administered by education authorities. It is for children who are nearing school starting age, usually 3–5 years of age.

- A *care* perspective which considers the paramount objective to be provision of child care for children of working mothers. The services tend to be provided by non-governmental organizations (NGOs) or private entrepreneurs, for children aged from birth to 5 years.
- A *health and welfare* perspective which considers that nutrition and child well-being are the paramount objectives, especially for undernourished or 'stunted' children, or children who are at risk in some way. Such programmes frequently try to co-opt or engage mothers in the activities undertaken because it is mothers who are seen to carry responsibility for ensuring their child's well-being, however harsh the circumstances in which they are bringing up their children.

These approaches tend to blur into one another. In the global south, the phrase 'early child development' is commonly used as shorthand to indicate that a holistic approach, combining all three perspectives, has been adopted, at least on paper. In ex-communist countries the kindergarten system did indeed operate like this, even in very poor countries such as Mongolia. It was presumed that women would work, and that education services would also encompass child care *and* health services. The food was carefully graded for nutritional content, children had regular health check-ups, doctors were assigned to kindergartens, and all kindergartens had recreational and exercise facilities. Despite over-regulation and control, kindergartens were popular with parents from all walks of life (Penn, 2005). However, the collapse of communism led to the collapse of many state-sponsored services, including kindergartens, and a disregard for the systems developed under communism (Alexander, 2000).

Some European countries, including all Nordic countries, have combined care and education. They frequently offer 25–30 hours a week of state-financed education and care in a single setting, with the possibility of additional care in the same setting to cover working hours. But in English-speaking countries the service most commonly offered is part-time nursery education, and/or private day care. Working mothers in these countries typically have a patchwork arrangement for their children that combines informal care by relatives, some paid care in private settings, and, when the children are old enough to be eligible, some nursery education (although not necessarily in a publicly funded education institution). While there may be many health and welfare projects within this patchwork, there is little systematic attention to it. There are many hybrid arrangements; in fact in English-speaking countries early childhood education and care (ECEC) is characterized by hybridity. Choice for parents in effect means choosing a way through whatever local arrangements are available, in order to find what is convenient and affordable. For children this results in discontinuities, as they move from place to place. Education is potentially a redistributive measure, if *all* children can access it on an equal basis. Yet early education (and care) in English-speaking countries is rarely distributive in this way.

It is the English-speaking model of early childhood education and care that mainly serves as the context for research, including the economic research discussed in this chapter. This research in turn is interpreted as offering universal messages, and research findings are exported to the global south through international agencies and donors such as the World Bank, UNICEF and leading charities. It is a particular irony that the holistic model adopted in so many policy statements by countries in the global south is undermined by the delivery models that are adopted (Penn, 2008b).

Human capital theory and early childhood

Human capital theory is about the economic productivity of individuals over time and the situations in which it might be maximized. Human capital theory has undoubtedly contributed to a rethinking of macroeconomic policies for education, and in particular for early education. Heckman, a leading theorist of human capital theory argues that investment in early childhood brings greater returns than investment in any other stage of education (for example Heckman, 2000; Heckman and Masterov, 2005). Heckman has highlighted early childhood intervention as being an especially effective economic investment and his views have been influential with international organizations such as the World Bank.

Heckman bases his analysis principally on three longitudinal cost–benefit studies (where longitudinal was taken as fifteen years or more, that is, the progress of a child into adulthood) of high quality[2] early interventions with poor and vulnerable children. These are the Perry High Scope (Barnett, 1996; Schweinhardt, 2003); the Abecedarian (Ramey et al., 2000); and the Chicago Child–Parent Centres (Reynolds, 2000). These interventions took place in the 1960s, 1970s and 1980s and were carried out in disadvantaged/poor areas in the United States. The populations investigated were overwhelmingly African American and Hispanic. The Abecedarian study investigated a particularly deprived population. The Perry High Scope Project and the Abecedarian were randomized controlled trials, although some queries have been raised about the randomization of the Perry study. The Chicago study in contrast used a control/experimental design.

Each of these three intervention studies has spawned a series of papers over the decades. The argument is basically that if the life chances of the poorest and most vulnerable children can be demonstrably improved by early education, then targeting such children can lead to substantial savings in the negative costs they may incur when they are older or become adults (for example, with less remedial education needed, less reliance on social housing, less crime being committed).

The three interventions differed from each other in their aims, the age ranges of the children, the length of time of the intervention, the role played by mothers, the outreach facilities available, and in various other ways. The cost–benefit calculations based on the studies follow broadly similar and acceptable economic procedures. They are, however, reliant on specific local school models for their costings (repeat years, nature of remedial assistance) and use US databases to make other financial projections, for instance related to juvenile offending rates and crime compensation.

Each study reported significant and positive longitudinal outcomes for the intervention group. All three studies reported an improvement in school performance for the intervention group, with less repetition and remedial assistance rates. The Abecedarian study reported a marginally significant difference in the education rates of teenage mothers of participants, and a marginally significant difference in the type of employment of all mothers. The major finding was that the Perry High/Scope and the Chicago study reported a significant difference in juvenile crime rates between the intervention and control groups, although at the minimal level of significance. The Abecedarian intervention group showed no difference. Crime reduction in the intervention group forms the major part of the saving in the Perry High Scope and Chicago studies. However, costs of crime in the United States are very high. The three strikes law means that levels of incarceration in the United States are the highest in the developed world, and black males in particular stand a high chance of incarceration. Victim compensation is also uniquely high in the United States because of the incidence of gun-related crime there (Aos et al., 2001). It is unlikely that savings of the order reported from early intervention in these two studies would accrue in any other country.

Each study made an overall estimate of the ratio of dollars spent to dollars saved, taking long-term projections of benefits into account. The Perry High Scope claimed an overall ratio of $7.16 saved for every dollar spent; the Child–Parent Centres $7.14 saved per dollar spent, and the Abecedarian $3.78 saved for every dollar spent. The size of the effect varies considerably according to the instruments used, and the attribute being measured. The figures are open to interpretation although, unsurprisingly, the most favourable figures are generally used as a basis for extrapolation (Penn, 2005; Penn and Lloyd, 2007).

The attraction of the studies to economists is that, as randomized or carefully controlled longitudinal studies they appear to present rigorous and irrefutable evidence, although as indicated above the methodology and conclusions are not consistent. The studies have become iconic and their findings have become endlessly recycled in the economic and child care literature. The most recent report from the Rand Corporation *The Economics of Early Childhood Policy* again bases its argument on the calculations from the three studies (Kilburn and Karoly, 2008). Yet even in a United States context the analysis of early childhood based on human capital theory presents many difficulties. Making long-range predictions on the basis of the data remains problematic, yet this kind of use is widespread.

One problem is that definitions of 'poor and vulnerable' overlap with race and class. For example, the Perry High Scope intervention referred originally to its sample of children as 'functionally retarded, culturally deprived, Negro, pre-school children' (Weikart, 1967: 57). This description has been modified over time, so that the participants are now described as being 'low-income children'. The possibility that racism may have distorted the results, and their subsequent interpretation, is only marginally addressed by the Abecedarian study (Campbell and Ramey, 1995) and is not raised by the other studies. However, other authors, especially black authors writing about this period of American history, describe the racism as overwhelming (Heath, 1983, 1990; Rosaldo, 1993). Johnson et al. (2003) suggest that research in child development has downplayed the importance of context and largely ignored or misunderstood the position of poor blacks and Hispanics in the United States. Perry and Albee (1994) also express concern with prevention programmes and their analyses which focus exclusively on micro-level interventions and ignore wider societal issues.

This human capital approach to early childhood takes inequity for granted, or at worst ignores it. It emphasizes that poverty is a problem only when it generates additional costs that could be avoided. The costs of disorder and incarceration are chief among those costs that could be lessened or avoided by early intervention. However, this approach does not raise questions regarding social justice in analysing the situation of poor children, nor does it consider redistribution as part of the possible solutions/redress. Instead, it generally leads to a policy option which recommends high quality targeted interventions for poor children to avert the worst consequences of poverty. This approach has been treated with some scepticism by some leading US commentators. For example, Brooks-Gunn (2003) commented in her evidence to a US Senate committee, that the evidence suggests that early intervention is important *but not sufficient* on its own to change life chances. Zigler, a leading US researcher, remarks:

> Are we sure there is no magic potion that will push poor children into the ranks of the middle class? Only if the potion contains health care, childcare, good housing, sufficient income for every

family, child rearing environments free of drugs and violence, support for parents in all their roles, and equal education for all students in schools. Without these necessities, only magic will make that happen.

(Zigler, 2003: 12)

Applying human capital theory in early childhood to the global south

To critique human capital theory is not to throw the baby out with the bathwater. There is now a body of large-scale aggregate studies of early childhood education and care (ECEC), especially in the global south countries where early intervention is a relatively new phenomenon, and as a new introduction its impact can be more easily measured. These studies, without exception, demonstrate a relationship between early intervention and improved school performance, although the size of the effect and its continuity into later school life may vary and costing models are much more conjectural than those from the three United States cost–benefit studies (Berlinski et al., 2007). It is *indisputable* that quality early education produces some cognitive and emotional gains for children, which may be long-lasting, and to which economic value can be assigned. The question is what kinds of intervention are most appropriate, and, more critically, who should deliver them and how can their efficacy be measured?

The limited policy of targeted interventions for poor children, based on a human capital theory analysis, is to an extent controversial in the United States. It is much more controversial when it is extrapolated beyond the communities in the United States where the investigations were undertaken. It is already a problematic assumption that intervention in early childhood will produce changes in the distant future, whatever dynamic and unforeseen shifts in societies and in global economies might take place. Societies in the global south are undergoing rapid change for a number of reasons, and most are experiencing major population shifts from rural to urban areas (UNFPA, 2007). Forms of governance and delivery of education in the global south often bear little resemblance to that of the global north (Steiner Khasi, 2004). To make long-range predictions based on three US studies in the global south is more than problematic, yet it continues to be carried out and justified. As a result, all kinds of misleading claims are made about future profits and losses in the countries of the global south, as well as in the global north. Further, loans are provided and justified on the basis of such evidence.

For example, human capital theory, and the particular US studies on which investment in early childhood is promoted, is the centrepiece in the World Bank early childhood development lending policy in education. This might be expected of a bank concerned with investment returns on loans. The information has been extrapolated from the United States context without caveats, and applied to Africa and other regions (Garcia et al., 2008). As mentioned above, the World Bank has funded the development of an early child development (ECD) calculator to enable countries to calculate the profits of investment in programmes per 1,000 children:

> The ECD calculator allows you to calculate the Net Present Value of an ECD program that results in increased school enrollment and improved school-achievement of a cohort (the 'targeted group') of 1,000 newborns. It is assumed that the ECD program improves the survival chances, the nutritional status, and/or the cognitive development of the target group. This results in better schooling outcomes. The latter is translated into increased lifetime productivity. The program provides the Present Value of this increase in lifetime productivity, net of the additional schooling costs. The end result, the Net Present Value, is the maximum amount one can invest in an ECD program for 1,000 children and still break even.
>
> (http://go.worldbank.org/KHC1NHO580)

The background paper which supports this analysis ignores the caveat of 'quality' which was part of the US studies model. It assumes that ECD programmes can be unproblematically broken down into specific components such as age groups of children receiving the intervention, programme types, parent training, for example. An aggregate average cost can be put on each component. The country using the calculator has to factor in national data about child mortality and school attendance. Then the cost of each of the components can be offset against the likely gains in productivity when the child becomes an adult. The components are simplistic, and the costs and benefits are entirely speculative, but the arithmetic is impeccable.

The World Bank rationales have in turn influenced many other donors. For example, UNICEF begins its rationale for ECEC with the title *A Sevenfold Return on Investment* and claims that

> numerous studies have shown that every dollar invested in ensuring children the best start yields $4–$7 return in the long run to children, their families and the taxpayer ... [ECEC] develops human capital and catalyzes economic growth.
>
> (www.unicef.org/earlychildhood/files/
> CARD_early_childhoodENG.pdf)

The 2007 annual report of the Bernard van Leer Foundation emphasizes the need to promote

the compelling cost–benefit case for investment in early childhood
... to expose high profile business leaders to the well-established evidence that increased evidence in quality early childhood programs
delivers handsome long-term profits for society.

(Bernard van Leer Foundation, 2007: 11)

Save US claims that

Children who participate in ECD programs when compared with
children who don't are more likely to enrol in school, plan their
families, become more productive adults and educate their own children. They are less likely to repeat a grade, drop out of school or
engage in criminal activities.

(http://www.savethechildren.org/programs/education/early-
childhood-development.html)

One issue in the transposition of findings from the USA to the global
south is that the models of provision being advocated by these international
non-governmental organizations (INGOs) and charities have been taken
from the 'high quality' provision deemed essential to produce long-term
cost advantages in the United States, to community self-help and small-
entrepreneur models in the new context. Much of the provision in the global
south, especially in Africa (ADEA, 2008) is in the hands of small profit-making
entrepreneurs, and in this situation quality is directly related to cost. The more
the parent can afford, the better the quality of provision; the less the parent
can afford the worse the quality. Sometimes it is extremely poor, with many
children being crammed into a very small space with inadequate carers and
few, if any, resources. Under these circumstances, far from offering a positive
and equalizing experience to children, social inequality is amplified, not
reduced, by ECEC services (Penn, 2008a).

A study carried out by Haihimbo et al. (2005) provides an example of this
mismatch between rhetoric and reality. The authors carried out research
into the sustainability of ECEC community-based projects in the rural areas
in Namibia, and commented on their 'here today, gone tomorrow' nature
and the 'benign neglect' which characterized care for vulnerable children
at the same time as the World Bank was promoting such services as part of
their productivity arguments for ECEC in its sector-wide education plan
for the country (Marope, 2005). The World Bank early childhood initiative
in Namibia explicitly favoured small entrepreneurs and/or community-based
interventions which rely heavily on parents and volunteers; precisely those
interventions that local research suggested were least sustainable and of
the poorest quality. The reliance on entrepreneurial and small-scale voluntary

initiatives, rather than exploring the possibility of governmental programmes, typifies much of the advocacy from INGOs and charities.

One of the appeals of the often repeated human capital theory argument, in relation to ECEC, is that investing in early childhood results in *future* productivity. The burden of proof regarding success or failure is then located far into the future. In fact, as Daniel (2008) suggests, aid agencies are heavily obliged to present a positive slant on their activities, and to downplay negative findings. The human capital theory arguments provide a kind of carte blanche for doing this. Who will know or remember in twenty years' time that a particular ECEC programme promised positive long-term payoffs?

Other rationales for ECEC

There are many other arguments besides human capital theory for introducing comprehensive ECEC systems and most OECD countries (not the United States) have already accepted them (OECD, 2006). The arguments used by economists assume that all ECEC costs are an *additional* burden on expenditure, and must be justified as a special case. In many European countries, some of which, for example Belgium and France, have had full-time nursery education for a majority of children aged 3–5 for more than a hundred years, and full coverage for all children for fifty years, ECEC costs are viewed as integral to state expenditure, in the same way as drains or bridges are regarded. Such services are seen as promoting social integration and citizenship and it would be inconceivable not to provide them. The current European debate is mainly about the extent of services for children under 3 years. The EU, in its Barcelona summit in 2002, set a target of services for 33 per cent of children under 3 years. This target was put forward in order to promote women's labour market participation by providing child care (EACEA, 2009; EU/NESSE, 2009).

Gender and working mothers

Jenson (2008) argues (in relation to the European Union) that human capital theory, with its emphasis on lifelong learning and on the economic contribution of successful and productive individuals, by default ignores, or downplays, the particular conditions and circumstances of women and children – which are very different from those of men in the various contexts and cultures. Structural issues are of less importance in human capital theory than the encouragement of individual striving. Yet women have legitimate concerns, for example regarding the care provided for the very young and elderly, and these may appear to be at odds with the need to succeed in a competitive economy. This gender blindness is multiplied when human capital theory is applied to the global south.

Heymann (2003, 2006) has carried out large-scale studies of working mothers in four very different countries in the global south. She suggests that around 29 per cent of young children are left alone or with young or unsuitable carers while their mothers work. She also noted that this frequently results in very high child accident levels. Women tend to work in the informal labour market, as hawkers, or servants or in other unregulated jobs. Consequently, there is unlikely to be any employment law protection for them. Child care for working mothers is an important issue. As noted above, one of the most significant demographic changes in the South is migration-urbanization, where men and women from the countryside migrate to towns and cities. Stripped of their rural support networks, women struggle to make a living and bring up children in the shanty towns which surround most big cities in the global south (UNFPA, 2008).

Children living in extreme circumstances

The situation for young children is still worse where HIV/AIDs is prevalent, and grandmothers are left caring for the young children of their deceased children, with little or no financial or any other kind of support. Similarly in situations of war and conflict, the situation of young children who are isolated and distressed means that the establishment of normal routines is important to their lives (Lloyd et al., 2005). In these situations ECEC provision can offer some relief to stressed carers, and some security to children. Although, of course, ECEC can only be effective as a small part of a wider amelioration package to dislocated and highly disadvantaged children living in extreme circumstances.

Inequity

A recent tranche of reports (for example OECD, 2008; UNICEF, 2008; UNESCO, 2009) suggest that equity and governance are crucial issues in predicting outcomes for education in all countries, whether in the global north or global south. Yet equity is rarely a stated goal in financial plans for the global south, because it can only be achieved by the regulation and taxation of externally held wealth. Africa has some of the highest gini coefficient (inequality) ratings in the world. The most unequal country of all, the one with the highest gini rating of over 0.70 is Namibia (the UK, itself an unequal country among developed nations, has a gini rating of 0.32). This is a legacy of Namibia's colonial apartheid past when the best land and the natural mineral resources were commandeered by German, English and South African expatriates. SWAPO (South West Africa People's Organization, the government of Namibia) adopted a hopeful rhetoric of equality and redistribution when it assumed office in 1990 after years of South African rule, but it has been unable to control ownership of assets or to shift inequality. The sector-wide education plan for Namibia, drawn up on the basis of a World Bank analysis (Marope, 2005) does not mention the inequality that exists. The European/OECD position that a universalistic approach to ECEC can reduce inequality and promote social mobility is of no technical interest. Instead, human capital theory posits that *individuals* can succeed – or rather, fail less often – if they are sufficiently primed when young.

Child rights

There is no INGO or charity that does not subscribe to the notion of child rights, and one, UNICEF, has a particular remit to promote them. However, the Convention on the Rights of the Child (CRC) is an aspirational document, and the interpretations of protection, provision and participation rights of young children are still being developed (Freeman and Veerman, 1992; Freeman, 2000, 2004, 2007). A recent update of the CRC (UN Committee on the Rights of the Child, 2005) has elaborated on the ways in which the concept of rights might apply to preschool-age children. CRC considers that young children have *entitlements* to basic services, to protection, to provision and to active participation in the lives that they lead.

This notion of entitlement challenges conventional understandings of young children as passive bystanders. Unlike the technocratic interventionist approach of human capital theory, and unlike a developmental approach which assumes that children only gradually become full human beings, and need to be both stimulated and protected to function fully, the CRC approach argues for a more radical stance. If every child has basic entitlements, *all children* should have access to basic facilities such as education, health care, shelter, clean water and sanitation. A child rights' approach puts emphasis on the lives of children as competent citizens, and sees the provision of ECEC services in that wider context of equitable services for *all* children. This approach is partly adopted in the UNESCO *Education for All Global Monitoring Report 2007*, which was mainly devoted to ECEC (UNESCO, 2007).

However, at the present time approximately 60 per cent of the world's children are denied basic rights to the facilities that are deemed necessary for ordinary everyday life in the global north (Gordon et al., 2003). A child rights' approach, although much espoused by INGOs working in the field of education, also raises the fundamental question of equity: what can be done in the here and now to make a difference when the gap between rich and poor is so great?

Most donors concerned with early childhood shirk the socio-economic and moral questions raised by the child rights debate, and instead regard child rights as a kind of extended support for individual children. Donors have to be very wary and tread a narrow path between intervention and interference (UNESCO, 2007). Human capital theory offers an apparently neutral position; by focusing on individual effort and interventions with young children, it posits that poverty can be overturned. But the idea of 'intervention' sits uneasily with the child rights discourses. The agenda of children's rights is arguably the one with the most potential for disruption of current discourses on ECEC.

Summary

In short, human capital theory is used as a simplistic explanation for complex situations where more nuanced and more challenging analysis and policy implementation are required. In situations of rapid societal change, especially in the global south, as Jones and Vilar (2008: 45) suggest, 'it is critical to unpack culturally specific understandings of core cultural concepts . . . (such as "children" "family" and "work") and how these are subject to competing interpretations and reinterpretations in societies undergoing rapid social, political, economic and demographic transitions'.

As discussed here, partly for ideological reasons on the part of major donors, and partly for lack of resources, present arrangements for ECEC in many countries, and certainly in most African countries, is ad hoc. Centre-based provision is mostly commercial and the standard of quality varies according to fees charged. Those few parents paying the highest fees tend to get a service on a par with European provision. Those who can afford only limited fees get the poorest provision, and this is often very grim for the children (Penn, 2008a,b; Penn and Maynard, 2009). Donors have also supported some centre-based provision but on an ad hoc basis, either a one-off from a very small charity or as part of a programme from a well known donor such as UNICEF. But all donors have to face the problem of continuity and sustainability. Donor priorities change and develop, and very few donors support projects for a long time, with devastating consequences for the projects left high and dry once the donor departs (Penn and Maynard, 2009).

In order to save costs, there are many programmes which are based on semi-volunteering, in which the volunteers – mothers or community activists – are offered a small incentive to participate, or offered an additional benefit such as nutritional supplements for their child if they accept an intervention (Engle et al., 2007; Grantham-McGregor et al., 2007). But volunteering programmes rarely succeed and remain sustainable without continuous support, especially in poor communities. Further, the volunteers, who see the volunteering as a first step to more lucrative employment, are often frustrated, and turnover tends to be high (Penn and Maynard, 2009).

Human capital theory was seized upon by early childhood activists because at last it seemed as though there were respectable and unsentimental explanations for promoting ECEC. As one leading economist in the field of ECEC stated: 'How can you disagree with human capital theory' (Garcia, 2008, personal communication). Yet, the consequences of adopting such a narrow economic-oriented approach has also been highly problematic. Poverty and inequity are marginalized and children are often regarded as creatures to be manipulated. The basic assumption is that it is possible to provide interventions for young children that directly, or indirectly, teach them how to compete and succeed, and this in turn will lead to poverty reduction. Originally, as outlined by Sen (1999), human capital theory provided an argument for investment in education and health in the global south, rather than, or as well as, infrastructural investment such as roads and machinery. However, the emphasis within human capital theory has shifted to a neoliberal approach of enabling *individual* success and striving, rather than any kind of vision of a welfare partnership between individuals and the state. This rationale is in direct contrast to, for example, the way in which ECEC has been developed in many European countries.

This chapter has attempted to show how human capital theory, already flawed in its assumptions about ECEC, has been misused to provide a ragbag of justifications for various kinds of low-cost ECEC initiatives in the global south. It has enabled donors to avoid more fundamental discussions around poverty and inequity.

In resource-poor environments, all expenditure is problematic. But a more positive approach would be to directly tackle the problems on their own terms; to use donor aid to review education systems in order to include early childhood education, to do something about the children left alone or placed in poor care by mothers struggling to feed their families and survive, to provide for children in extreme circumstances, to acknowledge the importance of child rights discourses, and above all to try to address the consequences of inequity and marginalization. Countries like South Africa are already working along these lines. Framing ECEC in terms of human capital theory hinders rather than enhances progress.

Notes

1. The division of 'North' and 'South' has itself been criticized as conceptually inadequate, because of inequity within countries as well as between countries, and because of the number of countries that do not fit into either category. It distorts perceptions of social justice which affect virtually every state in the world (Tinker, 2007). An alternative would be a 'commonalities' approach which stresses how particular issues affect people wherever they are. As 'North'

and 'South' still have considerable currency in the development literature they are used here, but with acknowledgement of this critique.
2. Generally assumed as good staff child ratios, trained staff and a well-worked out cognitively based curriculum.

References

ADEA (2008) Working Group on ECD. http://www.adeanet.org/workgroups/en_wgecd.html

Alexander, R. (2000) *Culture and Pedagogy: International Comparisons in Primary Education.* Oxford: Blackwell.

Aos, S., Phipps, S., Barnoski, R. and Lieb, R. (2001) *The Comparative Costs and Benefits of Programs to Reduce Crime.* Washington, DC: Washington State Institute for Public Policy.

Barnett, W.S. (1996) *Lives in the Balance: Age-27 Benefit–Cost Analysis of the High/Scope Perry Preschool Program.* Ypsilanti, MI: High/Scope Foundation.

Berlinski, S., Galiani, S. and Manacorda, M. (2007) Giving children a better start: preschool attendance and school-age profiles, *Journal of Public Economics*, 92 (5/6): 1416–1440.

Bernard van Leer Foundation (2007) Annual Report 2007. The Hague: BVL.

Brooks-Gunn, J. (2003) Do you believe in magic? What we can expect from early childhood intervention programs, *Social Policy Report*, XVII(1): 3–7.

Campbell, F.A. and Ramey, C.T. (1995) Cognitive and school outcomes for high-risk African-American students at middle adolescence: positive effects of early intervention, *American Educational Research Journal*, 32(4): 743–772.

Daniel, M.L. (2008) The hidden injuries of aid: Unintended side effects of humanitarian support to vulnerable children in Makete, Tanzania. Paper presented at 'Child and Youth Research in the 21st Century: A Critical Appraisal', First international conference organized by the International Childhood and Youth Research Network, Cyprus, 28–29 May.

EACEA (Education, Audiovisual and Culture Executive Agency) (2009) *Tackling Social and Cultural Inequalities through Early Education and Care in Europe*, Eurydice Report. Brussels: EACEA.

Engle, P., Black, M., Behrman, J., Cabral de Mello, M., Gertler, P., Kapiriri, L., Martorell, M., Eming Young, M. and the International Child Development Steering Group (2007) Strategies to avoid the loss of developmental potential in more than 200 million children in the developing world, *The Lancet*, 369: 229–242.

EU/NESSE (2009) *Early Childhood Education and Care – What we Know from Research – What Education Policy Makers Need to Know.* Paper prepared for the EU by Helen Penn on behalf of NESSE, Brussels (forthcoming).

Freeman, M. (2000) The future of children's rights, *Children and Society*, 14(4): 277–293.

Freeman, M. (ed.) (2004) *Children's Rights*, vols 1 and 2. Farnham: Ashgate Dartmouth.

Freeman, M. (2007) *A Commentary on the United Nations Convention on the Rights of the Child. Article 3: The Best Interests of the Child*. The Hague: Martinus Nijhoff.

Freeman, M. and Veerman, P. (1992) *The Ideologies of Children's Rights*. The Hague: Martinus Nijhoff Publishers.

Garcia, M., Pence, A. and Evans J. (eds) (2008) *Africa's Future, Africa's Challenge: Early Childhood Care and Development in Sub-Saharan Africa*. Washington, DC: World Bank.

Gordon, D., Nandy, S., Pantazis, C., Pemberton, S. and Townsend, P. (2003) *Child Poverty in the Developing World*. Bristol: Policy Press.

Grantham-McGregor, S., Cheung, Y.B., Glewwe, P., Richter, L., Strupp, B. and the International Child Development Steering Group (2007) Developmental potential in the first five years for children in developing countries, *The Lancet*, 369: 60–70.

Haihambo, C., Mushaandja, J. and Hengari, J. (2005) *Situation Analysis on IECD Provision in Karas, Kavango, and Omusati Regions of Namibia*. Consultative Workshop, Ministry of Gender Equality and Community Work, December 2005.

Heath, S.B. (1983) *Ways with Words: Language, Life and Work in Communities and Classrooms*. Cambridge: Cambridge University Press.

Heath, S.B. (1990) The children of Trackton's children: spoken and written language in social change. In J. Stigler, R. Shweder and G. Herdt (eds), *Cultural Psychology: Essays on Comparative Human Development* (pp. 496–519). Cambridge: Cambridge University Press.

Heckman, J. (2000) *Invest in the Very Young*. Chicago: University of Chicago Harris School of Public Policy Studies.

Heckman, J. and Masterov, D. (2005) *The Productivity Argument for Investing in Young Children*. http://jenni.uchicago.edu/human-inequality/papers/heckman_final_all_wp_2007-03-22c_jsb.pdf

Heymann, J. (2003) *The Role of ECCE in Ensuring Equal Opportunity*, Policy brief no 18. Paris: UNESCO.

Heymann, J. (2006) *Forgotten Families: Ending the Growing Confrontation of Children and Parents in the Global Economy*. Oxford: Oxford University Press.

Jenson, J. (2008) Writing women out, folding gender in: the European Union 'modernises' social policy, *Social Politics*, 15(2): 131–153.

Johnson, D., Jaeger, E., Randolph, S., Cauce, A., Ward, J. and the National Institute of Child Health and Human Development Early Child Care Research Network (2003) Studying the effects of early child care experiences on the development of children of color in the United States: towards a more inclusive research agenda, *Child Development*, 74(5): 1227–1244.

Jones, N. with Villar, E. (2008) Situating children in international development policy: challenges involved in successful evidence-informed policy making, *Evidence and Policy*, 4(1): 31–51.

Kilburn, M. and Karoly, C. (2008) *The Economics of Early Childhood Policy: What the Dismal Science has to say about Investing in Children*, Labour and Population Series Occasional Paper. Santa Monica, CA: The Rand Corporation.

Lloyd, E., Penn, H., Barreau, S., Burton, V., Davis, R., Potter, S. and Sayeed, Z. (2005) *How Effective are Measures Taken to Mitigate the Impact of Direct Experience of Armed Conflict on the Psychosocial and Cognitive Development of Children Aged 0–8?* Research Evidence in Education Library. London: EPPI-Centre, Social Science Research Unit, Institute of Education.

Marope, M.T. (2005) *Namibia: Human Capital and Knowledge Development for Economic Growth with Equity*. Africa Region Human Development Working Paper Series no. 84. Washington, DC: World Bank Africa Region Human Development Department.

OECD (2006) *Starting Strong II: Early Childhood Education and Care*. Paris: OECD.

OECD (2008) *Growing Unequal? Income Distribution and Poverty in OECD Countries*. Paris: OECD.

Penn, H. (2005) *Unequal Childhoods: Young Children's Lives in Poor Countries*. London: Routledge.

Penn, H. (2008a) Working on the impossible: early childhood policies in Namibia, *Childhood*, 15(3): 378–398.

Penn, H. (2008b) *Early Childhood Education and Care in Southern Africa: A Perspective Piece*. Reading: CfBT Educational Trust.

Penn, H. and Lloyd, E. (2007) Richness or rigour? A discussion of systematic reviews and evidence based policy in early childhood, *Contemporary Issues in Early Childhood*, (8)1: 3–18.

Penn, H. and Maynard, T. (2009) *Siyabonana: We All See One Another. Early Childhood in South Africa*, International Perspectives series. Edinburgh: Children in Scotland (forthcoming).

Penn, H., Burton, V., Lloyd, E., Mugford, M., Potter, S. and Sayeed, Z. (2006) *Systematic Review of the Economic Impact of Long-Term Centre-Based Early Childhood Interventions*. Research Evidence in Education Library. London: Social Science Research Unit, Institute of Education. www.eppi.ioe.ac.uk

Perry, M. and Albee, G. (1994) On the science of prevention, *American Psychologist*, 49(12): 1087–1088.

Ramey, C.T., Campbell, F.A., Burchinal, M., Skinner, M.L., Gardner, D.M. and Ramey, S.L. (2000) Persistent effects of early intervention on high-risk children and their mothers, *Applied Developmental Science*, 4: 2–14.

Reynolds, A.J. (2000) *Success in Early Intervention: The Chicago Child–Parent Centers*. Lincoln, NE: University of Nebraska Press.

Rosaldo, R. (1993) *Culture and Truth: The Remaking of Social Analysis*. London: Routledge.

Save US (2008) *Our Programs around the World: ECD*. http://www.savethechildren.org/programs/education/early-childhood-development.html

Schweinhart, L.J. (2003) Benefits, Costs and Explanation of the High/Scope Perry Pre-school Program. Paper presented at the biennial meeting of the Society for Research in Child Development, Tampa, Florida, April 2003.

Sen, A. (1999) *Development as Freedom*. Oxford: Oxford University Press.

Steiner Khasi, G. (2004) *The Global Politics of Educational Borrowing and Lending*. New York: Teachers College Press.

Tinker, J. (2007) Should we dump the North–South lens?, *Drum Beat 401*, 2 July. www.comminit.com/drum_beat401.html

UN Committee on the Rights of the Child (2005) *Implementing Child Rights in Early Childhood*, General Comment No. 7. New York: United Nations.

UNESCO (2007) *Education for All Global Monitoring Report 2007: Strong Foundations*. Paris: UNESCO.

UNESCO (2009) *Education for All Global Monitoring Report 2009: Overcoming Inequality: Why Governance Matters*. Paris: UNESCO.

UNFPA (United Nations Population Fund) (2007) *State of the World's Population. Unleashing the Potential of Urban Growth*. New York: UNFPA.

UNFPA (United Nations Population Fund) (2008) *State of the World's Population 2008. Reaching Common Ground: Reconciling Culture, Gender and Human Rights*. New York: UNFPA.

UNICEF (2003) *The Best Start for Every Child*. www.unicef.org/earlychildhood/files/CARD_early_childhoodENG.pdf

UNICEF (2007) *Innocenti Report Card 2007. Child Poverty in Perspective: An Overview of Child Well-Being in Rich Countries*. Florence: UNICEF/IRC.

UNICEF (2008) *Innocenti Report Card 2008. The Childcare Transition: A League Table of Early Education and Care in Economically Advanced Countries*. Florence: UNICEF/IRC.

Weikart, D.P. (ed.) (1967) *Preschool Interventions: Preliminary Results of the Perry Preschool Project*. Ann Arbor, MI: Campus Publishers.

World Bank (2008) *ECD Calculator*. http://go.worldbank.org/KHC1NHO580

Zigler, E. (2003) Forty years of believing in magic is enough, *Social Policy Report*, XVII(1): 10.

5 Reframing rights: poverty discourse and children's lives in the United States

Valerie Polakow

> Where, after all, do universal human rights begin? In small places, close to home – so close and so small that they cannot be seen on any map of the world. Yet they *are* the world of the individual person: the neighborhood he lives in; the school or college he attends; the factory, farm or office where he works. Such are the places where every man, woman, and child seeks equal justice, equal opportunity, equal dignity without discrimination. Unless these rights have meaning there, they have little meaning anywhere.
> – Eleanor Roosevelt, address to UN Commission on Human Rights, 1958

It is ironic that the United States, represented by Eleanor Roosevelt, played such a critical and determinative role in creating the Universal Declaration of Human Rights on 10 December 1948 – articulating and affirming the inalienable rights and freedoms of all human beings across the globe. Yet, more than a half-century later, the United States has still not ratified the central human rights treaty affirming children's rights, the United Nations Convention on the Rights of the Child (CRC) adopted in 1989. With the highest child poverty rates among wealthy, industrialized countries, the United States has failed to recognize fundamental provisions of the CRC, affirming children as 'rights-bearers': specifically economic, social, and cultural rights (article 4), children forming and expressing their own views (articles 12 and 13), the establishment of institutions, facilities, and social programmes for support of children, and the right to child care (article 18), rights and access to services for *all* children with special needs (article 23), access to and quality of health care (article 24), rights to social insurance and social security (article 26), equality of opportunity in education (article 28), and rights to youth justice, with an explicit ban on life imprisonment for children under 18 (article 37) (United Nations, 1989).

While the focus of this chapter is on poverty and children's rights, with particular emphasis on policies and practices within the United States, poverty is a global crisis of acute proportions. Yet, it is apparent that the field of early childhood pays relatively little attention to poverty and how it is manifested in the lives of young children and their families. Discussions around poverty have made few inroads into the progressive educational literature on educational change, the critical analysis of race and class, post-structuralist interrogations of power, identity and curriculum, and the work of the reconceptualists. However, it is essential that material and social conditions are understood in the daily context of young lives; for poverty maps the pathways of childhood, shaping terrains of possibility, or violated rights and eroded human capabilities.

Poverty in global context

Global poverty is an acute crisis facing more than 1 billion people – 1.2 billion live on less than $1 a day – fully 22 per cent of the world's population (United Nations, 2000). For women and children, the crisis is particularly acute, as poverty continues to be a gendered crisis in many parts of the world. Women's lives are inextricably bound *by* and *to* their children's lives; thus, confronting female poverty also reduces child poverty. The *Global Study on Child Poverty and Disparities* (UNICEF, 2007) reports that women and children are frequently left out of development initiatives, and women's struggles to juggle both work and child care responsibilities have not been recognized as priority agendas in the global fight to eradicate poverty and illiteracy. Further, the *Global Study* stresses the importance of targeted support for families, prioritizing social protection measures that promote family stability and economic survival, and emphasizes the role that childhood plays in the development of human capabilities which, in turn, shape national human capital. Nussbaum, who frames global justice and the rights of women in terms of a human capabilities approach, points out that whenever 'poverty combines with gender inequality, the result is acute failure of central human capabilities' (Nussbaum, 2000: 3).

In the case of children – whose human capabilities are in formation and whose development is threatened by vast gaps in inequality and consequent lack of resources for daily living – becoming an agent of one's life requires rights and, when those rights are absent, human capabilities cannot be fully realized. The global commitment by UNICEF to prioritize child poverty and advocacy for children's rights is shaped by the CRC, and the current *Global Study* encompasses forty countries, analysing the impact of economic and social policies on child outcomes grounded in context-specific evidence (UNICEF, 2007).

Child poverty rates in wealthy industrialized countries are also sobering, with the United States ranking last among the 24 OECD nations (Innocenti Research Centre, 2007). The UK ranks a close 23rd, and, despite the Labour government's pledge under former Prime Minister Tony Blair to end child poverty by 2020 and to cut child poverty by half by 2010, that goal is far from being met. However, the 2003 Green Paper *Every Child Matters* and the Children's Act of 2004 do create an explicit recognition and commitment to a public policy agenda that calls for accountability in meeting those goals – a commitment that, currently, just does not exist in the United States. While globalization and the development of neoliberal market-based policies and rising xenophobia towards immigrants and the Roma have impacted policy and practice in Europe, core children's policies remain embedded in EU legislation. The European Forum on the Rights of the Child has made distinctive efforts to craft social and educational policies, including early childhood and youth policies, in close alignment with the CRC. At the second meeting in Brussels in 2008, the European Forum's focus was on child poverty and social exclusion and the development of coordinated EU actions with comprehensive national plans to safeguard the rights of children with a stated intent of 'overcoming children's invisibility and marginalization and in achieving tangible progress in the realization of their rights' (Pais, 2008). The Social Protection Committee on Child Poverty and Child Well-Being addresses the urgency of child poverty and argues that child poverty has an 'inherent relationship' with citizenship and the realization of democracy, noting that a total of 19 million children live under the poverty threshold in the 27 countries of the EU (EU Task-Force, 2008: 13).[1] Among EU countries, Sweden, Denmark and Finland come out on top, with the most successful outcomes in combating child poverty, whereas Italy, Portugal, Romania, Lithuania and Poland have the highest child poverty rates, with Poland's close to 30 per cent (EU Task-Force, 2008). Poverty is particularly marked among immigrant, refugee, and Roma children as well as in isolated rural areas.

While the EU has made concerted efforts in addressing child poverty across the 27 member states, there has not been adequate attention paid to the 'multidimensional facets' of poverty; for poverty should not only be viewed as income related, but it also needs to be understood in terms of the all-encompassing impact on children's lives. It is also important that children's own perceptions of their material conditions and well-being are taken into account, in order to develop a children's rights framework for the understanding and analysis of poverty (Pais, 2008).

The Nordic countries, with their strong equality commitments and comprehensive social care infrastructures, promote child well-being and the balancing of work and family life, with clear benefits for women and children. These countries also rank at the top of OECD nations, with the lowest child poverty rates among 24 wealthy, industrialized nations (Innocenti Research Centre, 2007: Ostner and Schmitt, 2008).

There is a growing awareness across the globe that children's well-being is integrally intertwined with the well-being of their mothers, and that changing gender roles herald greater promise of reducing family and child poverty. In wealthy, industrialized societies, particularly among OECD countries, employed women create greater long-term stability for families, investing them with social insurance through insurance-based benefits and social supports such as child care and maternity and parental leave. Based on the 2002 European Council of Barcelona recommendations, explicit priorities were developed for child care expansion of facilities serving infants through school-age children. Scandinavia's family and child entitlements are consistently cited as a model of workable universalism, and demonstrate long-term, positive consequences for children in terms of their well-being and their educational achievement. Universal access to child care, after-school care, and child and youth interventions, shaped around the central precepts of the CRC, create a set of fundamental social rights for children, despite global countervailing trends towards increasing privatization.

Social citizenship rights and poverty discourse

Rights of universal access, frequently referred to as 'social citizenship' rights, are considered the foundation upon which sustainable policies and practices are built that best serve vulnerable populations. As British sociologist T.S. Marshall wrote in the late 1940s, *all* citizens should have a claim to 'the social heritage' and 'an absolute right to a certain standard of civilization' (1963: 72, 98), and his principles of social citizenship are embedded in the social and economic rights of modern welfare states. Yet, the United States has never embedded social and economic rights in federal public policy. Roosevelt's 1944 proposed Second Bill of Rights argued for economic security and 'freedom from want', stating that the nation 'cannot be content . . . if some fraction of our people – whether it be one-third or one-fifth or one-tenth – is ill-fed, ill-clothed, ill-housed, and insecure' (quoted in Sunstein, 2004: 12). Yet Roosevelt's Second Bill of Rights, which, in essence, was an economic Bill of Rights, never came to fruition in the United States. Most of what was embedded in Roosevelt's Second Bill of Rights was, ironically, enacted in Europe after the Second World War, and assisted in large measure by US funds from the Marshall economic recovery programme, also known as the Marshall Plan.[2]

But, as Fraser and Gordon (1992) point out, social citizenship has never found a foothold in the United States – with its communitarian ideals of social solidarity and entitlement to a set of universal services and provisions that guarantee a minimally decent life. Social citizenship rights are also critical gendered rights; for such rights guarantee 'a positive state' for women and their children (Hobson and Lister, 2002) through the creation of policies that sustain families such as universal child care and paid family leave policies, making possible the combining of work and family life. Esping-Andersen (1990) characterizes social citizenship rights in advanced capitalist societies by their degrees of *decommodification*, the extent to which citizens are not dependent on the vicissitudes of the market, but rather are protected by stable and universal entitlements within their own societies.

Yet, in contrast to most countries in northern and western Europe, Canada, Australia and New Zealand, in the United States there is no commitment to the establishment of social citizenship rights, or to the affirmative obligations engendered by the CRC. The EU emphasis on social inclusion, equality, and expanded access to child care services for infants and children in alignment with the CRC is absent; as is any public discourse about social citizenship rights. At the time of writing, health care as a right versus the 'right' to health insurance, is being hotly debated in the United States. Yet despite the promise of transformative change by the incoming Obama Administration, health care as a right may well disappear into the corporate tentacles of the health insurance industry that is currently lobbying hard, together with Republicans and some 'centrist' Democrats, against any notion of a public plan (*New York Times*, 2009). Health care, like child care and paid maternity and parental leave, is part of an explicit commitment to children's rights and well-being, but we, in the United States, take little public responsibility for children. Left to the ravages of the 'free' marketplace, poor families and their children either sink or swim depending on the geography of poverty and its reach.

Davis and Powell (2003) argue that US domestic policies, deeply embedded in US 'exceptionalism', transgress international norms, making the United States an outlier in the community of nations. Such policy care deficits stand in stark contrast to 'universal childcare and paid parental leaves, available to parents in other countries around the globe . . . the United States has yet to make a commitment to U.S. families by enacting policies that adequately address the care of children' (Davis and Powell, 2003: 711).

In the absence of any framework for social citizenship rights, the United States has long been trapped in a 'charity versus contract' discourse (Fraser and Gordon, 1992); and the discourse about poor people and poor women in particular has been framed around a rhetoric of dependence. Prior to the draconian PRWORA welfare legislation of 1996,[3] pernicious debates about single mothers' alleged promiscuity and work-averse behaviour were the wellspring of public discourse, and led to brutal proposals of family caps (no more welfare assistance for additional children born to women on welfare), and welfare-to-work legislation – a form of indentured servitude – as poor single mothers were forced into the workplace in many states when their infants were just 12 weeks old, in order to collect benefits (Kahn and Polakow, 2004). As Mink remarked, the 1996 legislation 'remove[d] poor single mothers from a welfare state to a police state' (1998: 133) and, during the 1990s, a racialised discourse of shaming and blaming constructed single mothers as the face of the new family values/moral threat. If only better mothering were in place, less promiscuity, a greater work-ethic, more taking of personal responsibility – poor children, it seemed, would cope with their poverty in more compliant and adaptable ways. A clear demarcation was drawn between the deserving and the undeserving poor. Women receiving welfare clearly fell into the latter category, whereas their children occupied a dubious, middle space.

Tainted as the unsuitable heads of undeserving families, with charity or indentured servitude as their due, welfare-reliant mothers of poor children have been the targets of increasingly vicious public attacks variously depicted as 'the locus of a kind of moral rot' (Piven, 1995: xiii). Hence made-in-America poverty was transformed into an interpersonal or psychological pathology; but absent was any serious, structural critique of inequality, the terrors of neighbourhood violence, the traumas of homelessness, the lead-poisoning in dilapidated urban tenements, the lack of access to any resources, the utility shut-offs, the evictions, the punitive welfare sanctions that cut off assistance, the low-wage jobs that despite full-time work kept a family in poverty, the lack of child care – all this and more was ignored in favour of a punitive and retributive discourse that was soaked in a toxic 'othering' – with a striking resemblance to the construction of the colonized, subaltern other.

Poor children, described as innocent and in need of better parenting, yet viewed as future predators and potential criminals, have been commodified by an instrumentalist cost–benefit discourse that dominates policy decision making about poverty and child care in the United States. Hence assistance and intervention for children have never been premised on rights or on children's daily existential needs, but rather on a crass and heartless instrumentalism – 'invest now or pay later' is the dominant mantra for early intervention. Nobel economist Heckman argues for early intervention to remediate the 'constellation of pathologies' associated with young, uneducated teen mothers, and suggests that redirecting funds away from K-12 education to early intervention represents a 'sound investment in the productivity and safety of our society' (Heckman and Masterov, 2004: 17, 3). The plethora of early childhood studies (Barnett, 1998; Helburn, 1995) citing the positive outcomes of early childhood education for children also stress the 'investment and prevention' aspect, claiming that longitudinal results (see Schweinhart, 2004) decrease crime, reduce teen pregnancy and alleviate a host of other social ills.

There is no doubt that investing in the social and educational capital of poor children yields positive outcomes; but should that be the dominant motive? And if there are no tangible positive outcomes that can be quantified, is it then not worth investing in the early lives of other people's poor young children? Should not *all* children have rights to a safe, nurturing, educationally enriching environment that affirms and celebrates their development? Spaces for play and exploration and freedom to express their growing understanding and give meaning to their world? Spaces that affirm their rights? Until child poverty eradication and access to child care in the United States are framed around a concept of rights, budget exigencies and state shortfalls will always wipe out social programmes; for they are the first to be cut, as reflected in the deepening current crisis (Lav and McNichol, 2009).

Rapidly increasing unemployment (now almost 10 per cent), widespread mortgage foreclosures, rising homelessness and destitution, and loss of health care all continue to hit American families. President Obama's massive $787 billion stimulus package has created wide-ranging opportunities for housing and foreclosure relief, infrastructure development, and $44 billion to states and local communities for educational reform (US Department of Education, 2009). However, the stimulus package is considered too little and too business-friendly by many critics on the left, who are urging the Obama Administration to take further bold steps, despite the pervasive anti-regulatory and anti-big-government rhetoric (Krugman, 2009). The unwillingness to publicly call for a radical redistribution of wealth amid soaring inequality is a far cry from Roosevelt's fundamental belief that 'increasing the opportunities and wealth of poor people, might be necessary to protect rights' (Sunstein, 2004: 28).

Child poverty and its reach in the United States

Child poverty constitutes a public assault on children; and in a wealthy power-ful nation such as the United States, a persistent shaming of democratic ideals. Over 13 million children live in poverty – with 5.8 million living in extreme poverty in households with incomes less than half of the federal poverty line (Children's Defense Fund, 2008a); and almost 29 million live in low-income families. Because of the artificially low and outdated US poverty measure (Lin and Bernstein, 2008; Fass, 2009), families with incomes between 100 per cent and 200 per cent of the federal poverty line are not officially classified as poor, although by European standards of relative poverty (less than 50 per cent of the national median) they clearly would be.

The 2009 federal poverty line is calculated at $18,310 for a family of three, and $22,050 for a family of four (US Department of Health and Human Services, 2009); yet family budget measures, developed by the Economic Policy Insti-tute, are a far more accurate indicator of poverty, and roughly correspond to 200 per cent of the federal poverty line. High numbers of children live in single female-headed households, with 57.1 per cent of single parents with three children, and 33.8 per cent with two children below the federal poverty line. But, as Lin and Bernstein (2008) show, if more realistic family budget measures were used, the actual percentage of single-parent households in poverty would be closer to 92 per cent and 74.7 per cent respectively; hence the widespread feminization of poverty in the United States.

Children of colour are also disproportionately poor: 60 per cent of Black and Latino children, and 57 per cent of American Indian children live in low-income families in comparison to 26 per cent of White children and 30 per cent of Asian children. Being an immigrant child also increases the risk of poverty: 58 per cent of children whose parents are immigrants, live in poverty. Age is also a clear risk factor, with 43 per cent of infants and toddlers under 3 years living in low-income households (Fass and Cauthen, 2009). With 12.4 million children estimated to be hungry or living on the edge of hunger, and 23 per cent of homeless children not attending school on a regular basis, children and youth have become the most vulnerable subgroup in the United States, and chronic poverty threatens their well-being and healthy development (Fass and Cauthen, 2008; Food Research and Action Center, 2008; National Coalition for the Homeless, 2008).

Child care and poverty

As demand for child care increased exponentially following the PRWORA welfare legislation of 1996, poor women were forced into the low-wage workforce with few good choices for child care, as state welfare-to-work programmes engaged in a race to the bottom to provide the cheapest of subsidized care (Boushey and Wright, 2004; Carlson and Sharf, 2004; Kahn and Polakow, 2004; Polakow, 2007). Since the recession in the United Sates, many of these low-wage jobs have dried up – leaving poor women as single heads of households with few resources in a radically altered de-welfared state. Hence young children in poverty face an acute unmet crisis of child care needs. Low-income mothers face cost and access barriers; they have few good affordable choices in poor neighbourhoods, and, due to their odd-hour work schedules which are characteristic of low-wage jobs, stable and good-quality child care arrangements are difficult to come by (Presser and Cox, 1997; Chaudry, 2004). One-third of employed mothers with incomes below the poverty line, and over 25 per cent of employed mothers with incomes below $25,000, have non-traditional odd-hour shifts, including weekends (Vandell and Wolfe, 2000).

In my own recent research on the national child care crisis, low-income (mostly single) mothers struggled to juggle work and parenting and frequently encountered inflexible workplaces leaving them to craft desperate and unsatisfactory child care arrangements for their young children. One mother in my study, whose 4-year-old daughter was cycled through four low-quality child care settings within a year and expelled from another centre due to behavioural 'meltdowns', was under constant threat of losing her job and destabilizing her family. With few good choices to make in the best interests of her daughter, Chiquila was forced to maintain unmanageable hours at a fast-food chain remarking that Wendy's (the restaurant chain) was not 'a job that had any compassion' (Polakow, 2007: 98) as she struggled to work a full-time odd-hour schedule, including Friday and Saturday evenings from 4 pm to 1 am, requiring another set of unstable secondary child care arrangements which further traumatized her young daughter. In yet another story of the bitter struggle to find affordable child care, Kim, a working solo mother attending college with dreams of becoming a lawyer, just could not make it as she worked and struggled to attend college: 'Everybody loses ... I mean the bottom line here is that you don't get adequate child care because you can't afford it – that's poverty – that's just a domino effect of poverty (Polakow, 2007: 59).

With no national child care system in place, and large numbers of women with children in the labour force: 74.3 per cent of mothers with children aged 6–17 years, 59.6 per cent with children under 6 years, and 55.4 per cent with children under 3 years (US Department of Labor, 2008a,b), child care is both a children's rights issue and a women's rights issue. With over 12 million children in some form of public or private child care, including 6 million under 3 years, the crisis of affordable, quality child care adversely affects the development of infants and children, as well as the economic independence and well-being of their mothers. Only 14 per cent of income-eligible families actually receive state child care subsidies to pay the high costs of care, which range from $4,000 to $15,000 a year for full-time infants and toddlers, and close to $11,000 a year for preschool children. Child care costs are so high that they exceed the cost of college tuition in over thirty states at most public universities (Children's Defense Fund, 2005, 2008b; National Association of Child Care Resources and Referral Agencies, 2008). Subsidies, pegged at 75 per cent of market rates, do not pay the full cost of quality care and there are thousands of children on subsidy waiting lists across the United States (Carlson and Sharf, 2004; Schulman and Blank, 2005; Children's Defense Fund, 2008b). While costs are considerably cheaper in small family day care homes, many of these facilities are unlicensed, and lack of regulation and monitoring substantially increases the risks for young children (Helburn and Bergmann, 2002; Polakow, 2007).

The developmental damage to young children caused by indifferent or abusive care is yet to be documented; but the reports that have been published are not encouraging. The Cost, Quality, and Child Outcomes study (Helburn, 1995) conducted in the 1990s, raised red flags about poor quality care; yet over a decade later the problems persist for the majority of poor children. In that study, only 8 per cent of infant centres were rated as good, and over 40 per cent were evaluated as *less than minimal quality*. Of particular concern is the care meted out to infants and toddlers who are most susceptible to early damage. The formation of healthy and stable relationships with caregivers, language and motor development, identity and agency, are all impacted by shoddy and inferior care. Toxic experiences in early childhood that combine the stresses of poverty with indifferent or damaging care have the potential to produce long-lasting damage to social, emotional, cognitive and physiological health (National Scientific Council on the Developing Child, 2007). Conversely, the positive outcomes of high quality interventions in the lives of vulnerable, poor children have been documented for decades, and point to long-term benefits in terms of social, emotional, and academic development (Barnett, 1998; Peisner-Feinberg et al., 1999; Schweinhart, 2004).

While high quality 'Cadillac' care can be purchased on the private market for affluent children, child care deficits produce early and long-lasting inequalities for the children of the poor. As 'cheap' children, they frequently spend their days in the worst of child care settings, with over one-third in the unregulated sector (Helburn and Bergmann, 2002). Access to public programmes is also restricted – as demand exceeds supply, and availability is regulated by cost constraints so that only 15 per cent of income-eligible 3-year-olds and 38.8 per cent of 4-year-olds are enrolled in Head Start, pre-kindergarten or special education early intervention programmes (Children's Defense Fund, 2008b).

For school-age children, life in impoverished communities may mean enduring the daily dangers of street and community violence, under-resourced and inferior schools, and isolation from networks of support, creating further conditions of social toxicity (Garbarino, 1995). School-age children and youth are less likely to be enrolled in after-school programmes, limiting their exposure to after-school activities, clubs, sports and enrichment activities which play a large role in building social capital among isolated and marginalized children, leading to enhanced academic achievement, a sense of well-being and connectedness, and positive peer and adult relationships (Maeroff, 1998; Children's Defense Fund, 2003). But the school lives of poor school-age children and youth (particularly those of colour) are characterized by high drop-out rates, low graduation rates, disproportionate expulsions and unmet special education needs. As growing numbers of youth (disproportionately African American and Latino) enter the criminal justice systems to face 'adult time for adult crime', prison budgets have increased with corresponding decreases in education and mental health budgets, resulting in the development of an unprecedented youth incarceration industry (Zweifler and DeBeers, 2002; Barton, 2005; Human Rights Watch and Amnesty International, 2005).

It is, after all, a question of which children matter? Poor children certainly count for less. Poor children have no *rights* to a decent life – neither their human capabilities nor their social citizenship rights are affirmed or enshrined in current US policies – and there are no binding legal restraints to prevent the redirection of scarce resources away from those who are most in need. In short, there is little redress for poverty as a violation of human rights. As Paul Krugman comments: 'Now we have another, even more compelling reason to be ashamed about America's record of failing to fight poverty . . . To be poor in

America today, even more than in the past, is to be an outcast in your own country' (Krugman, 2008).

Whither children's rights in the United States?

Davis (2005) argues that international treaties such as the Convention on the Rights of the Child, the Convention on the Elimination of All Forms of Discrimination, and the Universal Declaration of Human Rights, have the potential to produce paradigm shifts in the way we think about poverty and rights and to create possibilities for realization of those rights in both local and legal contexts. Despite not having ratified the Convention on the Rights of the Child, the US Supreme Court nevertheless found the death penalty unconstitutional for juveniles, citing the influence of international treaties. Davis also points out that many state constitutions, unlike the federal constitution, contain affirmative obligations, such as positive rights to education and welfare, and, in some states, a right to health care (Davis, 2005). Similarly, she argues that international treaties could be used to hold states accountable for protecting basic human rights. This strategy, now in its early stages, has been used by the Kensington Welfare Rights Union, the Economic Human Rights Documentation project and others, with a focus on bringing poverty to international visibility (Davis, 2005; Neubeck, 2006). Furthermore, the doctrine of human rights is universal and transcends national boundaries and sovereignty. Those countries that have ratified international human rights treaties take seriously the affirmative obligations and commitments to rights engendered by such treaties.

As we think about reframing the field of early childhood, we might ask why issues of child poverty and children's rights have not featured as a central and urgent focus of concern? Here, I reflect specifically on the reconceptualizing movement in the United States where, with some notable exceptions – such as the work of colleagues Beth Swadener and Lourdes Diaz Soto who have made social justice and rights, including poverty, a central theme of their work – there has been little emphasis on poor and vulnerable children and youth. This needs to change, and we must ask how we can advance the social justice agenda for all children, particularly those who are most vulnerable to the ravages of poverty.

The dominant discourses in early childhood, including the reconceptualist narrative, have failed to take account of the centrality of poverty in young children's lives on a global scale. Deconstructing interventionist discourses, for example, may speak to the surveillance technologies of a postmodern neoliberal welfare state; but what about the consequences of an absence of intervention in a radically de-welfared state such as the United States? There needs to be a recognition of the centrality of human rights and of what it means for children and their childhoods when their fundamental rights are violated.

How does one fight for children's rights without intervention discourses when intervention and advocacy are inextricably woven together? How does one use one's 'expert' power on behalf of, *with* and *for* those who have been disempowered? Creating networks of allies to fight for fundamental rights requires a critical interrogation and transformative set of practices that move beyond current post-structuralist, reconceptualizing and decolonizing theories. Clearly, the question of rights is mired in clashes between the emancipatory and the traditional, and the legacies of colonialism and western democratic liberal ideals of individual rights. But cultural and religious values and national sovereignty are not sacrosanct; they are also used as covers for patriarchal control of women and children – child trafficking, genital cutting, child marriage, lack of education for girls, economic and domestic oppression of women – issues that extend far beyond the scope of this chapter; yet these are issues that also require critical interrogation as part of children's rights.

Poverty matters. Discourses matter. Policies matter. Reframing discourses about poverty and creating momentum for recognition of children's rights are central to the transformation of the early childhood field in the United States. Recognition and affirmation of children's rights require that urgent attention be paid to poverty and the social suffering of the young. International human rights law and the commitments to social and global justice are a place to begin the transformative struggle for the realization of rights. Poverty is central to that struggle.

As John Steinbeck so powerfully reminds us in *The Grapes of Wrath*:

> The decay spreads over the State, and the sweet smell is a great sorrow on the land . . .
>
> (Steinbeck, 1967 [1939]: 384)

Child poverty has no place in wealthy, industrialized nations. Affirming children as 'rights bearers' requires an on-the-ground universal commitment to respecting and dignifying childhood as a landscape of voice and agency. Reframing current poverty discourse in a language of rights is an urgent policy agenda for the United States and other nations across the globe; for economic and social rights are central to democracy's as yet unrealized ideals. Children's rights do, indeed, begin in 'small places, close to home'.

Notes

1. In the EU the 'poverty risk threshold is set at 60% of the national median equivalised household income' (EU Task-Force, 2008: 12).

2. George C. Marshall was President Truman's Secretary of State.
3. The Personal Responsibility and Work Opportunity Reconciliation Act, referred to as welfare reform, was signed into law 26 August 1996 by President Clinton.

References

Barnett, W.S. (1998) Long-term effects on cognitive development and school success. In W.S. Barnett and S.S. Boocock (eds), *Early Care and Education for Children in Poverty: Promises, Programs, and Long-Term Results* (pp. 11–44). Albany, NY: State University of New York Press.

Barton, P. (2005) *One-Third of a Nation: Rising Dropout Rates and Declining Opportunities*. Washington, DC: Educational Testing Service Policy Information Center. http://ets.org/Media/Education_Topics/pdf/onethird.pdf (accessed 10 July 2009).

Boushey, H. and Wright, J. (2004) *Working Moms and Child Care*, No. 3. Washington, DC: Center for Economic and Policy Research. http://www.cepr.net/index.php/publications/reports/working-moms-and-child-care/ (accessed 10 September 2008).

Carlson, B. C. and Scharf, R. (2004) *Lost in the Maze: Reforming New York City's Fragmented Child Care Subsidy System*. New York: Welfare Law Center.

Chaudry, A. (2004) *Putting Children First: How Low-Wage Working Mothers Manage Child Care*. New York: Russell Sage Foundation.

Children's Defense Fund (2003) *School-Age Child Care: Keeping Children Safe and Helping Them Learn while their Families Work*. Washington, DC: Children's Defense Fund.

Children's Defense Fund (2005) *Child Care Basics 2005*. http://www.childrens-defense.org/site/DocServer/child_care_basics_2005.pdf (accessed 10 November 2008).

Children's Defense Fund (2008a) *Children in the United States*. http://www.childrensdefense.org/child-research-data-publications/data/state-data-repository/cits/children-in-the-states-2008-all.pdf (accessed 5 July 2009).

Children's Defense Fund (2008b) *The State of America's Children 2008*. http://www.childrensdefense.org/child-research-data-publications/data/state-of-americas-children-2008-report.html (accessed 5 July 2009).

Davis, M. (2005) International human rights from the ground up: the potential for subnational, human rights-based reproductive health advocacy in the United States. In W. Chavkin and E. Chesler (eds), *Where Human Rights Begin: Health, Sexuality, and Women in the New Millennium* (pp. 235–269). Piscataway, NJ: Rutgers University Press.

Davis, M. and Powell, R. (2003) The international convention on the rights of the child: a catalyst for innovative child care policies. *Human Rights Quarterly*, 25(3): 689–719.

Esping-Anderson, G. (1990) *The Three Worlds of Welfare Capitalism*. Cambridge: Polity Press.

EU Task-Force on Child Poverty and Child Well-Being (2008) *Child Poverty and Well-Being in the EU: Current Status and Way Forward*. Brussels: European Commission. http://ec.europa.eu/employment_social/spsi/docs/social_inclusion/2008/child_poverty_en.pdf

Fass, S. (2009) *Measuring Poverty in the United States*. National Center for Children in Poverty. http://www.nccp.org/publications/pub_876.html (accessed 10 July 2009).

Fass, S. and Cauthen, N. (2008) Who are America's poor children? National Center for Children in Poverty. http://www.nccp.org/publications/pub_843.html (accessed 10 July 2009).

Fass, S. and Cauthen, N. (2009) *What is the Nature of Poverty and Economic Hardship in the United States*? National Center for Children in Poverty. http://www.nccp.org/publications/pub_829.html (accessed 10 July 2009).

Food Research and Action Center (2008) *Hunger in the US*. http://www.frac.org/html/hunger_in_the_us/hunger_index.html (accessed 7 July 2009).

Fraser, N. and Gordon, L. (1992) Contract versus charity: why is there no social citizenship in the United States? *Socialist Review*, 22, 45–68.

Garbarino, J. (1995) *Raising Children in a Socially Toxic Environment*. San Francisco: Jossey-Bass.

Heckman, J.J. and Masterov, D.V. (2004) *The Productivity Argument for Investing in Young Children*, No. 5. Washington, DC: Committee for Economic Development.

Helburn, S.W. (ed.) (1995) *Cost, Quality and Child Outcomes in Child Care Centers*, Technical Report ED 386 297. Denver, CO: Center for Research in Economic and Social Policy, University of Colorado.

Helburn, S.W. and Bergmann, B. (2002) *America's Child Care Problem: The Way Out*. New York: Palgrave Macmillan.

Hobson, B. and Lister, R. (2002) Citizenship. In B. Hobson, J. Lewis and B. Siim (eds), *Contested Concept in Gender and Social Politics* (pp. 23–54). Cheltenham: Edward Elgar.

Human Rights Watch and Amnesty International (2005) *The Rest of their Lives: Life without Parole for Child Offenders in the United States*. http://hrw.org/reports/2005/us1005/ (accessed 9 January 2009).

Innocenti Research Centre (2007) *Child Poverty in Perspective: An Overview of Child Well-Being in Rich Countries*. www.unicef-irc.org (accessed 15 September 2008).

Kahn, P. and Polakow, V. (2004) That's not how I want to live: student mothers fight to stay in school under Michigan's welfare-to-work regime. In V. Polakow, S. Butler, L. Deprez and P. Kahgn (eds), *Shut Out: Low Income Mothers and Higher Education in Post-Welfare America* (pp. 75–96). Albany, NY: State University of New York Press.

Krugman, P. (2008) Poverty is poison, *New York Times*, 18 February. http://www.nytimes.com/2008/02/18/opinion/18krugman.html (accessed 20 September 2008).

Krugman, P. (2009) The stimulus trap, *New York Times*, 9 July. http://www.nytimes.com/2009/07/10/opinion/10krugman.html (accessed 9 July 2009).

Lav, I.J. and McNichol, E. (2009) *State Budget Troubles Worsen*. Washington, DC: Center on Budget and Policy Priorities. http://www.cbpp.org/cms/index.cfm?fa=view&id=711 (accessed 10 July 2009).

Lin, J. and Bernstein, J. (2008) *What We Need to Get By*, Briefing Paper No. 224. Washington, DC: Economic Policy Institute. http://www.epi.org/content.cfm/bp224 (accessed 1 November 2008).

Maeroff, G. (1998) *Altered Destinies: Making Life Better for Schoolchildren in Need*. New York: St Martins Griffin.

Marshall, T. H. (1963) Citizenship and social class. In *Sociology at the Crossroads and Other Essays* (pp. 66–127). London: Heinemann.

Mink, G. (1998) *Welfare's End*. Ithaca, NY: Cornell University Press.

National Association of Child Care Resources and Referral Agencies (NACCRRA) (2008) *Parents and the High Price of Child Care: 2008 Update*. http://www.naccrra.org/ (accessed 21 November 2008).

National Coalition for the Homeless (2008) *How Many People Experience Homelessness?*, NCH Fact Sheet No. 2. http://www.nationalhomeless.org/publications/facts/How_Many.html (accessed 20 November 2008).

National Scientific Council on the Developing Child (2007) *The Science of Early Childhood Development: Closing the Gap between What we Know and What we Do*. http://www.developingchild.net/ (accessed 29 June 2009).

Neubeck, K.J. (2006) *When Welfare Disappears: The Case for Economic and Human Rights*. New York: Routledge.

New York Times (2009) Editorial: A public health plan, 20 June. http://www.nytimes.com/2009/06/21/opinion/21sun1.html (accessed 1 July 2009).

Nussbaum, M. (2000) *Women and Human Development: The Capabilities Approach*. Cambridge: Cambridge University Press.

Ostner, I. and Schmitt, C. (2008) *Family Policies in the Context of Family Change: The Nordic Countries in Comparative Perspective*. Göttingen: VS Verlag für Sozialwissenschaften.

Pais, M.S. (2008) *Second Meeting of the European Forum on the Rights of the Child*, 4 March. http://www.unicef-irc.org/homepages/files/documents/f_33.pdf (accessed 30 June 2009).

Peisner-Feinberg, E.S., Burchinal, M.R., Clifford, R.M., et al. (1999) *The Children of the Cost, Quality, and Outcomes Study go to School: Executive Summary*. Chapel Hill: University of North Carolina at Chapel Hill, Frank Porter Graham Child Development Center.

Piven, F.F. (1995) Foreword. In S. Schram, *Words of Welfare: The Poverty of Social*

Science and the Social Science of Poverty (pp. ix–xv). Minneapolis: University of Minnesota Press.

Polakow, V. (2007) *Who Cares for Our Children? The Child Care Crisis in the Other America*. New York: Teachers College Press.

Polakow, V., Butler, S., Deprez, L.S. and Kahn, P. (eds) (2004) *Shut Out: Low Income Mothers and Higher Education in Post-Welfare America*. Albany, NY: State University of New York Press.

Presser, H. and Cox, A.G. (1997) The work schedules of low-educated American women and welfare reform, *Monthly Labor Review*, 120(4): 25–34.

Roosevelt, E. (1958) *In Your Hands*. Address to United Nations Commission on Human Rights, New York, 27 March 1958. http://www.udhr.org/history/inyour.htm (accessed 3 July 2009).

Schulman, K. and Blank, H. (2005) *Child Care Assistance Policies 2005: States Fail to Make up Lost Ground, Families Continue to Lack Critical Supports*. Washington, DC: National Women's Law Center.

Schweinhart, L.J. (2004) *The High/Scope Perry Preschool Study through Age 40: Summary, Conclusions, and Frequently Asked Questions*. Ypsilanti, MI: High/Scope Educational Research Foundation.

Steinbeck, J. (1967 [1939]) *The Grapes of Wrath*. New York: Penguin.

Sunstein, C. (2004) The *Second Bill of Rights: FDR's Unfinished Revolution and Why We Need It More than Ever*. New York: Basic Books.

United Nations (1989) Convention on the Rights of the Child. New York: United Nations Office of the High Commissioner for Human Rights. http://www.unhchr.ch/html/menu3/b/k2crc.htm (accessed 10 July 2009).

United Nations (2000) *Millennium Report of the Secretary-General*. http://www.un.org/millennium/sg/report/key.htm (accessed 1 July 2009).

UNICEF (2007) *Global Study on Child Poverty and Disparities 2007–2008*. http://unicef.globalstudy.googlepages.com/UNICEFGlobalStudyGuide.pdf (accessed 3 July 2009).

US Department of Education (2009) *$44 billion in stimulus funds available to drive education reforms and save teaching jobs*. http://www.ed.gov/news/pressreleases/2009/04/04012009.html (accessed 9 July 2009).

US Department of Health and Human Services (2009) *The 2009 HHS Poverty Guidelines*. http://aspe.hhs.gov/poverty/09poverty.shtml (accessed 11 July 2009).

US Department of Labor, Bureau of Labor Statistics (2008a). Employment status of the population by sex, marital status, and presence and age of own children under 18, 2006–07 annual averages, *Economic News Release*, 30 May, table 5. http://www.bls.gov/news.release/famee.t05.htm (accessed 20 November 2008).

US Department of Labor, Bureau of Labor Statistics (2008b) Employment status of mothers with own children under 3 years old by single year of age of youngest child and marital status, 2006–07 annual averages, *Economic News Release*,

30 May, table 6. http://www.bls.gov/news.release/famee.t06.htm (accessed 20 November 2008).

Vandell, D.L. and Wolfe, B. (2000) *Child Care Quality: Does it Matter and Does it Need to be Improved?*, No. 78. Madison, WI: Institute for Research on Poverty.

Zweifler, R. and DeBeers, J. (2002) How zero tolerance impacts our most vulnerable youth, *Michigan Journal of Race and Law*, 8(1): 191–220.

6 The displaced early childhood education in the postcolonial era of Hong Kong

Gail Yuen

Introduction

Early childhood education in Hong Kong has expanded considerably since the Second World War (Sweeting, 1993) as a result of steady demand for provision and also an increase in the appetite for demonstrably high quality services as society has become more affluent. Chen and Wong (1999) attribute transformational changes in social practices and the resulting expectations of childhood to the blossoming of the economy that occurred in the 1970s. All services, whether they are kindergartens (for ages 3–6) under the Education Bureau, or child care centres (for ages 0–3) under the Social Welfare Department, are privately operated but mostly non-profit-making in nature. While attempting to cope with the issues brought forth by rapid economic growth and service expansion, as well as making an effort to respond to the increased regulatory control imposed on their operations, early childhood educators have been campaigning, since the British colonial era, for direct public funding to sustain and improve provision. Resource allocation for early childhood education continues to be the most contested area of concern after the establishment of Hong Kong as a Special Administrative Region (SAR) of China in 1997 (Yuen, 2008). It is a policy issue, as it involves 'disagreements about how given problems should be approached and solved' (Heck, 2004: 1).

Various contentions on the relationship between cost and quality have resulted in a number of changes in the mode of subsidy implemented by both the colonial and SAR governments. These changes, sometimes introduced alongside other policy initiatives, describe how early childhood education in Hong Kong has been shaped into a modernist project. From the early adoption of different subsidy schemes, to the recent introduction of a voucher scheme, the postcolonial period seems to demonstrate, on the part of the government, an increasing faith in the globally circulated notion of quality.

Why were certain modes of subsidy chosen over others? How did the various subsidy schemes come about? Can these schemes address the core issues or the root of the problem as expressed by educators? All of these are important and complex questions for early childhood education in Hong Kong.

This chapter contributes to the discussion by exploring how early childhood education may have been marginalized by local resource allocation policy in the light of the power politics embedded in the colonial and postcolonial contexts of governance. Through examining the historical and contemporary issues around resource allocation policy, it foregrounds the particular path travelled by policies under both political periods and identifies patterns of official responses to voices from the field. A critical examination of this policy trajectory uncovers ethical issues that highlight the various ways in which early childhood education in Hong Kong has been reshaped. The discussion is regarded as a personal journey to unravel the professional and cultural struggles resulting from having lived in two politically different spaces. Engaging in postcolonial theory is considered a daring endeavour and one which will enable me to break away from the boundaries framed by my own experiences in Hong Kong. Fully aware of the potential risk of being perceived as a defiant voice 'standing in the way of progress' (Viruru, 2007: 51), I wish to see new possibilities in my work with young children and students so as to open up alternative spaces for constructing more liberated and humanized visions of childhood and early childhood education.

Colonization: a legacy that lingers?

Because of its century-old connection with Britain, Hong Kong by default has a history of colonization. The year 1997 signified the official conclusion of the colonial legacy. Unlike Singapore, the decolonization of Hong Kong did not result in an independent state: with the departure of British officials, the Chinese government reclaimed sovereignty. Nevertheless, the influence of colonization continues to demonstrate its presence in society. Colonialism has manifested itself in another form in the postcolonial period, as distinct from the past where there was the physical existence of a western ruling regime. The growing economic prominence achieved by the SAR government represents an ardent response to the current thrust of globalization. Mok and Welch (2002) suggest that globalization 'bears the strong imprint of American political and economic power' (p. 24). To understand colonialism in the Hong Kong context, therefore, one must travel between temporal boundaries in addition to critiquing its impact and searching for possibilities from the postcolonial perspective.

With reference to the critical works of Radhika Viruru and Gaile Cannella (for example Cannella and Viruru, 2002, 2004; Viruru, 2005, 2007) in examining the powerful interplay of colonization with early childhood education,[1] colonialism can be described as the 'will to power' in order to 'essentialise diverse societies into one universal form, and to impose a narrow economic path on cultures that conceptualised not only economics but also human experiences, from a range of diverse perspectives' (Viruru, 2005: 8). It can be achieved directly through colonizing a territory or indirectly through colonizing the minds of citizens. Cannella and Viruru (2004) maintain that the latter is far more problematic since it was 'pioneered by so-called rationalists, who believed in advancing thought in backward lands, liberals who hoped to save the world, and modernists who believed they were bringing order and civilisation to places that both lacked and needed enlightened civilisation' (p. 65). Viruru (2007) thus asserts colonialism as a psychological state in which control and influence are present yet covert and that it is derived from the social consciousness that instigates it. Colonialism is closely connected with imperialism, which involves the colonizer's desire to rule over others through expanding its outward influence. While imperialism results in colonialism, it can exist in the absence of colonies (Cannella and Viruru, 2004). This is exactly the concern of postcolonialism, that is, the western imperialist project which has left 'nations and peoples living under one form of imperialist political and economic domination that is spreading to include power over identity(ies) and intellect' (Cannella and Viruru, 2004: 19). As Viruru (2007) suggests, a postcolonial critique aims to challenge domination, ensure equity, as well as create collective political and cultural identities.

Not being a permanent colony in the usual sense, Hong Kong served as a source of diplomatic, economic and military support to the British Empire (Ng, 1984). To resolve uncertainties over the future of the city resulting from the change of sovereignty, the Basic Law, adopted in the early 1990s, states: 'The socialist system and policies shall not be practised . . . and the previous capitalist system and way of life shall remain unchanged for 50 years' (Government of the People's Republic of China, 1990: article 5). As Cheung (2002) explains: 'the whole logic of Hong Kong's political transition . . . has assumed minimum change and maximum continuity of the previous system of governance under an executive-led administration' (p. 64). During the years of British colonization, the executive-led machinery of governance was a means to secure the centralized power of the colonial regime whereas the consultative system (Cheng, 1998) and the apolitical school curriculum (Tse, 1997) were used as built-in mechanisms to reduce resistance. In other words, they constituted the structure of colonialism (Viruru, 2007).

By adopting a consultative autocracy (Cheng, 1998), the British government was able to legitimize colonialism and showcase its commitment to an apparent openness to liberalism and intellectual pluralism (Viruru, 2007). The rational approach it took to deal with issues (that is to say, it was in search of the best solutions) resonated with local residents' specific social and cultural characteristics (such as rationality, lack of public spirit, achievement orientation, and pragmatism) (Ng, 1984; Sweeting, 1995; Cheng, 1998). It supported the illusion that there was a reciprocal relationship between colonizer and colonized. The partial consent of the needs and values of the colonizer which this produced among the colonized, achieved particularly through education, served to consolidate its hegemonic dominance (Cannella and Viruru, 2002). Tsang (2006) remarks, when analysing the proposed aims of education, that the three-stage consultation process launched in 1999 to gather territory-wide suggestions for formulating the reform blueprint was much like the past practice of *administrative absorption politics*.

Because of Hong Kong's status as a territory on temporary lease to Britain, officials and business people were more interested in attaining tangible returns from the territory than settling and enculturating the local residents (Sweeting, 1995). With the colonial government's adoption of a laissez-faire approach to education, the introduction of compulsory basic education and quantitative expansion of other types of provision were regarded as a source of pride for the city at the time (Cheng, 2002a). A more determined agenda to reform the education system did not actually come about until the 1990s. Christopher Patten, the last British governor, repeatedly stressed his concerns about the increasingly competitive and rapidly changing economic situation and identified the quality of education as a long-term challenge (Governor, 1995, 1996). The role of education in economic development was further emphasized by the first chief executive of the SAR government (Chief Executive, 1997). Foreshadowed by the Asian financial crisis and the city's fear of losing its international position in the light of increasing regional competition (Cheng, 2002a), the reform blueprint submitted to the government by the Education Commission revealed the obvious connection with economic impact: 'In a knowledge-based society, people must keep on learning. Many countries have already adopted "lifelong learning" as their national policies [sic]' (Education Commission, 2000: 27).

Global economic situations have brought about enormous challenges to local education systems. In effect, a particular notion of quality used to improve the education system in Hong Kong had already emerged during the colonial period. Patten articulated it explicitly by saying that 'we must also ensure we are getting good value for money. Quality assurance focuses on whether funds are spent efficiently and effectively and how budget holders can be made more accountable to the public' (Governor, 1995: 83). Since the 1980s, the neoliberal way of thinking about quality has spread from business to public service, and from the United States to the rest of the world. It epitomizes the modernist thirst for order, objectivity, quantification, and certainty (Dahlberg et al., 2007). Just as the concept of lifelong learning is oriented towards economic interests (Dahlberg et al., 2007), the quality discourse has been viewed as a western imperialist project (Cannella and Viruru, 2004) that intends to privilege rationality and the market over subjectivity and humanity, and shape the colonized into economic subjects rather than political and cultural intellects. As mentioned earlier, the SAR government inherited the executive orientation of the colonial legacy (Cheung, 2002). Policy makers show a tendency to view educational matters in a purely technical sense (Cheng, 2002a). Such an approach was in fact highlighted as an area of concern as early as the 1980s (Llewellyn, 1982). While Mok and Currie (2002) point out that the SAR administration favours business practices to a greater extent, Cheng (2002b) criticizes policy makers for their blind faith in managerial accountability when improving education provision.

In brief, the neoliberal notion of quality is used as a form of regulatory control to ensure the progress of mankind. From British colonization to recent globalization, the structure of governance has continued to enhance the political and economic domination of the West. The politics of power and economics has created, in the minds of local people, a consciousness enabling them to rationalize their thoughts and actions as if a truth really exists and to do so in favour of the priorities which have been set for survival and prosperity. This consciousness not only allows the resistance of the colonized to be contained, but also justifies certain kinds of social oppression. As a case in point, the trajectory of resource allocation for early childhood education in Hong Kong can offer insights into this mechanism of colonialism.

Official resistance to an aided early childhood education

The development of early childhood education in Hong Kong has followed a path similar to that found in many parts of the colonized world. It started out as a private enterprise undertaken by missionary or voluntary organizations. This self-supporting mode of operation, however, is highly prone to volatile economic performance and other factors such as an ageing population and low birth rate. With an increasing demand for quality provision, early childhood institutions found it relatively difficult to sustain themselves financially.

Until the late 1970s, there was not much by way of organized effort to pressure the colonial government to improve the provision of early childhood education. Over the years, many organizations and groups have pressed for immediate attention to the problems of increasing financial assistance for families, designing reasonable salary scales to give adequate recognition to kindergarten and child care personnel, subsidizing these salaries, and formulating a plan to include early childhood education in the aided sector.[2] Without adequate government support to create the impetus for paying comparable salaries and upgrading professionalism, the vicious cycle that had troubled the field for years could not be stopped because the only other way to afford higher salaries for qualified teachers was to raise tuition fees. This was perceived by early childhood institutions as undesirable, since they relied heavily on student enrolment for survival, and they were committed to making their services affordable to families.

Given the laissez-faire approach to education, the concentration on quantitative and qualitative development of the education system in the 1980s and 1990s respectively, and the focus on economic return, it was no surprise to see that the response of the colonial government to the demands of early childhood educators was at best indifferent. The temporary status of Hong Kong as a British colony gave the government a good reason to limit its benevolence to the poor. This helps explain why the development of child care services in the early days was better resourced. Such services, framed in terms of welfare policy, were aimed at those families who were unable to care for their own children. Non-profit child care operators received financial support in the form of land allocation, accommodation, fitting-out costs, rent and rates reimbursement, as well as a recurrent subvention (Hong Kong Government, 1981).

By comparison, kindergartens had received only the rates reimbursement from the colonial government prior to the 1980s. As a result of public pressure and policy makers' actions in response to demands from the field, different modes of subsidy were then introduced. For needy families (including those using the basic child care services), the government offered a means-tested fee assistance scheme (later renamed the fee remission scheme) (Hong Kong Government, 1981). For non-profit operators, the government provided rent and rates reimbursement (Hong Kong Government, 1981), a recommended salary scale (Education Commission, 1986), and the kindergarten subsidy scheme (later known as the kindergarten and child care centre subsidy scheme) (Governor, 1995). Still, these new changes could not satisfactorily answer the questions which had been posed about the effectiveness of different modes of subsidy and other related policies in resolving the dilemma between cost and quality and improving the welfare of early childhood educators (Hong Kong Educational Information Centre, 1989, 1993, 1997). By choosing less expensive ways of subsidizing the field and focusing on professional upgrading and curriculum issues (Governor, 1995), policy makers of the colonial period claimed that they were improving quality and were able to avoid the direct subsidy issue with regard to teacher salaries and early childhood education.

The colonial government's lack of interest in early childhood education closely resembled developments in Britain at the time. Moss and Penn (1996) comment on the British experience in the early days: 'When it comes to early childhood services, Britain suffers a poverty of expectation and a low level of awareness of issues, arising from years of neglect and indifference' (p. 24). The policy debates on early childhood education in Britain, especially concerning the roles of women, have lasted for more than a century (Tizard et al., 1976; Moss and Penn, 1996). In the 1980s, the colonial government in Hong Kong positioned early childhood education as the sole responsibility of the family and private sector, seeing it as something designed 'to achieve an expansion of pre-primary education in accordance with demand, at a price that people can afford and offering a suitable range of facilities and programmes' (Government Secretariat, 1981: 198). This position was unmistakably the same as the one noted in the 1960s: 'For the time being, it will be necessary to rely on voluntary organisations and private enterprise to provide education at this level' (Hong Kong Government, 1965: 2); and the one articulated immediately before Hong Kong reverted to China: 'to promote the development of high-quality kindergarten education in the private sector' (Governor, 1996: 92). Apparently, taking care of young children was perceived as a main job of the mother.

In spite of the rhetoric of giving more support to working parents, mothers in particular, prevailing patriarchal forces had restrained the colonial government's commitment to the universal provision of early childhood education. Reflecting the scientific orientation of colonialism, 'the logic of Enlightenment/modernism that has been forced on the colonised is a linear, male-constructed form of reason and hierarchical power that reinforces the notion one group is superior to another' (Cannella and Viruru, 2004: 21). By categorizing women or the marginalized in biological and binary terms, their work (such as educating young children and caring for others) is made invisible and not valued as real work or seen as capable of delivering a finished commodity in the Eurocentric and capitalist sense (Cannella and Viruru, 2004). This kind of linear, stereotypical orientation asserts a continuous and profound influence on the policy process pertaining to early childhood education in the postcolonial era.

Seeing the possibility of new hope by virtue of the change of circumstances instigated by the handover, early childhood educators continued their vocal demand for changes in both service provision and quality improvement, asserting that equal access to quality education should be given to all children.[3] Regardless of the high hopes and concerted efforts being made in the field, the SAR government only recognized early childhood education as the foundation of lifelong learning in the reform blueprint while accepting the Education Commission's (2000) recommendation not to provide either a full subsidy for the sector or a partial subsidy for teacher salaries. The reasons given were that 'the provision of full subsidy does not necessarily ensure the quality of early childhood education' (Education Commission, 2000: 55); it was proposed that quality would be better achieved through enhancing professional competence, strengthening quality assurance and monitoring mechanisms, and promoting parental choice.

The strong objection expressed by policy makers of the colonial and SAR governments to a full subsidy for early childhood education, or a partial subsidy for teacher salaries, has led many to wonder why there is such a remarkable reluctance to offer more support to young children. This is particularly questionable in the light of the growing international call for increased investment in the education and care services during the early years (OECD,

2006). Having completed reviews in twenty countries, the OECD (2006) suggests that equal access and quality would be more effectively ensured if direct subsidy is provided for operators instead of parents. It is just as hard to believe that official resistance to direct subsidy for early childhood education is happening in a Chinese context, where education very much matters to the local community. The high enrolment rate in early childhood education is a good reflection of this cultural practice. One may think the return of Hong Kong to Chinese sovereignty would have turned the tide, but paradoxically, this is not the case.

As mentioned previously, the managerial and technical approach to education policy is an important force in shaping why and how a particular policy is made in the Hong Kong context. It is the basis through which policy makers reason for themselves and others the choice of preference, thus maintaining the status quo. It is not uncommon to hear them say that turning early childhood education into an aided sector involves too much money and that resources are limited (Hong Kong Educational Information Centre, 2000, 2001). In preparing the reform blueprint, the Education Commission had made clear the official position: the quality of basic education had to be attended to first. This was presented as a question of making choices about different needs, rather than as meaning that the government did not recognize the importance of early childhood education (Hong Kong Educational Information Centre, 1997). As a matter of fact, similar rationalizations of priority, in the form of the view that limited resources have to be first spent on other levels of education, had already surfaced in the 1960s and have been repeated continually since then (Yuen, 2008). This long-standing argument seems to have produced a sound justification for playing down the essential role of public funding in ensuring quality provision and applying the neoliberal vision of the marketplace to early childhood education.

Both the colonial and the SAR governments have indicated rhetorically that they would be prepared to review the possibility of early childhood education becoming an aided sector if there are social needs for this (Hong Kong Government, 1981; Yuen, 2008). Unfortunately, from the first public consultation conducted by the colonial government in 1980 to the territory-wide consultation for envisioning the millennium education reform under the SAR administration, there has been no change to the official stance of keeping early childhood education in the private sector. The conscious attempt to avoid the direct subsidy issue reflects an organized system of resistance that points to the uncontestable nature of the power relationships vested in the autocratic governance structure. Typically, a pattern is observed after a new subsidy scheme has been introduced. That is, policy makers keep expanding or improving the scheme while relaxing tuition fee control and adjusting salary scales. At first, this only involved the fee assistance scheme. With the kindergarten subsidy scheme in operation, policy makers resorted to the same strategy by modifying the fee remission scheme, tuition fee control and salary scales simultaneously. Likewise, the SAR government changed the calculation method of the kindergarten subsidy scheme a number of times in order to keep conflicts and dissatisfaction in check. To ensure that 'no children will be deprived of early childhood education due to lack of financial means' (Education Commission, 2000: 55) while relying on tuition fee increases to cover the rising costs of operation, policy makers had continually to relax the eligibility criteria for the scheme so as to avoid public criticism about issues of equality and equity. By redirecting the focus to professional upgrading (Yuen, 2008), both governments were also able to claim that they had taken one of the most effective measures to raise the quality of early childhood education provision in Hong Kong. Decades of debates over the subsidy schemes and the numerous detours taken by policy makers have provided potent evidence for the invisible system which has been built in to enable the evasion of full financial responsibility.

Evidently, the autocratic structure of governance and built-in mechanisms of resistance are actively at work to control how given problems should be perceived and dealt with by policy makers. In return, an objective reality – the legitimization of early childhood education in the marketplace due to more efficient management of resources and more effective improvement of quality – is being produced to silence the voices of those who have been intensively governed. The ongoing negotiations between policy makers and educators in the field did lead to some policy changes in the mode of subsidy, as previously stated. Understanding why and how these changes have come about helps us find a way to interrogate the oppressive forces embedded in the structure of governance during the two political periods. *Civilized oppression* is identified by Harvey as being most common in western industrialized societies (cited in Viruru, 2005), thus prompting an examination of 'the mechanisms through which power is wielded, how perceptions and information are controlled, as well as the kinds of harm that are done' (Viruru, 2005: 19). Invisible forms of oppression, according to Viruru (2005), 'are no less destructive than overt forms, they are just elusive and harder to isolate, in that simplistic conclusions about causes and effects are harder to draw' (p. 20). Hong Kong is not a western industrialized society in the strictest sense. But its experiences with colonialism, and its success in developing as a centre of commerce and capitalism, enable comparisons to be made.

Whereas Britain moved away from the short-lived voucher system to universal provision in 1997, Hong Kong has gone the opposite way by introducing a first-of-its-kind voucher scheme to early childhood education in 2007. This is also a contrast to the OECD's assertion that quality would be improved if operators received direct subsidy (OECD, 2006). The new policy was framed in the context of the reform direction to build a quality culture and prioritize resource allocation for parents (Education Commission, 2000). The scheme symbolizes the policy makers' wholehearted adoption of a complete market approach to early childhood education serving children from 3 to 6 years of age. It reflects their intention to 'preserve the market responsiveness of the sector and to enhance quality at the same time' (EMB, 2006b: 3). The SAR government indicated it had no intention of changing the private mode of operation (EMB, 2006b), insisting that 'increasing resources alone cannot enhance the quality of education' (EMB, 2006a: 2). While parents receive more financial assistance through the voucher scheme, non-profit early child-hood institutions serving children from the ages of 3 to 6 years can no longer benefit from the kindergarten and child care centre subsidy scheme. For child care centres serving children between birth and the age of 3, the subsidy arrangements remain unchanged (EMB, 2006b).

Meanwhile, policy makers maintained that all early childhood institutions 'should enjoy full discretion in determining salaries for teachers and principals, subject to market forces' (EMB, 2006b: 6). As a result of this, the recommended salary scale was abolished. The government believed that the new mode of subsidy would provide early childhood institutions with 'enhanced flexibility and capacity to adjust salaries commensurate with enhanced professional upgrading' and the required disclosure of operational information could guarantee that reasonable salaries were paid (EMB, 2006b: 5). To ensure accountability in terms of the efficient and effective use of public funding, policy makers have increased the transparency of operations and implemented a more stringent quality assurance mechanism (based on performance indicators, self-evaluation and external inspection). Early childhood institutions can remain in the scheme only when they have met the desired standards. By reshuffling resources from operators to parents and controlling operations remotely through a structure of technical measures, the SAR government is able to reduce complex educational issues to simple steps which will satisfy its thirst for an orderly, measurable and standardized reality (Dahlberg et al., 2007).

Although the *no worse off* principle is applied to all eligible students with the introduction of the voucher scheme, other actions such as withdrawing the kindergarten and child care centre subsidy, imposing tuition fee caps as an eligibility requirement, setting an equal voucher value for both half- and full-day services, subsuming the amount of tuition fee subsidy into the voucher value, and maintaining the same fee remission ceilings for 5 years (EMB, 2006b), have all led to serious concerns about the fairness of the new policy. The voucher scheme tends to disadvantage children from low-income families that have applied for the fee remission scheme and use a full-day service. Letting the market mechanism determine teacher salaries is also a surprising U-turn from the position in colonial history. Thus, not just children from needy families but also teachers from early childhood institutions are worse off under the new policy.

It is still not clear how the voucher scheme may have improved the quality of provision. But a market-driven notion of quality is becoming evident, one which has been vigorously constructed by the interaction between the various forces operating within the official effort to keep early childhood education in the private sector, parents' choice of service, and practices in the field (Yuen and Grieshaber, 2009). Making the *how* of services the priority (Dahlberg et al., 2007), the quality discourse has been comfortably positioned as the best approach to dealing with educational issues. Ironically, the pressure to increase tuition fees to cover rising operational costs has persisted even after the implementation of the voucher scheme. Will the vicious cycle, which has troubled the field for years, continue to exist as before? Can the voucher scheme bring financial stability and thus sustainable development to early childhood education? Can quality be truly enhanced using this new mode of subsidy? The voucher scheme has aggravated issues of equality and equity, which in turn may lead to more social stratification. If it does, can this really be called a quality provision?

In summary, the return of Hong Kong to China in 1997 had brought new hope to early childhood education since the colonizer or *Other* (from the insider's point of view; see Cannella and Viruru, 2002, for an explanation of the term) was now gone and had been replaced by the colonized, with the *Us* being Chinese (Yuen, 2008). That hope, however, has not taken us very far in terms of resource allocation and improving quality and opportunities for the field. In reality, the Us is also the colonizer. Policies relating to different modes of subsidy have allowed oppressive forces to reproduce the colonized identity of early childhood education through seemingly civilized mechanisms of resistance. As always, 'how we think about our problems determines both what we see and what we fail to see' (Heck, 2004: 28). This explains why Hong Kong today still has no public provision of early childhood education as its privatized present is essentially connected with its colonial past.

Official resistance as a way of normalization

In Viruru's (2007) view, colonialism has the capacity to enhance control by 'appropriating systems of classification and refashioning them according to "reason", transforming relatively fluid categories . . . into firm structures' (p. 44). It consciously creates, in both the colonizer and colonized, systems of reasoning to define membership and discipline bodies. As a result, the regulatory power, which constructs what is regarded as being normal through laws and legislative measures, is much harder to confront and challenge (Cannella and Viruru, 2004).

Specific resource allocation policies in Hong Kong, especially the latest voucher scheme, have reproduced the significant inequalities in power, enabling policy makers to govern and regulate operators with greater ease and without coercion. These policies regard early childhood education as 'a natural good of the private sphere over the public' (Bloch et al., 2003: 22). Because of policy makers' overwhelming resistance to the idea of early childhood education becoming a publicly funded sector, they have successfully encouraged the field to manage on its own. A *perfect* market model has thus been produced. The private nature of the operation has given freedom to early childhood institutions to manoeuvre their own resources and develop innovative practices. In contrast to the questionable performance of publicly funded basic education, the significant improvement made in curriculum development in the field of early childhood education has further reinforced policy makers' beliefs in the neoliberal notions of privatization, progress and quality, as well as their determination to keep the provision in the private sector. The fact that early childhood educators have acknowledged the good practices produced by a competitive market (Yuen, 2008) illuminates the self-regulating forces at work. The new voucher scheme only adds more significance to self-regulation of this kind. Lee (2008) describes vouchers as a socio-cultural governing practice which has become the dominant reasoning logic by which to (re)constitute educational norms in Hong Kong.

Effectively, official resistance has legitimized the normalization of early childhood education as a private responsibility, a marketplace, a production of a lifelong-learning-oriented and competitive workforce, and an exemplary representation of a progressive policy in a modern society. As a form of disciplinary and regulatory power, resource allocation policy has served to normalize the ways that early childhood education is understood and practised. By means of constructing it as a private good, early childhood education has been pushed further away from the publicly funded education system. In 2007, a year after the announcement of the voucher scheme, the chief executive indicated the intention to expand the period of free basic education from nine to twelve years to include three years of senior secondary education rather than early childhood education. Having been defined as different from its publicly funded counterparts, early childhood education has been placed totally in the private market, leading to its simultaneous, natural exclusion from the public structure. Such an inclusion–exclusion practice in turn reproduces existing power relationships or the pecking order of education and marginalizes early childhood education to a still greater extent.

Whatever the policy priority, it is a simple economic principle that a 4-year-old can understand: we all need to share because there is not enough. The question is whether this is a fair share. In response to the disparities between early childhood education and other levels, Opper (1993) refers to kindergarten education as the Cinderella of the education system that 'remains in the kitchen, neglected and despised, gleaning the meagre droppings that fall from the . . . table' (p. 88). When compared with the past, early childhood education has definitely received more official attention of late. Nevertheless, its relationship with other levels of education has seldom been built on an equal and equitable basis. As Rigby et al. (2007) note, policy choices concerning early childhood services can give rise to not only short-term effects but also long-term socio-political consequences.

Resisting the official resistance

Obviously, policy makers in the postcolonial period of Hong Kong still see young children as members of the family in a private space rather than as citizens of society in the public place. This patriarchal frame of thinking has prevented early childhood education from playing an essential role in achieving the political, social and economic goals of national development. The increasing prevalence of business management and market practices in the field (Dahlberg et al., 2007) has further eroded the government's ability to acculturate its members at this level. As a modernist project, early childhood education primarily concerns the children of *tomorrow* instead of *today*. It is closely associated with ideas about how the future should be constituted, thus making its constructions of childhood highly susceptible to the impact of globalization and severely limiting the opportunities for young children.

In any case, allowing civilized oppression to prevail and create market domination in favour of humanity and democracy can only leave many urgent and ethical issues unexamined. Soto and Swadener (2002) critique the relatively weak enculturation of social justice and equity in the field of early childhood education. For policy and practice to take on a discourse that embraces social transformation, we have to recognize the political nature of the field and, as Canella and Viruru (2004) propose, take note of 'the systematic power to silence, reconstruct as invisible, and remarginalise' (p. 75). As Viruru (2007) argues, postcolonial theory can potentially offer 'a place to go to find unusual meanings and understandings that contradict and disrupt the discourses that one can so easily be surrounded and overwhelmed by' (p. 41). Only when we actively look for ways to resist the resistance, as she suggests, can we actually contest the domination of western imperialism and turn early childhood education into a cultural project of meaning making.

Acknowledgement

I would like to express my gratitude to both Radhika Viruru and Alan Pence for giving me the inspiration and courage to adopt the postcolonial lens to understand and interpret my experiences.

Notes

1. Their scholarship is based on a wide variety of perspectives, including feminism, and also including those of Michel Foucault and other scholars such as Ashis Nandy, Ania Loomba and Robert Young. The discussion in this chapter reflects the ideas of some of these scholars.
2. See Yuen (2008) for a more elaborated discussion.
3. See Yuen (2008) for a more elaborated discussion.

References

Bloch, M.N., Holmlund, K., Moqvist, I. and Popkewitz, T. (2003) In M.N. Bloch, K. Holmlund, I. Moqvist and T. Popkewitz (eds), *Governing Children, Families, and Education: Restructuring the Welfare State* (pp. 3–31). New York: Palgrave Macmillan.

Cannella, G.S. and Viruru, R. (2002) (Euro-American constructions of) education of children (and adults) around the world: a postcolonial critique. In G.S. Cannella and J.L. Kincheloe (eds), *Kidworld: Childhood Studies, Global Perspectives, Education* (pp. 197–213). New York: Peter Lang.

Cannella, G.S. and Viruru, R. (2004) *Childhood and Post-Colonization: Power, Education and Contemporary Practice.* New York: Routledge.

Chen, E.K.Y. and Wong, T.Y.C. (1999) Socioeconomic transformation and child development. In N.A. Pryde and M.M. Tsoi (eds), *Hong Kong's Children: Our Past, Their Future* (pp. 23–61). Hong Kong: Centre of Asian Studies.

Cheng, K.M. (1998) The policymaking process. In G.A. Postiglione and W.O. Lee (eds), *Schooling in Hong Kong: Organisation, Teaching and Social Context* (pp. 65–78). Hong Kong: Hong Kong University Press.

Cheng, K.M. (2002a) Reinventing the wheel: educational reform. In S.K. Lau (ed.), *The First Tung Chee-hwa Administration: The First Five Years of the Hong Kong Special Administration Region* (pp. 157–174). Hong Kong: Chinese University Press.

Cheng, K.M. (2002b) The quest for quality education: the quality assurance movement in Hong Kong. In J.K. Mok and D.K. Chan (eds), *Globalisation and Education: The Quest for Quality Education in Hong Kong* (pp. 41–65). Hong Kong: Hong Kong University Press.

Cheung, B.L.A. (2002) The changing political system: executive-led government or 'disabled' governance? In S.K. Lau (ed.), *The First Tung Chee-hwa Administration: The First Five Years of the Hong Kong Special Administration Region* (pp. 41–68). Hong Kong: Chinese University Press.

Chief Executive (1997) Speech by the Chief Executive the Honorable Tung Chee-hwa at the ceremony to celebrate the establishment of the Hong Kong

Special Administrative Region of the People's Republic of China. http://hwww. info.gov.hk/ce/speech/cesp.htm (accessed 15 April 2003).

Chief Executive (2007) *Policy Address 2007–08*. Hong Kong: Government Printer.

Dahlberg, G., Moss, P. and Pence, A. (2007) *Beyond Quality in Early Childhood Education and Care: Postmodern Perspectives*, 2nd edition. London: Falmer Press.

Education Commission (1986) *Education Commission Report No. 2*. Hong Kong: Government Printer.

Education Commission (2000) *Learning for Life. Learning through Life: Reform Proposals for the Education System in Hong Kong*. Hong Kong: Government Printer.

EMB (Education and Manpower Bureau) (2006a) *Review on Pre-primary Education*. http://www.info.gov.hk/gia/general/200605/10/P200605100160.htm (accessed 13 May 2006).

EMB (Education and Manpower Bureau) (2006b) *Item for Finance Committee*. http://hwww.legco.gov.hk/yr06–07/english/fc/fc/papers/f06–29e.pdf (accessed 13 March 2008).

Government of the People's Republic of China (1990) *The Basic Law of the Hong Kong Special Administrative Region of the People's Republic of China*. Hong Kong: Consultative Committee for the Basic Law of the Hong Kong Special Administrative Region of the People's Republic of China.

Government Secretariat (1981) *The Hong Kong Education System: Overall Review of the Hong Kong Education System*. Hong Kong: Government Secretariat.

Governor (1995) *1995/96 Policy Address*. Hong Kong: Government Printer.

Governor (1996) *1996/97 Policy Address*. Hong Kong: Government Printer.

Heck, R.H. (2004) *Studying Educational and Social Policy: Theoretical Concepts and Research Methods*. Mahwah, NJ: Lawrence Erlbaum Associates.

Hong Kong Educational Information Centre (1989) *Educational News Clippings on Pre-primary Education 1985–1989*. [Chinese]. Hong Kong: Hong Kong Educational Information Centre.

Hong Kong Educational Information Centre (1993) *Educational News Clippings on Pre-primary Education 1990–1993*. [Chinese]. Hong Kong: Hong Kong Educational Information Centre.

Hong Kong Educational Information Centre (1997) *Educational News Clippings on Pre-primary Education 1994–1997*. [Chinese]. Hong Kong: Hong Kong Educational Information Centre.

Hong Kong Educational Information Centre (2000) *Monthly educational news clippings 2000*. [Chinese]. Hong Kong: Hong Kong Educational Information Centre.

Hong Kong Educational Information Centre (2001) *Monthly educational news clippings 2001*. [Chinese]. Hong Kong: Hong Kong Educational Information Centre.

Hong Kong Government (1965) *Education Policy*. Hong Kong: Government Printer.

Hong Kong Government (1981) *White Paper on Primary and Pre-primary Services*. Hong Kong: Government Printer.

Lee, I.F. (2008) Formations of new governing technologies and productions of new norms: the dangers of preschool voucher discourse, *Contemporary Issues in Early Childhood*, 9(1): 08–82.

Llewellyn, J. (1982) *A Perspective on Education in Hong Kong: Report by a Visiting Panel.* Hong Kong: Government Printer.

Mok, J.K. and Currie, J. (2002) Reflections on the impact of globalisation on educational restructuring in Hong Kong. In J.K. Mok and D.K. Chan (eds), *Globalisation and Education: The Quest for Quality Education in Hong Kong* (pp. 259–277). Hong Kong: Hong Kong University Press.

Mok, J.K. and Welch, A.R. (2002) Economic rationalism, managerialism and structural reform in education. In J.K. Mok and D.K. Chan (eds), *Globalisation and Education: The Quest for Quality Education in Hong Kong* (pp. 23–40). Hong Kong: Hong Kong University Press.

Moss, P. and Penn, H. (1996) *Transforming Nursery Education.* London: Paul Chapman.

Ng, L.H. (1984) *Interactions of East and West: Development of Public Education in Early Hong Kong.* Hong Kong: Chinese University Press.

OECD (Organisation for Economic Co-operation and Development) (2006) *Starting Strong II: Early Childhood Education and Care.* Paris: OECD.

Opper, S. (1993) Kindergarten education: Cinderella of the Hong Kong education system. In A.B.M. Tsui and I. Johnson (eds), *Teacher Education and Development,* Education Paper No. 18 (pp. 80–89). Hong Kong: University of Hong Kong, Faculty of Education.

Rigby, E., Tarrant, K. and Neuman, M.J. (2007) Alternative policy designs and the socio-political construction of childcare, *Contemporary Issues in Early Childhood*, 8(2): 98–108.

Soto, L.D. and Swadener, B.B. (2002) Toward liberatory early childhood theory, research and praxis: decolonising a field, *Contemporary Issues in Early Childhood*, 3(1): 38–66.

Sweeting, A. (1993) *A Phoenix Transformed: The Reconstruction of Education in Post-war Hong Kong.* Hong Kong: Oxford University Press.

Sweeting, A. (1995) Hong Kong. In P. Morris and A. Sweeting (eds), *Education and Development in East Asia* (pp. 41–77). New York: Garland.

Tizard, J., Moss, P. and Perry, J. (1976) *All Our Children: Preschool Services in a Changing Society.* London: Maurice Temple Smith.

Tsang, W.K. (2006) The discourse on the education reform of the Hong Kong Special Administrative Region: Introduction. In W.K. Tsang (ed.), *Education Blueprint for the 21st Century? Discourse on the Education Reform in the Hong Kong Special Administrative Region* (pp. 3–26) [Chinese]. Hong Kong: Chinese University of Hong Kong.

Tse, K.C. (1997) Civic and political education. In M. Bray and R. Koo (eds), *Education and Society in Hong Kong and Macau: Comparative Perspectives on Continuity and Change* (pp. 151–169). Hong Kong: Hong Kong University Press.

Viruru, R. (2005) The impact of postcolonial theory on early childhood education, *Journal of Education*, 35: 7–30.

Viruru, R. (2007) Resisting resistance in postcolonial theory: implications for the study of childhood, *International Journal of Equity and Innovation in Early Childhood*, 5(1): 40–59.

Yuen, G. (2008) Education reform policy and early childhood teacher education in Hong Kong before and after the transfer of sovereignty to China in 1997, *Early Years: An International Journal of Research and Development*, 2(1): 23–45.

Yuen, G. and Grieshaber, S. (2009) Parents' choice of early childhood education service in Hong Kong: a pilot study about vouchers, *Contemporary Issues in Education*, 10(3): 263–279.

7 National 'treasures': the Aotearoa New Zealand child

Judith Duncan

Children are not little bundles of innocence: they are little bundles of depravity . . . and can develop into unrestrained agents of evil . . . unless trained and disciplined. Selfishness, violence, lying, cheating, stealing and other such manifestations of rebellion, are just the child unpacking some of this sinful foolishness from the vast store in his heart.

– Smith, quoted in Wood et al. (2008: 102)

The constructions of children and childhood in society at any given time demonstrate not only perceptions that adults hold of children, but also the discursive positions that are available for children to experience their lives. While membership in childhood itself is constantly changing, 'childhood' as a category is a significant and permanent part of all social structures (Qvortrup et al., 1994), and does not exist outside of culture, class, gender or ethnicity (Woodhead and Faulkner, 2000). Looking at the discourses of childhood in Aotearoa New Zealand positions children in both the cultural context of Aotearoa New Zealand and also in the global context of childhoods, particularly those in the western world ('minority world'[1]), since children share the same market resources and access to technologies as those in other countries (Buckingham, 2004).

Christensen and Prout (2005) argue that childhood cannot be conceptualized in the absence of an adult 'just as it is impossible to picture the adult and his or her society without positing the child' (p. 43). This relationship between adult and child is a dominant one within society, and one with multiple tensions and complexities, as demonstrated in the quote above. One would be forgiven for thinking that the opening quote was from a medieval text on the ills of childhood. However, it is a view of children that was published in 2005 by the leader of a New Zealand organization called Family Integrity. This group entered the debate in New Zealand to oppose the repeal of a section of the Crimes Act 1961. This section of the Act enabled parents to defend themselves from prosecution for using physical punishment to 'correct the behaviour' of, or to 'discipline', their children (Wood et al., 2008). The description is a powerful image that demonstrates the range of competing and conflicting images of children that any society can hold at any time, across time, and at particular given historical moments. These interrelationships between adult and child, and childhoods across countries, offer contested positions both for children's lives and for the adults who live and/or work with children. In addition complexities of images of children and childhoods also differ given the ethnicity of the child (for example Māori, Chinese, European), the age of the child (the 'terrible toddler', the 'surly adolescent'), and the location of the child (the 'rural' child, the 'mall rat'). Each and every one of these images and descriptions shapes the society in which children spend their lives. Burman describes how discourses of childhood are central to

> The ways we structure our own and others sense of place and position. They are part of the cultural narratives that define who we are, why we are the way we are and where we are going.
> (Burman, 1994: 48)

Drawing on the theoretical ideas of the French philosopher Michel Foucault, this chapter begins with an examination of the discourses and the resultant discursive practices surrounding images of children and childhood. The first part of the chapter considers the study of childhood and describes how the discourses of childhood relate to individuals and society – how children and childhood have been described and researched. The second part looks at examples from Aotearoa New Zealand early childhood policy and draws on the findings of two research projects (undertaken by the author with colleagues) capturing the discursive constructions of childhood and the resultant discursive pedagogy and constructions of childhood in the early years (Duncan, 2004, 2005a,b, 2009; Smith et al., 2005; Duncan et al., 2006, 2008).

Childhoods: discursive images, discursive practices

Theoretical and empirical developments in the study of childhood have contributed to discourses of 'childhood' as social constructions (Burman, 1994, 2005; James and Prout, 1997; James et al., 1998; Bloch and Popkewitz, 2000; Farquhar and Fleer, 2007). This is in sharp contrast to earlier research in the 1970s where childhood was understood to be 'an interpretive frame for understanding the early years of human life', that is, human immaturity (James and Prout, 1997). There are numerous commentators who, drawing on the paradigm of childhood studies, have traced how western childhood has been described historically (Aries, 1962; Cannella and Viruru, 2004). Commentators have discussed how constructions of childhood have ranged from images of the child as the 'empty vessel' (awaiting the more knowledgeable to fill), the child of 'nature', the child as 'labour market supply factor' (Dahlberg et al., 2007), and as a 'consumer' (Langer, 1994; Kincheloe, 2002; Hughes, 2005). Kehily (2004), in tracing the history of childhood, identifies the 'lost child' who needs to be protected from harm at all costs. Kjørholt (2005) links childhood with constructions of individualization and the autonomous, self-determining subject in the late modern societies. Most recently, children themselves are now described as the new consumer market – this includes products designed for children to be bought by adults, as well as products designed for children to buy, collect and have for themselves (Langer, 1994; MacNaughton and Hughes, 2000; Feedman Lustig, 2004; Hughes, 2005; Nyland and Rockel, 2007). Woodhead, reflecting on his own work in child psychology, critiqued his vision of children which had described them as 'becoming' rather than 'being', thus reinforcing both the discourse and the discursive practices around children that position them as 'needy' and 'immature' (Woodhead and Faulkner, 2000).

Similarly, notions and images of children and childhoods have often been constructed in ways that fit with the economic and social discourses of the time, and each and every one of these childhood images positions 'the child' very differently in terms of the child's sense of self, and the opportunities that become available for them. Rinaldi challenges these traditional discourses on children:

> [We can] continue to look at the child as property, as a private subject, as a needy child. But the child is the subject not of needs, but of rights … We want to support the child from birth as strong and rich, as having curiosity, as being wise, as having tools of living, as full of wonder and amazement. The child is powerful from birth. A six-day-old child is powerful because he wants to learn, because he wants to live with us.
>
> (Rinaldi, quoted in Nyland and Rockel, 2007: 77)

Discourses of children as individuals with rights, and as active 'co-constructer(s) of knowledge, identity and culture' (Dahlberg et al., 2007: 48) present very different experiences for children. This 'postmodern' child is described as a child who is capable and competent in their own right (Smith, 2000a,b, 2002; Anning et al., 2009), as a citizen with full participatory rights (Alderson, 2003, 2004; Alderson et al., 2005), and a child in the 'here and now' rather than as a 'becoming' adult (Woodhead, 2000; Woodhead and Faulkner, 2000).

How childhood is understood and constructed in contemporary society is worth considering, as these understandings shape children's experiences and day-to-day lives at multiple levels. Society's ideas about childhood are funda-mental to the enhancement of children's lives and the public provisions that are made for them (Qvortrup et al., 1994; Moss and Petrie, 2002). Negative understandings of childhood in society can be detrimental to children and threaten their rights and their own sense of possible selves and experiences; as demonstrated in the opening quote in this chapter. Importantly, the study of children and childhood, not just in relation to the adult they will become, is now an established field in multiple disciplines, for example: sociology (James and Prout, 1997; James et al., 1998; Cannella and Viruru, 2004), health (Alderson et al., 2005), education (Cannella and Kincheloe, 2002; Bird, 2003; Bodine, 2003; Buckingham, 2004; Burr, 2004), and psychology (Burman, 1994; Woodhead, 1997).

Discursive constructions of the Aotearoa New Zealand child: a national treasure

The theoretical arguments of Foucault provide useful tools for an examination of children and childhood. His theories are increasingly being utilized by writers in early childhood education (for example Cannella, 1997; Duncan, 2004, 2005a; MacNaughton, 2005). Foucault identified discourses as historic-ally specific ways of speaking knowledge and truth, that is, what is possible to speak at any given moment, who can speak and with what authority (Foucault, 1970, 1971, 1980a). Discourses then act as sets of rules and behaviours. In this way discourses are powerful. Accordingly, discourses are

> practices that systematically form the objects of which they speak . . . Discourses are not about objects, they do not identify objects, they constitute them and in the practice of doing so conceal their own invention.
>
> (Foucault, quoted in Ball, 1990: 2)

Thus, for Foucault, not only do discourses reflect what already exists, but they actually work to create this reality. Individuals act on the basis of their ideas of how the world should be and their position within that world. According to Foucault (1980a), human beings internalize the dominant discourses in society at any given time, and this provides individuals with the rules of what can and cannot be spoken, acted on, thought and participated in. He describes the interrelationships between discourse, the creation of subjectivity (or sense of 'selves'), and the conforming to power that discourses enable, as how modern societies shape and maintain control of their populations (Foucault, 1980b, 1982). One way that a population of children is maintained is through the discourses and images of childhood at any given time. The discursive practices that arise from these impact directly on children's lived experiences; for example, a discourse of 'an inherently evil child' leads to punitive parenting behaviours and harsh public reactions to children's behaviours, or a discourse of a 'majority-world needy child' can lead to a missionary zealot approach to 'save the disadvantaged' (Kessing-Styles and Sumison, 2007) which translates to western values of lifestyle and parenting (Smidt, 2006). Bloch and Popkewitz's (2000) discussion of the social administration of children draws on the ideas of Foucault by highlighting how 'stages of development, norms of achievement and growth that inscribed certain ways of thinking about children and their parents' (p. 10). They contend that these are linked to political modes of governing and self-governing principles enabling a peaceful management of the population – in this case of children and their parents (Bloch and Popkewitz, 2000). Modes of governing can be seen in the discourses expressed in popular media, and pedagogical practices targeting children and their families, as described in the following example from Aotearoa New Zealand.

National treasures in national messages in Aotearoa New Zealand

Repeal of section 59 of the Crimes Act 1961

Children as 'national treasures' is a contested position within Aotearoa New Zealand. 'National treasures' often hold idealist and nostalgic status in society. The term has been used as a provocation for this chapter, as the discursive positions experienced by children do not readily match with this nostalgic view of children. 'National treasures' are held as symbols – symbols of a culture or society that tell the rest of the world that this 'treasure' is valued and revered above all, often over time, and holds a historical as well as current significance. Commentators have linked the notion of a 'national treasure' to those of romantic nostalgia – demonstrating a link between a symbol, its ideology and its connection to a shared culture (Cannella and Viruru, 2004; Smidt, 2006). Conceptualizing children as a national treasure has not arisen from Aotearoa New Zealand's colonial past but from its indigenous Māori history. The arrival of European settlers in the 1800s in Aotearoa New Zealand introduced views on children and childhood, of 'evil' children and the role of 'physical punishment in the pursuit of "godly child-rearing" ' (Wood et al., 2008). These changing images and descriptions created discursive positions for children that differed significantly from indigenous Māori traditional experiences with their *tamariki* (children) (Wood et al., 2008: 91).

The debates that raged in Aotearoa New Zealand over the Repeal of Section 59 of the Crimes Act 1961 demonstrated how images, constructions and discourses about children had not shifted from the earlier colonial settlement days of Aotearoa New Zealand: for example, children seen as needing attendance at kindergarten to compensate for the lack of care, discipline and guidance they received in their homes and to ensure the growth of a 'healthy nation' (Duncan, 2001, 2008).

The relevant section of the Act read:

> 59 Domestic discipline
> (1) Every parent of a child ... is justified in using force by way of correction towards the child, if the force used is reasonable in the circumstances.

The change, legislated 2 May 2007, repealed this section and replaced it with a specific ban on the use of force for the purpose of correcting children, but provided for parents to restrain their children for the child's or another's safety (for example, running out onto the road). To soothe opponents to the change, a clause was added that affirmed that the police would have discretion not to prosecute minor parental assaults on children (Wood et al., 2008).

The arguments that shaped the debate over this legislation ranged from discourses of children as an extension of their parent – not a citizen or human by right – to a child who has human rights: rights to be loved, cared for and raised in a non-violent environment.

Wood et al. (2008) highlight how arguments which positioned children with 'rights' separate from those of their parents, became an unacceptable argument within Aotearoa New Zealand and was dropped from being the leading campaign argument for changing the law. They argue that the role of the media in the debate became pivotal to both sides of the debate (for and against), and in raising the complexity of the issues:

> Supporters of reform were challenging a deeply ingrained parenting habit that a large proportion of parents had previously used and a lesser proportion currently did. It was inevitable that efforts to change parental attitudes and behaviours as well as reform the law would be controversial and divisive ... Most of the public debate about the place of physical punishment and the desirability or otherwise of law reform therefore occurred in the mainstream media.
>
> (Wood et al., 2008: 166)

Media headlines from this time demonstrate the conflicting discursive positions for children:

> Children 'seen as not fully human'
>
> (*Dominion Post*, 7 April 2007)

Why you just can't beat a good caning
(*Otago Daily Times*, 30 May 2007)

Be afraid parents, your children will dob you in
(*NZ Herald*, March 2007)

Smacking police will not be on your doorstep
(*Otago Daily Times*, 11 April 2007)

Misconceptions over parental control
(*Otago Daily Times*, 10 May 2007)

'Sparing the rod' continued to be seen as 'spoiling the child', and parental rights to physically abuse children were defended by opponents to the changes by drawing on the discourses that: (a) physical punishment by a 'loving parent' is unrelated to other areas of violence in society, and (b) no law should interfere in families and in parenting in particular (Wilkstedt and Murachver, 2006; Wood et al., 2008). These debates positioned children as owned by parents, who legally and morally should have the right to treat their children in any way they feel is appropriate.

Positioning 'children against parents' demonstrates the historical legacy of child ownership by parents and the difficulties in constructing a discourse of childhood that challenges this in the context of parenting.

Marketing treasures

The images that dominated Aotearoa New Zealand over this legislation change are in sharp contrast to the discursive constructions of the very young child used for marketing purposes. Children's images have been used for marketing purposes for many years – promoting early childhood centres and schools, toys and clothing designed for children, fast-food outlets and entertainment venues targeting children. More recently, children have been used in advertisements for selling family cars, telecommunication products and 'popular stationary images' (Aitken and Kennedy, 2007; Nyland and Rockel, 2007). Advertisements that have 'cute, adorable' children catch the eye and send a message – the anticipated sale of a product most usually. But what do these images mean for the construction of childhood? Are they simply 'nice' photos, which 'warm the heart'? While advertising is designed to sell a product, the question to ask is, how does this position children within their own daily lives?

In 2007 the magazine *Little Treasures* celebrated twenty-one years of publication. This Aotearoa New Zealand bimonthly magazine purports to be the country's most popular parenting magazine, with a circulation of 34,000 – 6.3 per cent of target age group – and a readership of over 200,000 (ACP Media,

2009). The magazine is aimed primarily at parents of babies and preschoolers, but looking at their reader profile the readers are in high-income brackets, mid-thirties age group and 'compared with typical New Zealand mums with kids under-5 *Little Treasures* readers are more likely to: Attend a night class; spend a lot of money on clothes; be financially comfortable; entertain at home; [and] feel optimistic about the future' (ACP Media, 2009).

On the cover of each magazine is a child 'model'. Parents can send in photos of their child, through the magazine's website, and children (preschoolers) fill the front cover with overlaid text highlighting the key stories inside the magazine. An interesting feature of the cover of these magazines is the juxtaposition of the image in comparison to the overlaid text. The images of the children on the covers are angelic in pose, very clean and bright-eyed, with designer-label clothes. The children range in age from small babies to 5-year-olds. In most cases the children are looking directly into the camera – directly at you the reader. The text, overlaying the photos on the cover often tells a different story about managing or coping with children as a new parent: 'Terrible twos: wise ways to handle tears and tantrums' (June/July 2004); 'Are daycare kids different? How your working life affects your child' (August/ September 2004); ' "I do more than you": when a new baby sparks a couple crisis' (February/March 2005; 'Fat-proof your kids' (August/September 2006); 'Why parents are so broke!' (February/March 2007); 'Stop shopping tantrums' (February/March 2008); 'Are you feeding your child too much?' (August/ September 2008); 'Non-stop screamers: what to do when your baby won't stop crying' (February/March 2009). This contrast between the 'cute, adorable' child and the attention-grabbing headlines demonstrates the constant tensions around discourses of childhood. While the magazine is designed to capture its buyers with a combination of both lovely images of children and startling headlines, these headlines emphasize either the difficulties of parenting or, increasingly, the issues to do with children that parents worry most about: for example, childhood obesity has become the new focus of western countries (replacing poverty, hunger and social injustice experiences for children). The circulation of *Little Treasures* is wide and, arguably, the magazine plays a key discursive role in new parents' understanding of childhood – how my child should look, behave, and 'what I should be worried about or trying to change'. A reliance on the use of magazines and the internet for parenting advice exposes new parents to discourses of childhood which are shaped and manufactured from consumerism, often with outdated understandings of child development and based solely on western styles of parenting. Where does early childhood education fit within the visions of children and childhood?

The construction of childhood and early childhood education

The development of both a national curriculum – Te Whāriki – (Ministry of Education, 1996) and a ten-year strategic plan for early childhood services (Ministry of Education, 2002) has provided vision and coherence to the early childhood sector in Aotearoa New Zealand, and focused on social and educational areas of greatest need. The strength of both of these documents is that, until recently, they have had support from the major political parties,[2] thus enabling progress to be made in the early childhood sector over a nine-year period without constant disruptions or changes which had hampered the growth and quality of services in early childhood education over the 1990s (Duncan, 2001). Interestingly, these documents, while supporting the provisions of quality early childhood services, are not without discursive tensions themselves.

Aotearoa New Zealand has an early childhood curriculum, which applies across all the early childhood sector. In Aotearoa New Zealand early childhood centres provide education and care for children between birth and 5 years of age.[3] Therefore, children from birth until they reach school age, no matter which early childhood setting they experience, have their learning positioned within the discourses and discursive practices created by the curriculum – Te -hāriki.[4] The opening aspiration statement of Te Whāriki sets out the discursive vision for New Zealand children:

> To grow up as competent and confident learners and communicators, healthy in mind, body and spirit, secure in their sense of belonging and in the knowledge that they make a valued contribution to society.
> (Ministry of Education, 1996: 9)

This statement has been a key influence in shaping Aotearoa New Zealand's teachers' visions for children in their early childhood settings (Alvestad and Duncan, 2006; Alvestad et al., forthcoming). The discourse of children as 'competent and confident' is a direct challenge to deficit-based developmental practices. Recent writings by Cannella (1997), Bloch and Popkowitz (2000) and Dahlberg et al. (2007) have all critiqued our reliance on child development, developmental psychology and age-based theories in early childhood. They argue that these modernist theories present children as organized and divided into categories (lacking and in the process of 'becoming' – see also Woodhead and Faulkner, 2000); provide norms which are perceived as universalized and natural (work to include and exclude children); present development as linear and compartmentalized (physical, intellectual, emotional, social); and use these ideas to explain children's behaviour and to describe appropriate and inappropriate practices and environments for children (NAEYC, 1997). While Te Whāriki offers a differing vision from these, *Pathways to the Future* – the early childhood ten-year strategic plan – is not without critiques as to the vision, or the discourse of children and childhood that it contains. Nuttall (2004) argues that while the document itself is a government policy and although it represents a 'shared sector vision' (Mallard, quoted in Nuttall, 2004: 3), it does not express the wishes of the early childhood sector. She highlights how the discourses of children in the document do not compare with the competent capable child of the curriculum document. She argues:

> The Plan makes repeated referent to two representations of New Zealand childhood in particular: a proportionately small but critical group of children who are 'currently missing out' on early childhood services (Ministry of Education, 2002, p. 6); and second, children as future contributors to the 'social, educational and economic health of the nation' (Mallard, 2002, p. 1). In portraying young children in this way, the Plan reflects a persistent concern of the current Government with the achievement of Māori and Pasifika children in schools and their under-representation in post-compulsory education.
>
> (Nuttall, 2004: 3)

Thus, the tensions between the two leading policy and curriculum documents in Aotearoa New Zealand early childhood education demonstrate the struggle between constructing and treating children as capable and competent, or targeting 'needy' children for 'future benefit', that is, 'becoming something better in the future'. Discourses of childhood matter within early childhood education as noted by Dahlberg et al.:

> [W]ho is the child on whom [early childhood] practice is centred? From our postmodern perspective, there is no such thing as 'the child' or 'childhood', an essential being and state waiting to be discovered, defined and realized, so that we can say to ourselves and others 'that is how children are, that is what childhood is'. Instead there are many children and many childhoods, each constructed by our 'understand-ings of childhood and what children are and should be'. Instead of waiting upon scientific knowledge to tell us who the child is, we have choices to make about who we think the child is, and these choices have enormous significance since our construction of the child and early childhood are *productive*, by which we mean that they determine the institutions we provide for children and the pedagogical work that adults and children undertake in these institutions.
>
> (Dahlberg et al., 2007: 43, italics in original)

Recent constructions of childhood within early years pedagogy in Aotearoa New Zealand have emerged from two research projects undertaken by the author in collaboration with other academic colleagues. Both of these projects provide examples of the contested images of children that are held by teachers and the resulting discursive pedagogical practices that children experience in the early years. The first is from a project examining the experiences of 2-year-olds in kindergartens (Duncan et al., 2006; Duncan, 2009), and the second compares the discourses over a transition of one child from early childhood to school (Duncan, 2005a).

Two-year-olds in kindergartens[5]

Duncan and Dalli carried out a two-year research project working with kindergarten teachers in Aotearoa New Zealand in order to reconceptualize 2-year-olds as capable and competent within the kindergarten environment (Duncan et al., 2006). Kindergartens in Aotearoa New Zealand have historically been provided for 3- and 4-year-old children and so the introduction of these younger children was a new challenge for the teachers. How the 2-year-old in Aotearoa New Zealand was perceived, and what teachers felt or believed was the best practice and the best environments for a 2-year-old, was shaped around the teachers' understanding about child development. One of the reasons for the anxiety and concern at 2-year-olds attending kindergarten was a common understanding of the abilities, or lack of abilities, of 2-year-olds which informed much of the thinking about children in this age group. Interestingly, while we were searching to compile our literature base for this study it became apparent that 2-year-olds disappeared into the 'black hole' between being an infant and toddler (0–2 years) and being a young child or preschooler (3–5 years). Information pertaining to specifics of being a 2-year-old, or directed at working with 2-year-olds, was not apparent. This raised an interesting point for reflecting on how the discourses of 'ages and stages' still dominate what constitutes 'good' or 'bad' practice – working as regimes of truth in early childhood education (Cannella, 1997; Duncan, 2005b, 2009). In New Zealand's own curriculum document, Te Whāriki (Ministry of Education, 1996), the 2-year-old sits within both the toddler and the young child categories, thus acknowledging the 'considerable variation amongst individual children' (p. 20). The curriculum document in its explanation of 'good practice' goes on to address the importance of the suitability of early childhood environments for children. While this *is* an important factor, it is often interpreted into age-related, and age-segregated, categories rather than responding to individual children and contexts.

'What are 2-year-olds doing at kindergarten?' is the question that began our research study. Through our observations and interviews we found that our eighteen case study 2-year-olds were doing what was expected of them in a kindergarten: accepting and adopting the discourse of 'being a kindy kid'. They were 'fitting' into the rules and routines of the environment; they were building up their skills and confidence and they were approaching social relationships with a variety of experience and enthusiasm. An interesting finding was that rather than the *age* of the child being the key variable for pedagogical successful experience, the *type* of previous experience of the child, with the kindergarten, impacted more on whether they were confident and became part of the 'community of practice' of the kindergarten smoothly or not. For example, children who had already experienced the kindergarten from an older sibling attending appeared to be at an advantage over the 'first timers'. Another interesting observation, which was unsurprising, was that the expectations of the teachers, and the resulting interactions and practices, shaped the experiences of the children. For example, if the child was seen to be 'too little to do that' then they didn't do it; but if it was expected that they would carry out the behaviour, or complete the routine, they would (Duncan, 2009). What *was* surprising was that age did not make a significant difference in the teacher's expectations; for example, the same perceptions of the children were applied to a beginning kindergarten child irrespective of their age at starting. Hence, it is timely to change our discursive understandings of children away from a developmental discourse that ties us to ages and stages and reflect on the pedagogical implications of 'being and becoming an early childhood centre child'.

Learning dispositions and social contexts[6]

In this second research example, 'being and becoming' a student in early childhood and primary school[7] was also a dominant discourse in another Aotearoa New Zealand early years research study. A team of six researchers, led by Anne B. Smith and Margaret Carr,[8] observed twenty-seven children in their early childhood centres and over their first year of schooling, to investigate learning dispositions. Each member of the research team was responsible for a number of case study children, and two of the four children that the author observed have been written about in other publications (see Duncan, 2005a; Duncan et al., 2008). One of these children, Sarah, is reported here as an example where the discursive constructions of Sarah structured both her early childhood experiences and her schooling experiences in ways that presented challenges to her learning and to her own positional subjectivities.[9]

Sarah

At the beginning of the research in 2002 Sarah was a 4-year-old who had been attending a full-day child care centre from the age of 2. Sarah's parents chose for her to attend the nursery section of the same early childhood centre complex which allowed Sarah to engage with other children who, at the age of 2, also moved into the full-day centre with her. The centre was part of a larger complex and was licensed for twenty-five children, which means that no more than twenty-five children can attend at any one time. The majority of the children attending the centre attended for 6–8 hours every day of the week, which created a very stable group of children. In 2003, Sarah attended her local primary school. This was a small school with three full-time teaching positions (but this was job-shared with additional staff), and sixty children. Sarah's class was grouped with children aged 5–6 years. Sarah had been attending the school for two ten-week terms at the time of her observations and interviews. As published elsewhere (Duncan, 2005a), the discursive constructions of Sarah as a 'perfect day-care child' by her early childhood teachers contrasted sharply with the primary teachers' descriptions of her as a schoolchild – 'What kind of learner is she? What kind is she as a person?' These differences reflect two competing discursive constructions of childhood (with regard to Sarah in particular): the 'competent, capable child' of the Te Whāriki curriculum document, and the 'child becoming' something in the future of more traditional constructions of childhood. This dichotomy is illustrated in the following two examples.

At the early childhood centre: Over the time that Sarah had been attending the centre the teachers could see that she had developed in confidence and, by the time she was about to start school, not only was she able to speak out competently but she also enjoyed telling long stories and speaking to the whole group of children at morning tea times, usually about events or shared experiences with her parents.

> EC Teacher X: She's always been what I would think a perfect day-care child. She gets on with people. She's enthusiastic about whatever you put out for them. And gets involved. She never caused strife or . . .
> (Duncan, 2005a: 55)

The early childhood staff were very positive in their discussion of Sarah's anticipated school move. They had felt that she would fit into the school setting in the same way as she had fitted into the early childhood centre. With her 'imagination', her 'creativity' and her long attention span when involved in activities, alongside her attention to rules and doing things right, they felt that she would do well at school. Would the perfect day-care child become the perfect school child?

At primary school:

Morning Teacher: [I]s this little girl a very tactile kind of learner? What kind of learner is she? *What kind – you know, is she as a person?*

(Duncan, 2005a: 56)

Sarah's teachers at her primary school shared some of the views of the early childhood teacher. They saw her as a child who was particularly skilled in oral and imaginative language. They felt that, in comparison with other children her age, she was able to provide more than a superficial response in class, and was able to make links, explore ideas in depth, and draw on her rich knowledge in her work in the class. As at the early childhood centre, the teachers described her social skills as inclusive of all children – girls and boys – and that she could relate easily and well to her peers in the classroom as well as work comfortably and happily independently. Sarah's morning teacher felt that Sarah had the qualities that 'ultimately are going to make her [a] very good learner and thinker'.

Conflicting discursive constructions

Sarah's ability to be focused on a task or to be 'self-contained' and 'just get on with it', as emphasized by the early childhood teachers, was presented in a very different discourse at school. Sarah was described as unfocused and easily distracted when it came to the formal learning tasks of the classroom. The teachers held out great promise for Sarah, as they could see the qualities and abilities that she brought to the school.

The positions offered to Sarah at the early childhood centre and at the school differed markedly. While the teachers in both settings described Sarah in very rich, positive and supportive ways, the 'images' they held of Sarah differed – as did the very different discursive practices of each educational setting. While Sarah was arguably not such a 'different child' from one setting to the other, the positions of being a 'day-care child' and a 'schoolchild' were conceptualized very differently in each environment, and thus the discursive practices which shaped her every day were dramatically different. The images and expectations that teachers hold of and for their students are powerful normalizing practices. This is the power of understanding how discourse and discursive practices act and interact with individual subjectivities and the images of children within their lived childhood, demonstrated in this example by Sarah's experiences in an early childhood centre and an early school years classroom.

Conclusions

This chapter set out a provocation: Aotearoa New Zealand children as national treasures. A discourse of 'treasures' positions children as sacred, special and to be taken care of. As discussed, images of children as healthy, active, clean and well presented, imitating adults, presenting images of what they will be in the future, has masked the position of childhood in Aotearoa New Zealand where children's experiences are still dominated by the colonial heritage that settled with the European immigrants in the 1800s. This context is one where some parts of society construct children as 'evil' (needing to be corrected), where being accorded rights positions a child in competition against their parents' rights; where teachers have been relying on dated developmental or learning theories to construct their discursive practices, their images of the child and the possibilities for who children can become, and who as teachers they can be.

The range of images that surround parents and teachers about the very young child serve the interests of those who depict them – be it for market gain, political or policy agendas, or for child advocacy and change. The examples in this chapter have demonstrated the tensions involved in images of childhood between official policy (education policy, curriculum, legislation), pedagogical practices (by teachers and parenting by parents), and marketing forces (promoting sales). What sense do parents and teachers make of these conflicting images and the resulting discursive practices? When children are constructed as 'capable and competent' it does not remove the place for guidance, support and encouragement from the adults in their lives, for example the principles and strands expressed in Te Whāriki (the early childhood curriculum) which set out clearly the roles and responsibilities of teachers to contribute to each and every child's learning. Nor does being new in a setting or context, or new at a skill mean that children are 'deficient' or 'lacking', as in the study of 2-year-olds in kindergartens. Similarly, our constructions of healthy, beautiful children on the covers of parenting magazines should not disguise the position of children who in Aotearoa New Zealand experience real daily poverty and violence (Fletcher and Dwyer, 2008). Examining the constructions and images of children and childhood that teachers, and parents, hold of the children they engage with daily will enable clearer understandings of the limitations that we place on children and provide opportunities to rethink new possibilities that can be promoted to enhance the lived experiences of children in the twenty-first century.

Notes

1. Dahlberg et al. (2007).
2. In 2008 the government changed. The incoming National government indicated that there would be a new plan for early childhood education but, at the time of writing, there were no official indications as to what this plan would look like or be.
3. Children attend compulsory education from their fifth birthday in Aotearoa

New Zealand (although they are not legally obliged to attend until they are 6 years old).

4. For further discussion on the history and development of Te Whāriki, see Podmore et al., 1977; Carr and May, 1993a,b; Reedy, 1993; Cubey and Dalli, 1996; Smith, 1996; Burgess, 1999; May and Carr, 1996, 2000; Nuttall, 2003.

5. This research was funded by the New Zealand Teaching and Learning Research Initiative, managed by the New Zealand Council for Educational Research. This research fund enables research into understandings around improved teaching and learning. The author thanks the TLRI for support in both undertaking the research and in disseminating the findings.

6. The research was funded by the Royal Society of New Zealand's Marsden Social Science Research Fund. The author wishes to thank Marsden Fund for the funding that made this research possible.

7. Children in Aotearoa New Zealand begin school at 5 years of age.

8. The whole Marsden team that carried out the three-year project were: Professor Anne B. Smith (University of Otago), Professor Margaret Carr (University of Waikato), Dr Judith Duncan (University of Otago); Carolyn Jones (University of Waikato), Wendy Lee (University of Waikato) and Kate Marshall (University of Otago).

9. Sarah's story is told in full in Duncan, 2005a.

References

ACP Media (2009) *Little Treasures*. http://www.acpmedia.co.nz (accessed 20 January 2009).

Aitken, H. and Kennedy, A. (2007) Critical issues for the early childhood profession. In L. Keesing-Styles and H. Hedges (eds), *Theorising Early Childhood Practice: Emerging Dialogues* (pp. 165–185). Castle Hill: Pademelon Press.

Alderson, P. (2003) *Institutional Rites and Rights: A Century of Childhood*. London: Institute of Education, University of London.

Alderson, P. (2004) The participation rights of premature babies, *International Journal of Children's Rights*, 13: 31–50.

Alderson, P., Hawthorne, J. and Killen, M. (2005) The participation rights of premature babies, *International Journal of Children's Rights*, 13: 31–50.

Alvestad, M. and Duncan, J. (2006) 'The value is enormous – It's priceless I think!' New Zealand preschool teachers' understandings of the early childhood curriculum in New Zealand – a comparative perspective, *International Journal of Early Childhood*, 38(1): 31–46.

Alvestad, M., Duncan, J. and Berge, A. (forthcoming) Aotearoa New Zealand early childhood teachers' perspectives on Te Whāriki: one aspect of a larger comparative study, *New Zealand Journal of Teachers Work*, 6(1).

Anning, A., Cullen, J. and Fleer, M. (eds) (2009) *Early Childhood Education: Society and Culture*, 2nd edition. London: Sage.

Aries, P. (1962) *Centuries of Childhood: A Social History of Family Life*. London: Jonathan Cape.

Ball, S.J. (1990) *Foucault and Education: Disciplines and Knowledge*. London: Routledge.

Bird, L. (2003) Seen and heard? Moving beyond discourses about children's needs and rights in educational policies, *New Zealand Journal of Education Studies*, 38(1): 37–47.

Bloch, M.N. and Popkewitz, T.S. (2000) Constructing the parent, teacher and child: discourses of development. In L. Diaz Soto (ed.), *The Politics of Early Childhood Education* (pp. 7–32). New York: Peter Lang.

Bodine, A. (2003) School uniforms and discourses on childhood, *Childhood*, 10(1): 43–63.

Buckingham, D. (2004) New media, new childhoods? Children's changing cultural environment in the age of digital technology. In M.J. Kehily (ed.), *An Introduction to Childhood Studies* (pp. 108–122). Maidenhead: Open University Press.

Burgess, F. (1999) Blending Te Whariki and the Taïala, *Early Childhood Folio*, 4: 16–19.

Burman, E. (1994) *Deconstructing Developmental Psychology*. London: Routledge.

Burman, E. (2005) Childhood, neo-liberalism and the feminization of education, *Gender and Education*, 17(4): 351–367.

Burr, R. (2004) Children's rights: international policy and lived practice. In M.J. Kehily (ed.), *An Introduction to Childhood Studies* (pp. 145–159). Maidenhead: Open University Press.

Cannella, G.S. (1997) *Deconstructing Early Childhood Education: Social Justice and Revolution*. New York: Peter Lang.

Cannella, G.S. and Kincheloe, J.L. (eds) (2002) *Kidworld: Childhood Studies, Global Perspectives and Education*. New York: Peter Lang.

Cannella, G.S. and Viruru, R. (2004) *Childhood and Postcolonization*. New York: RoutledgeFalmer.

Carr, M. and May, H. (1993a) Celebrating Te Whāriki. In NZEI Te Riu Roa (ed.), *Early Childhood Education: Papers presented at the CECUA National Curriculum Conference* (pp. 10–19). Wellington: NZEI Te Riu Roa.

Carr, M. and May, H. (1993b) Choosing a model. Reflecting on the development process of Te Whāriki: National Early Childhood Curriculum Guidelines in New Zealand, *International Journal of Early Years Education*, 1(3): 7–21.

Christensen, P. and Prout, A. (2005) Anthropological and sociological perspectives on the study of children. In S. Greene and D. Hogan (eds), *Researching Children's Experience: Approaches and Methods* (pp. 42–60). London: Sage.

Cubey, P. and Dalli, C. (1996) *Quality Evaluation of Early Childhood Education Programmes: A Literature Review*, Occasional Paper No. 1. Wellington: Institute for Early Childhood Studies, Victoria University of Wellington.

Dahlberg, G., Moss, P. and Pence, A. (2007) *Beyond Quality in Early Childhood Education and Care: Languages of Evaluation*, 2nd edition. London: Routledge.

Duncan, J. (2001) Restructuring lives: Kindergarten teachers and the education reforms 1984–1996. Unpublished thesis submitted for the degree of Doctor of Philosophy, University of Otago, Dunedin, New Zealand.

Duncan, J. (2004) Toddlers in kindergarten – expectations and experiences. Paper presented at the New Zealand Early Childhood Research Symposium, Wellington, November.

Duncan, J. (2005a) 'She's always been, what I would think, a perfect day-care child': constructing the subjectivities of a New Zealand child, *European Early Childhood Education Research Journal*, 13(2): 51–62.

Duncan, J. (2005b) Two year olds in kindergarten: What are they doing there?! *The First Years: New Zealand Journal of Infant and Toddler Education*, 7(2): 4–8.

Duncan, J. (2008) *Moving with the Times: Leaders in Education since 1908. 100 years of the Auckland Kindergarten Association*. Auckland: Auckland Kindergarten Association.

Duncan, J. (2009) 'If you think they can do it – then they can': two-year-olds in Aotearoa New Zealand kindergartens and changing professional perspectives. In D.C. Berthelsen, J. Brownlee and E. Johansson (eds), *Participatory Learning in the Early Years: Research and Pedagogy* (pp. 164–184). New York: Routledge.

Duncan, J., Dalli, C., Becker, R., Butcher, M., Foster, K., Hayes, K., et al. (2006) *Under Three-year-olds in Kindergartens: Children's Experiences and Teachers' Practices*. Wellington: Teaching and Learning Research.

Duncan, J., Jones, C. and Carr, M. (2008) Learning dispositions and the role of mutual engagement: factors for consideration in educational settings. *Contemporary Issues in Early Childhood Education*, 9(2): 107–117.

Farquhar, S. and Fleer, M. (2007) Developmental colonisation of early childhood education in Aotearoa/New Zealand and Australia. In L. Keesing-Styles and H. Hedges (eds), *Theorising Early Childhood Practice: Emerging Dialogues* (pp. 27–49). Castle Hill: Pademelon Press.

Feedman Lustig, D. (2004) Baby pictures: family, consumerism and exchange among teen mothers in the USA, *Childhood*, 11(2): 175–193.

Fletcher, M. and Dwyer, M. (2008) *A Fair Go for All Children: Actions to Address Child Poverty in New Zealand*. Wellington: Office of the Children's Commissioner.

Foucault, M. (1970) *The Order of Things: An Archeology of the Human Sciences*. London: Routledge.

Foucault, M. (1971) Orders of discourse, *Social Science Information*, 10(2): 7–30.

Foucault, M. (1980a) *The History of Sexuality. Vol. 1: An Introduction*. New York: Pantheon Books.

Foucault, M. (1980b) Truth and power. In C. Gordon (ed.), *Power/Knowledge: Selected Interviews and Other Writings, 1972–1977: Michel Foucault* (pp. 109–133). Hemel Hempstead: Harvester Press.

Foucault, M. (1982) Afterword: The subject and power. In H.L. Dreyfus and

P. Rabinow (eds), *Michel Foucault: Beyond Structuralism and Hermeneutics*, 2nd edition (pp. 208–228). Chicago: University of Chicago Press.

Hughes, P. (2005) Mickey and Barbie and strawberry shortcake: children playing in promotional webs, *International Journal of Equity and Innovation in Early Childhood*, 3(2): 98–117.

James, A. and Prout, A. (eds) (1997) *Constructing and Reconstructing Childhood: Contemporary Issues in the Sociological Study of Childhood*, 2nd edition. London: RoutledgeFalmer.

James, A., Jenks, C. and Prout, A. (1998) *Theorizing Childhood*. Cambridge: Polity Press.

Kehily, M.J. (2004) Understanding childhood: an introduction to some key themes and issues. In M.J. Kehily (ed.), *An Introduction to Childhood Studies* (pp. 1–22). Maidenhead: Open University Press.

Kessing-Styles, L. and Sumison, J. (2007) Connections, dissension and dialogue: the role of teacher education in promoting social justice. In L. Kessing-Styles and H. Hedges (eds), *Theorising Early Childhood Practice: Emerging Dialogues* (pp. 211–230). Castle Hill: Pademelon.

Kincheloe, J.L. (2002) The complex politics of McDonald's and the new childhood: colonizing kidworld. In G.S. Cannella and J.L. Kincheloe (eds), *Kidworld: Childhood Studies, Global Perspectives and Education* (pp. 75–121). New York: Peter Lang.

Kjørholt, A.T. (2005) The competent child and the 'right to be oneself': reflections on children as fellow citizens in an early childhood centre. In A. Clark, A.T. Kjørholt and P. Moss (eds), *Beyond Listening: Children's Perspectives on Early Childhood Services* (pp. 151–174). Bristol: The Policy Press.

Langer, B. (1994) Born to shop: children and consumer capitalism. In F. Briggs (ed.), *Children and Families: Australian Perspectives*. St Leonards: Allen & Unwin.

MacNaughton, G. (2005) *Doing Foucault in Early Childhood Studies: Applying Poststructural Ideas*. London: Routledge.

MacNaughton, G. and Hughes, P. (2000) Take the money and run? Toys, consumerism and capitalism in early childhood conferences. In L. Diaz Soto (ed.), *The Politics of Early Childhood Education* (pp. 85–98). New York: Peter Lang.

May, H. and Carr, M. (1996) The ideals and realities of the implementation of the New Zealand National Early Childhood Curriculum. Paper presented at 'Weaving Webs: Collaborative Teaching and Learning in the Early Years Curriculum', University of Melbourne.

May, H. and Carr, M. (2000) Empowering children to learn and grow – Te Whāriki: the New Zealand Early Childhood National Curriculum. In J. Hayden (ed.), *Landscapes in Early Childhood Education* (pp. 153–169). New York: Peter Lang.

Ministry of Education (1996) *Te Whāriki: Early Childhood Curriculum. He Whāriki Matauranga mo nga Mokopuna o Aotearoa*. Wellington: Learning Media.

Ministry of Education (2002) *Pathways to the Future: Nga Huarahi Arataki. A 10-year Strategic Plan for Early Childhood Education*. Wellington: Ministry of Education.

Moss, P. and Petrie, P. (2002) *From Children's Services to Children's Spaces: Public Policy, Children and Childhood*. London: RoutledgeFalmer.

NAEYC (National Association for the Education of Young Children) (1997) *Developmentally Appropriate Practice in Early Childhood Programs*. Washington, DC: NAEYC.

Nuttall, J. (ed.) (2003) *Weaving Te Whāriki: Aotearoa New Zealand's Early Childhood Curriculum Document in Theory and Practice*. Wellington: New Zealand Council for Educational Research.

Nuttall, J. (2004) What's my line? Exploring personal and political identities in early childhood education through the stories we tell. Paper presented at 'The Politics of Early Childhood Education', University of Auckland, Auckland.

Nyland, B. and Rockel, J. (2007) Infant-toddler care and education in Australia and Aotearoa/New Zealand: in search of status. In L. Keesing-Styles and H. Hedges (eds), *Theorising Early Childhood Practice: Emerging Dialogues* (pp. 71–95). Castle Hill: Padamelon Press.

Podmore, V., May, H. and Mara, D. (1997) Evaluating early childhood programmes using Te Whariki: a process of joint discoveries. Paper presented at the New Zealand Association for Research in Education, University of Auckland, Auckland.

Qvortrup, J., Bardy, M., Sgritta, G. and Wintersberger, H. (eds) (1994) *Childhood Matters*. Aldershot: Avebury.

Reedy, T. (1993) I have a dream. Early childhood education. Paper presented to the National Curriculum Conference, Christchurch.

Smidt, S. (2006) *The Developing Child in the 21st Century: A Gobal Perspective on Child Development*. London: Routledge.

Smith, A.B. (1996) The early childhood curriculum from a sociocultural perspective, *Early Childhood Development and Care*, 115: 51–64.

Smith, A.B. (2000a) Children's rights and early childhood education: the rights of babies and young children. In A.B. Smith, M. Gollop, K. Marshall and K. Nairn (eds), *Advocating for Children* (pp. 198–204). Dunedin: University of Otago Press.

Smith, A.B. (2000b) The rights of young children. Paper presented at the National Family Day Care Council Australia National Conference 'Our Future in our Hands', June.

Smith, A.B. (2002) Interpreting and supporting participation rights: contributions from sociocultural theory, *International Journal of Children's Rights*, 10: 73–88.

Smith, A.B., Duncan, J. and Marshall, K. (2005) Children's perspectives on their learning: exploring methods, *Early Child Development and Care*, 175(2): 473–487.

Wilkstedt, M. and Murachver, T. (2006) New Zealand policy on the discipline of children within the family, *Childrenz Issues*, 10(1): 40–45.

Wood, B., Hassall, I., Hook, G. and Ludbrook, R. (2008) *Unreasonable Force: New Zealand's Journey Towards Banning the Physical Punishment of Children*. Wellington: Save the Children New Zealand.

Woodhead, M. (1997) Psychology and the cultural construction of children's needs. In A. James and A. Prout (eds), *Constructing and Reconstructing Childhood: Contemporary Issues in the Sociological Study of Childhood*, 2nd edition (pp. 63–85). London: RoutledgeFalmer.

Woodhead, M. (2000) Towards a global paradigm for research into early childhood. In H. Penn (ed.), *Early Childhood Services: Theory, Policy and Practice* (pp. 15–35). Buckingham: Open University Press.

Woodhead, M. and Faulkner, D. (2000) Subjects, objects or participants? Dilemmas of psychological research with children. In P. Christensen and A. James (eds), *Research with Children: Perspectives and Practices* (pp. 9–35). London: Falmer Press.

8 *Investigating Quality project*: opening possibilities in early childhood care and education policies and practices in Canada

Alan Pence and Veronica Pacini-Ketchabaw

The hope [in early childhood education] is not generated by regulatory modernity's assumption of linear and inevitable progress through finding the one true way. Rather it lies in the possibility of a more dialogic, plural and democratic early childhood field.

– Moss (2008: 20)

Introduction

This chapter explores the activities and conceptual underpinnings of a large Canadian project entitled 'Investigating Quality in Early Childhood' (IQ) that is currently attempting to broaden and reposition early childhood discourses that have long dominated early childhood care and development practice, as well as programme and policy directions, in Canada and also throughout North America. Such dominant discourses are maintained through reinforcing synergies across systems and system levels. In order to effect change, such multiple system dynamics must be addressed, and the IQ project has attempted to do this.

The chapter begins with a brief overview of the contexts in which Canadian early childhood policies are enacted. On the one hand, Canadian early childhood policies and practices have long pursued reductionist approaches that overly simplify the nature of the child, quality, care and programming. On the other hand, Canadian policies and practices have grown to appreciate the complexities inherent in supporting cultural diversity, addressing challenges associated with immigration, and the importance of recognizing Indigenous rights. The schism that emerges from these two different

Canadian orientations provides a key background against which the IQ project is positioned.

The second part of the chapter provides a description of the multi-system planning behind the project, ways in which those systems and levels were engaged, and reflections on the degree to which the approach taken was effective. Central to the overall process has been a series of forums and presentations by respected leaders from various parts of the world who have played similar broadening and deepening roles in their own countries. Certain of those approaches were adapted to the Canadian IQ project with, for example, work with front-line early childhood educators proving to be effective. We hope that the processes described in the chapter are valuable for others to consider in their own contexts. The chapter concludes with a critical reflection on our work.

Background and contexts

Several international movements and publications have inspired the Investigating Quality project. Through the project, we were able to engage a Canadian jurisdiction with the ideas explored in *Valuing Quality* (Moss and Pence, 1994) and *Beyond Quality in Early Childhood Education and Care: Postmodern Perspectives* (Dahlberg et al., 1999). The project also drew significant inspiration from work that was initiated in the late 1980s and early 1990s in New Zealand (Meade, 1988; Carr and May, 1992), writings from the US-based reconceptualist movement commencing in the early 1990s (Kessler and Swadener, 1992; Cannella, 1997; Grieshaber and Cannella, 2001; Cannella and Viruru, 2004); from Australia (MacNaughton, 2000, 2003, 2005; Grieshaber and Cannella, 2001; Robinson and Diaz, 2006); practice, programme, training and policy development work in Sweden (Lenz Taguchi, 2006; Dahlberg et al., 2007); and in Italy (Edwards et al., 1998; Rinaldi, 2005, 2006) – the latter with a significant international following and a strong position of 'never again' with regard to the conditions of civil society that allowed a fascist regime to take root in Italy under Mussolini.

The intent of the IQ project was to simultaneously engage policy makers, government officials, early childhood instructors and early childhood front-line educators with critical perspectives that existed outside the established and 'normal' North American discourses, but to do so in a way that emphasized the 'do-ability', practicality and possibilities of these 'other' perspectives and practices for early educational contexts.

Early childhood education in Canada

Early childhood education in Canada is closely allied with its counterpart in the United States. Community child care studies undertaken in both countries, from the earliest ones in the late 1960s (see Pence and Benner, 2000), through to the present (Pence and Pacini-Ketchabaw, 2008), have been deeply influenced by modernist and reductionist understandings of the field. In neither of the countries have post-structural or critical theory approaches gained more than a marginal influence – insufficient to disrupt, more than momentarily, dominant narratives that include: remedially focused programming with concomitant cost–benefit analyses (Schweinhart and Weikart, 1999; US Department of Health and Human Services, Administration for Children and Families, 2005), developmentally appropriate practice (Bredekamp and Copple, 1997), and more recently conjoined neuro-development and economic development arguments (Shore, 1997; McCain and Mustard, 1999; Shonkoff and Phillips, 2000; Young, 2002).

Despite the emergence of such streams of research over time, there is a *plus ça change, plus c'est la même chose* quality to North American early childhood policies and research that has consistently viewed early childhood care and education through economic and social class lenses, never quite escaping its nineteenth century framing as 'failed motherhood'. The persistence of this stigma has hampered forward progress, and, not surprisingly, led both countries to failing grades near the bottom of a recent UNICEF report card on early childhood education in 'developed' countries (UNICEF, 2008). A failure for the public discussion to evolve is in some ways understandable given both countries' long histories of ambivalence regarding the role of women in society, with an emphasis on the singular importance of the nurturing bond between mother and child conflicting with women's roles in the paid labour force.

The failure of the academy, however, to significantly move beyond questions of quality first posed in the 1980s and 1990s is, we argue, more discouraging than the general public discourse. North American research engagements with issues of care and quality, specifically research currently published in major journals, fails to meaningfully engage, across a broad front, issues of diversity, difference, democracy and early childhood's key potential in influencing civil society, at the same time as research publications coming out of Europe, Australia and New Zealand have opened up new and innovative avenues for research and theory development. It was those *other* works that were of particular interest at the time that funding was made available for the Investigating Quality project.

Seeking innovative ways forward

As co-principals for the IQ project we shared strong interests in the critical, post-structural and postmodern literature that had come into early childhood education (ECE), early childhood care and development (ECCD) and child development starting in the mid-1980s with Walkerdine's critiques of child development theories (Walkerdine, 1984, 1985), followed by a surge of early childhood care and education literature in the early 1990s that continues to the present (Davies, 1993; Cannella, 1997; Dahlberg et al., 1999, 2007; MacNaughton, 2000, 2003, 2005; Grieshaber and Cannella, 2001; Moss and Petrie, 2002; Cannella and Viruru, 2004; Lenz Taguchi, 2006; Moss, 2007). We were also interested in the ways in which 'Reggio Emilia' had become a symbol for innovation and quality in North America, particularly given that its pedagogical infrastructure and conceptualization was largely at odds with the dominant literature in Canada and the United States (New, 2000, 2003). The adoption of Reggio-inspired ideas in Sweden was also of great interest (Dahlberg et al., 2007).

But perhaps of greatest interest were advances in Aotearoa/New Zealand that had not only spread, in a fairly short period of time, throughout the country and throughout the various systems and system levels of the country, but which had consciously and conscientiously sought to create an approach to ECE that was not only culturally sensitive but truly culturally inclusive (Carr and May, 1992, 2007; May, 1997, 2001, 2002; Carr, 2001; Carr et al., 2003, 2005; May and Hill, 2005). Aotearoa/New Zealand was not only of great interest for its innovative and comprehensive approach to ECE, but given its history as a former British colony, its form of government and its history of Indigenous relations and patterns of immigration, there was much that Canada could relate to. Thus, Aotearoa/New Zealand became one of the primary sources of inspiration for the IQ project.

From its inception, it was clear that if the project was going to achieve any level of impact or take-up, it would need a multi-systems approach. At its most basic this would need to include: front-line practice, programme delivery, in-service training, tertiary education, research, government engagement and policy development; and in each of these contexts sensitivity to issues of diversity would be paramount. Fundamental to work across all systems and levels was considering a means to introduce new approaches and understandings.

Opening opportunities for dialogue and conversations

In order to work across multiple systems and levels and broaden and deepen British Columbia's approaches towards early childhood education by considering diverse discourses currently found internationally, a series of symposia were launched. Overall, the symposia attempted to: bring together small groups of international leaders in early childhood studies who shared a perspective of young children as meaningful knowledge makers; explore ways to disseminate diverse understandings on 'quality' at policy, practice, research and training levels; support the development of a sophisticated and innovative early childhood education field at the provincial level; create meaningful links between policy makers, the early childhood field and researchers; and share these discussions with diverse early childhood stakeholder groups.

International scholars from different locations (primarily the four contexts mentioned above) who had experiences in broadening and deepening discussions around 'quality' within various systems and levels were invited to participate in each symposium. Although the delivery format of each symposium varied to meet diverse needs and opportunities, the symposia shared certain characteristics. First, small-group brainstorming and idea-sharing sessions (ranging from one to three days) were arranged. The purpose of these sessions was to create opportunities to engage in rich and meaningful dialogue that worked to capture the diverse aspects, concepts and knowledge systems of the selected topic. This was done as a way to move forward, within and across boundaries, in pursuit of new ideas about what constitutes 'good' early childhood education. Second, small-group consultations with various stakeholder groups took place with a format of brief presentations to raise issues, followed by discussions of those issues. The consultations focused primarily on forum guests' interaction with key individuals within governments, appropriate academics, tertiary educators, specific service groups and community representatives, and other key stakeholders. The purpose of the consultations was to provide information regarding postmodern approaches to the invited participants, and beyond the provision of information, there were opportunities to engage in meaningful dialogue regarding these issues and their implementation in the British Columbia (and sometimes broader) contexts. Third, the expertise and learning that our guests brought and the ideas that emerged from the small-group discussions and consultations were made accessible to the broader early childhood education community (including academic, Aboriginal and service communities, front-line practitioners, policy makers, politicians) through public presentations.

The inaugural symposium took place in 2006. Entitled 'International Perspectives on Indigenous Quality Early Childhood Care and Development', it addressed issues of policy, practice and training in relation to Indigenous communities (Rodriguez et al., 2007). Our second event, 'Developing Policies on "Quality" Early Childhood Care and Development', addressed the ways in which countries that have incorporated postmodern approaches in front-line practices have worked with policy development, implementation, regulation and assessment. The third symposium, 'Pedagogical Considerations on Quality Early Learning and Child Care' (Pacini-Ketchabaw and Pence, 2007), also held in 2006, focused on the development and implementation of meaningful, community-informed pedagogies and was specifically designed to address front-line and tertiary educators. The fourth symposium was 'Building Capacity in the Early Years: Discussion and Consultation with New Zealand Leaders'. This event allowed us to engage in an in-depth exploration of the ways in which New Zealand has moved forward with meaningful, community-informed policies and practices. With the specific purpose of engaging the early childhood community in British Columbia around discussions of child development perspectives that are responsive to different cross-cultural contexts, we organized the fifth symposium, Early Childhood Care and Development: Perspectives from the Majority World (Pence, 2008). The sixth symposium, Times for Innovation in ECE: Challenging Our Ways of Thinking About Educators' and Children's Learning, focused again on the experiences of one particular context – Sweden. We engaged in dialogue with scholars from Sweden regarding the development and implementation of early childhood spaces designed to focus on children's learning processes. The seventh symposium was co-sponsored with the provincial early childhood association. The purpose of the event was for educators and leaders of British Columbia to engage in focused discussions on issues regarding pedagogical documentation, social justice, diversity, and advocacy that build on postmodern approaches. The eighth, and most recent, symposium was made possible, in part, through support from the Society for Research on Child Development (SRCD). The first author has long worked with early child development (ECD) leaders in Africa and been troubled by the degree to which African 'voices' are not heard in the international child development literature. Marfo and Pence submitted a proposal to the SRCD in response to a call for the society to broaden its international relevance and were pleased to be one of four applicants (out of fifty-seven) to receive funding to host an SRCD/IQ symposium focused on that theme. Overall, the symposia have made visible 'new' ideas not necessarily well known within the Canadian context, as well as discussions around critical paths that lead to change.

The feedback received from participating audiences has been very positive. Important ripple effects are seen at the policy level, specifically around the recently published *British Columbia Early Learning Framework* (Government of British Columbia, 2007). The Framework incorporates postmodern approaches to early childhood education, drawing on innovative early childhood ideas developed in New Zealand, Sweden and Reggio Emilia (Italy). For example, a central idea in the Framework is a constructivist perspective on the child. For instance, the Framework refers to the image of the child:

> Whether one is aware of it or not, everybody has an image of the child that is rooted in their culture, knowledge, personal histories, and aspirations for the future. In many ways, the image of the child

reflects not only a person's beliefs about children and childhood, but also their beliefs about what is possible and desirable for human life at the individual, social, and global levels.

The particular image of the child held by people strongly influences their decisions about young children, the way they interact with children, and how they construct the environments where children grow, develop and learn ... Being aware of their own image of the child helps adults to reflect on and make conscious choices that foster children's early learning.

This framework supports the creation of a shared image of the child that can guide efforts to promote early learning at the local and provincial levels. It views young children as capable and full of potential; as persons with complex identities, grounded in their individual strengths and capacities, and their unique social, linguistic, and cultural heritage. In this image, children are rooted in and take nourishment from a rich, supportive ground, comprised of relationships with their families and communities, their language and culture, and the surrounding environment. As children grow and learn, they ask questions, explore, and make discoveries, supported by these roots and branching out to new experiences, people, places, and things in their environment. Within this complex ecology, every child belongs and contributes.

(Government of British Columbia, 2007: 4)

We think that this statement opens possibilities for alternative discourses in early childhood practices in British Columbia. For example, it invites us, as Moss and Petrie (2002) argue, to question our ideas of children's services and to work towards the creation of children's spaces:

as spaces – physical environments certainly, but also social, cultural and discursive – provided through public agency, places for civic life rather than commercial transactions, where children meet one another, and adults. They foreground the present, rather than the future: they are part of life, not just a preparation for it. They are spaces for children's own agendas, although not precluding adult agendas, where children are understood as fellow citizens with rights, participating members of the social groups.

(Moss and Petrie, 2002: 106)

To summarize, the engagement of British Columbia ECE and ECCD communities in the organized symposia highlighting culturally meaningful international practices created a space for change that was ultimately manifested in policy documents. Change, however, was also sought at the practice level as we attempted to create spaces for discussions with early childhood educators around what is involved in moving from children's services to children's spaces. In the next section, we discuss our work with educators.

Reconceptualizing practices

A second strategy was to work directly with front-line early childhood educators within the context of their programmes. Before we proceed to describe the processes and preliminary results of this component of the IQ project, we outline the reasons for linking issues of quality with the reconceptualization of local early childhood education practices. To engage in this discussion we revisit our views on and conceptualization of the concept of quality.

As mentioned above, the IQ project intends to move beyond definitions of quality that embrace prescriptive practice and universal measurements that detach quality from the everyday practices of early childhood institutions and from those who are involved in those institutions (Dahlberg et al., 1999; also see Pence and Pacini-Ketchabaw, 2008). We further suggested that we believe in working from the postmodern perspective of the discourse of 'meaning making':

> In the field of early childhood, the discourse of meaning making speaks first and foremost about constructing and deepening *understanding* of the early childhood institution and its projects, in particular the pedagogical work – to make meaning of what is going on . . . The discourse of meaning making calls for explicitly ethical and philosophical choices, judgments of value, made in relation to the wider questions of what we want for our children here and now and in the future . . . The discourse of meaning making therefore not only adopts a social constructionist perspective, but relates to an understanding of learning as a process of co-construction, by which in relationship with others we make meaning of the world.
>
> (Dahlberg et al., 1999: 106–107)

We felt that, to engage in the discourse of meaning making and challenge the taken-for-granted assumptions of the discourse of quality, it was important to engage in discussions *with* front-line practitioners directly involved with the pedagogical work that Dahlberg et al. (1999) refer to. From the perspective of the discourse of meaning making, change emerges from dialogue: 'To change a pedagogical practice, it is necessary to start by problematizing and deconstructing [dominant] discourses and to understand and demonstrate how they are related to what is going on in pedagogical practice' (Dahlberg et al., 1999: 131).

Within this framework, we engaged in working towards quality by promoting the active engagement of early childhood educators in British Columbia in discussions and actions that would lead to the formation of innovative, dynamic and sustainable early childhood environments for young children and in turn build capacity in and bring innovation to the field of early childhood education in the province. In response to our current context, and our interest in postmodern approaches, we worked towards creating opportunities for early childhood educators to network and critically reflect on their own practices through the use of pedagogical documentation and learning stories. A participatory action research approach (MacNaughton and Hughes, 2008) was used to reflect on knowledge, experiences and values embedded in the educators' own practices. Working relationally, pedagogies characterized by depth, meaning, purpose, engagement, discussions and dialogue were used to explore meaningful understandings of practices.

Our inspiration for the delivery aspect of this component of the project has been multifaceted. First, we drew again on New Zealand's experiences in developing and implementing curricula, assessment tools (learning stories), and professional development with early childhood teachers (Carr, 2001; Carr et al., 2003, 2005; Carr and May, 2007). Second, the work of MacNaughton and her colleagues at the University of Melbourne provided us with important insights into how we might engage in postmodern practices in early childhood classrooms (MacNaughton, 2000, 2003, 2005). Third, the practices of Reggio Emilia early childhood education programmes, as well as Swedish perspectives on Reggio Emilia approaches, inspired and broadened our work with early childhood educators, specifically the work conducted around pedagogical documentation (Rinaldi, 1998, 2001, 2005, 2006; Project Zero, 2004; Dahlberg et al., 2007). What inspired us was that these practices are contextual, interactive approaches that open up to local voices, celebrate diversity, provide encouragement to families and community members to participate meaningfully in the lives of children, and nurture a democratic process.

The work with educators occurred in three phases. Each involved participation in a series of learning circles, one sharing circle, online discussions, and site visits. Monthly learning circles provided opportunities for small groups of educators to share and discuss established and emerging practices as well as to become familiar with, reflect upon, discuss, struggle with, and challenge postmodern critical approaches to practice. Educators collected moments of their practice following pedagogical documentation (Project Zero, 2004; Dahlberg and Moss, 2005; Dahlberg et al., 2007) and learning stories (Carr, 2001; Carr et al., 2003, 2005; Carr and May, 2007) in their centres using journal writing, photography, video recording and audio recording, which were then shared with the group. During our learning circles, we critically reflected together on each educator's documentation and made visible how we might work with postmodern theories to extend their practices. Sharing circles took place annually and their purpose was to bring together all of the educators from the different learning circles to interact and share the work produced as a result of their involvement in the learning circles. The 'online space' was created and used by educators and researchers to communicate between circles and circulate materials of interest. In addition to facilitating the workshops, members of the research team provided individual support to each educator through visits to early childhood education centres, providing opportunities for one-to-one conversations between the educators and the researchers. In Phase I of the project, twenty-six early childhood educators completed the delivery. Phase II of the project invited the educators from the first phase to continue and added spaces for approximately forty more educators. To date, over seventy early childhood educators have participated in at least one phase of the circles.

Our work with educators is ongoing, but to provide the reader with a brief insight into what we are currently achieving we present some of our qualitative findings obtained from an open-ended written survey completed by participating educators in the second year of delivery. The IQ project works towards building capacity in, and bringing innovation to the field. This is of particular interest to us given the situation in which child care is positioned in British Columbia (for example low pay, high rates of turnover, difficulties recruiting new educators to the field and retaining those who are currently in the field). Through their participation in the IQ project, we found that educators began to value their work more and, more importantly, began to expand their horizons in relation to the possibilities of their work and the knowledge bases within the field. In the words of participating educators:

> Not only is my knowledge expanding with the analytical perspectives and current issues with ECE but also I participate differently because I feel more confident in my learning through the sessions.

> I feel that it was the ultimate pro-d [professional development] experience. I had the opportunity to read interesting and thought-provoking articles, discuss ideas with others, share in the projects that were going on at other centres and expand my knowledge and thinking.

> I have been more than satisfied; I have been enriched and challenged in a myriad of ways. This kind of exchange of ideas has been severely lacking in other professional development opportunities. In my mind it is imperative that we move our profession forward with this kind of dialogue. We have been stuck on 'how to' and we need to move to 'why'.

> I have always sought out new ideas and knowledge in the field of child care, and I felt confident in my practice. However my

involvement in IQ has broadened that knowledge, extended the theoretical base, reaffirmed much of what I do and challenged me to consider new ways of thinking and being with children. After participating in IQ I feel my level of professionalism has been raised. I am able to discuss ideas and theories of child care more knowledgeably, and relate those ideas and theories to my practice. I am more confident and reflective in my practice, and now have a burning desire to share what I've learned!

Critical reflection, as noted above, is a key component in the discourse of meaning making and therefore in our work with educators. MacNaughton (2003) argues that reflecting critically on our own practices opens up opportunities for learning and motivates us to make changes, when necessary, and also to be creative. In their work on effective professional development, Mitchell and Cubey (2003) argue that, 'if early childhood education centers are to be learning communities for teachers as well as children, parents and others, there need to be opportunities within the work environment for reflection, experimentation and planning' (p. xv). In the IQ project, we have introduced pedagogical documentation as a tool for reflection, planning and action within the discourse of meaning making. Our use of pedagogical documentation embraces the values of the early childhood system of Reggio Emilia, which regards the child as an active learner, values the role of the community and relationships in learning, and views learning and life as ongoing experimentation and research (Dahlberg et al., 2007). Educators have responded to the challenge of embracing other ways of understanding practice with great enthusiasm:

> This has been significant for me . . . I think the possibilities for creativity on the part of the caregiver could be enormous with this process which I think will create wonderful possibilities for children.
>
> I was not as familiar with pedagogical narrations before; however, participating in the IQ Project has considerably increased my knowledge about the different types and styles of pedagogical documentation.
>
> I have been able to incorporate some of my learning in my practice. I have changed the way I look at and do documentation. I have become more reflective and look for ways to make this reflection visible to others.
>
> I have appreciated the opportunity to engage in real discussions about quality education and childcare with like-minded supportive colleagues. I felt supported, listened to, and a great sense of camaraderie within our group. I have been searching for further educational

opportunities to find a deeper understanding, a more thoughtful academic approach, and was excited by what the IQ Project initially offered. Having now participated in the IQ Project I am more motivated than ever to continue the investigation and the learning. The IQ Project has exceeded all my expectations for professional development, and set me on a path for seeking new learning, sharing what I have learned thus far, and continuing to reflect, modify and expand my work with children. Thank you for giving me this amazing learning experience.

Educators' engagement in critical reflection, Lenz Taguchi (2006) reminds us, is a step towards changing practices:

> Once I revisit and revise what I 'know' about how children think and learn, or about what approach I should use to help them grow, then I may be ethically obliged to change what I actually do with them. Based on my new understandings, I cannot ethically continue with my old practices. And neither can I stop with my new understandings. I am ethically obligated to continue to examine my practices always looking for better ways to 'do good' for these particular children with whom I am working.
>
> (Lenz Taguchi, 2006: 260)

MacNaughton (2003) also argued that 'critical educators need to look carefully at how values construct the teaching and learning relationships, processes and products' (p. 196). Educators participating in the IQ project are deeply engaged in challenging their own established practices – as stated within the discourse of meaning making. By documenting critical incidents, they deconstruct taken-for-granted assumptions within the field in general as well as their own positions within dominant discourses. In the following quote, an educator refers to one of the ways in which she is 'unpacking' her own assumptions:

> I feel more compelled to step in when policing or less than respectful practice is sliding in . . . Is that our rule – where did it come from – is it appropriate?

Overall, the IQ project has provided a space for professional revitalization of educators by engaging in reflection and critical analysis and challenging each other to think differently about early childhood education issues. The opportunity to connect, participate, collaborate and grow with colleagues has been an invaluable component noted by many of the participants. They spoke about the importance of having the opportunity to network and make ongoing and meaningful connections with others working in the field. They indicated that they appreciated the various ideas that were introduced as well as the critical edge that the curriculum discussions involved. These critical discussions enabled them to view their work in alternative ways. The ongoing nature of the programme, as well as the time provided for thinking and reflecting outside of their time with children, made them feel empowered and valued as professionals.

Although the programme has been a valuable resource to the participating early childhood educators, as researchers and professionals we still face a multitude of challenges. We certainly bring these challenges as spaces for new possibilities and further learning. Given that participating educators valued the change that the project brought for them, the project needs to reach more early childhood educators to ensure changes in the entire field. Although we have also observed very positive results in our work with tertiary educators, there is still a need for more opportunities for students to be exposed to discourses beyond dominant developmental ones. Time is important, particularly if we are to open further spaces to give educators the opportunity to fully integrate the ideas into their practices, particularly those centres that have been working with prescriptive approaches for a long time. We are also to take into consideration the overall realities in which the centres work (for example under-staffed in a low-paid field). Many of the educators who have fully engaged in a transformation process through the IQ project are working outside of regular paid hours (beyond the time covered by the project) to engage in the discussions, reflections and collaboration that pedagogical documentation requires. Managers and governments need to consider the time demands that more meaningful and contextually supportive practices involve.

Final reflections

Working within the realm of postmodern discourses 'on the ground' presents challenges that require different ways of thinking and doing. However, as Moss (2006) points out, engaging in this work is ethically and politically necessary as local, diversified and culturally driven narratives become undermined through hegemonic globalization. The good news is, perhaps, that we have work to do!

> Those of us who wish to contest the discourse and transgress its norms need to dialogue more about how this might be done. What processes could be used, which alliances formed, and what other forms of resistance are possible? How can we proliferate a multiplicity of discourses to avoid replacing one dominant discourse with another? There are no easy or certain answers because the dominant

discourse draws strength from its denial of multiplicity and diversity. There is, according to this discourse, just one way of knowing, thinking, and practicing, the supreme task being to define and follow a particular way.

(Moss, 2006: 133)

Our work has focused on opening up towards diversity and multiplicity, towards responding to our local contexts rather than grand narratives of childhood. What we are engaged in with the Investigating Quality project can be conceptualized as a form of resistance in support of inherent diversities, in response to Moss's invitation to challenge dominant discourses. Dominant discourses 'can be subject to what Foucault terms practices of freedom' (Dahlberg and Moss, 2005: 144), and we feel that such practices are much needed in the world of early childhood.

One word of caution as we take seriously Moss's second question, 'how can we proliferate a multiplicity of discourses to avoid replacing one dominant discourse with another?'. We are not presenting our work as 'the way' to engage in resistance, rather as 'a way' informed by local knowledge and provisional truths. Neither are we claiming our work as having been outside of power/knowledge relations. 'Power relations are always present, as the means by which individuals try to determine the behaviour of others' (Dahlberg and Moss, 2005: 144). As a team, we are always shifting courses of actions, looking for ruptures in systems of knowledge production, and responding to emerging possibilities and to the doors that close. Foucault reminds us that resistance work is a dangerous enterprise and can never be an innocent activity. One of the authors, in collaboration with others, previously wrote: 'We do not have any guarantees. We have to see that risks and possibilities are not opposites, but exist at the same time . . . Considering the risks, we always have to pose questions concerning what right we have . . . what is ethically legitimate' (Dahlberg et al., 1999: 156). Through our work we attempt to create a forum for dialogue and learning.

The dialogue we are interested in generating through the IQ project symposia is dialogue across paradigms, that is, conversations between modernist and postmodernist ways of understanding the world. Moss (2008) argues that 'the absence of dialogue and debate impoverishes early childhood and weakens democratic politics' (p. 11), and 'marginalizes postfoundationalism, confining the increasing opus of work to a critical ghetto and denying the possibility of change' (p. 12). Drawing on Mouffe (2000), Moss (2008) presents the concept of 'agonistic pluralism' – a concept we find important in our work – as a possibility for dialogue in early childhood education.

A politics of agonistic pluralism is a condition for democracy. It recognizes and legitimates conflict arising from different interests, values and perspectives: it does not give up on or deny profound differences of perspective . . . It provides a framework for thinking about how to bring some people located in different paradigms and working with different discourses into some form of engagement without requiring domination by one camp or phoney consensus.

(Moss, 2008: 13)

References

Bredekamp, S. and Copple, S. (1997) *Developmentally Appropriate Practice in Early Childhood Programs*. Washington, DC: National Association for the Education of Young Children.

Cannella, G.S. (1997) *Deconstructing Early Childhood Education: Social Justice and Revolution*. New York: Peter Lang.

Cannella, G.S. and Viruru, R. (2004) *Childhood and Postcolonization: Power, Education, and Contemporary Practice*. New York: RoutledgeFalmer.

Carr, M. (2001) *Assessment in Early Childhood Settings: Learning Stories*. Thousand Oaks, CA: Sage.

Carr, M. and May, H. (1992) *National Early Childhood Curriculum Guidelines in New Zealand*. Hamilton: Waikato University.

Carr, M. and May, H. (2007) Te Whariki: curriculum voices. In R. Openshaw and J. Soler (eds), *Reading across International Boundaries: History, Policy, and Politics* (pp. 33–73). Charlotte, NC: Information Age Publishing.

Carr, M., Hatherly, A., Lee, W. and Ramsey, K. (2003) Te Whariki and Assessment: A Case Study of Teacher Change. In J. Nuttall (ed.), *Weaving Te Whariki: Aotearoa New Zealand's Early Childhood Curriculum Document in Theory and Practice* (pp. 187–214). Wellington: NZCER.

Carr, M., Jones, C. and Lee, W. (2005) Beyond listening: can assessment practice play a part? In A. Clark, P. Moss and A.T. Kjorholt (eds), *Beyond Listening: Children's Perspectives on Early Childhood Services* (pp. 129–150). Bristol, UK: The Policy Press.

Dahlberg, G. and Moss, P. (2005) *Ethics and Politics in Early Childhood Education*. London: RoutledgeFalmer.

Dahlberg, G., Moss, P. and Pence, A.R. (1999) *Beyond Quality in Early Childhood Education and Care: Postmodern Perspectives*. London: Falmer Press.

Dahlberg, G., Moss, P. and Pence, A.R. (2007) *Beyond Quality in Early Childhood Education and Care: Languages of Evaluation*, 2nd edition. London: Routledge.

Davies, B. (1993) *Shards of Glass: Children Reading and Writing beyond Gendered Identities*. Cresskill, N.J.: Hampton Press.

Edwards, C.P., Gandini, L. and Forman, G.E. (1998) Introduction, background and starting points. In C.P. Edwards, L. Gandini and G.E. Forman (eds), *The*

Hundred Languages of Children: The Reggio Emilia Approach – advanced reflections (pp. 5–26). Greenwich, CT: Ablex.

Government of British Columbia (2007) *British Columbia Early Learning Framework.* Victoria, BC: Ministry of Education, Ministry of Health, Ministry of Children and Family Development.

Grieshaber, S. and Cannella, G.S. (2001) From identity to identities: increasing possibilities in early childhood education. In S. Grieshaber and G.S. Cannella (eds), *Embracing Identities in Early Childhood Education: Diversity and Possibilities* (pp. 3–21). New York: Teachers College Press.

Kessler, S. and Swadener, B.B. (1992) *Reconceptualizing the Early Childhood Curriculum: Beginning the Dialogue.* New York: Teachers College Press.

Lenz Taguchi, H. (2006) Reconceptualizing early childhood education: challenging taken-for-granted ideas. In E. Johanna and J.T. Wagner (eds), *Nordic Childhoods and Early Education Philosophy, Research, Policy, and Practice in Denmark, Finland, Iceland, Norway, and Sweden* (pp. 257–287). Greenwich, CT: Information Age Publishing.

MacNaughton, G. (2000) *Rethinking Gender in Early Childhood Education.* London: Paul Chapman.

MacNaughton, G. (2003) *Shaping Early Childhood: Learners, Curriculum and Contexts.* Maidenhead: Open University Press.

MacNaughton, G. (2005) *Doing Foucault in Early Childhood Studies: Applying Post-structural Ideas.* London: Routledge.

MacNaughton, G. and Hughes, P. (2008) *Doing Action Research in Early Childhood Studies: A Step by Step Guide.* London: Open University Press.

May, H. (1997) *The Discovery of Early Childhood: The Development of Services for the Care and Education of Very Young Children, Mid Eighteenth Century Europe to Mid Twentieth Century New Zealand.* Wellington, NZ: Auckland University Press/Bridget Williams Books.

May, H. (2001) *Politics in the Playground: The World of Early Childhood in Postwar New Zealand.* Wellington, NZ: Bridget Williams Books with the New Zealand Council for Educational Research.

May, H. (2002) Early childhood care and education in Aotearoa–New Zealand: an overview of history, policy and curriculum. Unpublished manuscript, Wellington.

May, S. and Hill, R. (2005) Māori-medium education: current issues and challenges, *International Journal of Bilingual Education and Bilingualism*, 8(5): 377–403.

McCain, M. and Mustard, J.F. (1999) *Early Years Study.* Toronto, ON: Ontario Children's Secretariat.

Meade, A. (1988) *Education to be More,* Report of the Early Childhood Education and Care Working Group. Wellington, NZ: Government Printer.

Mitchell, L. and Cubey, P. (2003) *Best Evidence Synthesis: Characteristics of Professional Development linked to Enhanced Pedagogy and Children's Learning in Early*

Childhood Settings. Wellington, NZ: Ministry of Education Te Tahuhu o te Matauranga.

Moss, P. (2006) Early childhood institutions as loci of ethical and political practice, *International Journal of Educational Policy, Research and Practice: Reconceptualizing Childhood Studies*, 7: 127–136.

Moss, P. (2007) *Bringing Politics into the Nursery*. The Hague: Bernard van Leer Foundation.

Moss, P. (2008) Meeting the paradigmatic divide. In S. Farquhar and P. Fitzsimons (eds), *Philosophy of Early Childhood Education: Transforming Narratives* (pp. 7–23). Malden, MA: Blackwell.

Moss, P. and Pence, A.R. (1994) *Valuing Quality in Early Childhood Services: New Approaches to Defining Quality*. New York: Teachers College Press.

Moss, P. and Petrie, P. (2002) *From Children's Services to Children's Spaces*. New York: RoutledgeFalmer.

Mouffe, C. (2000) *The Democratic Paradox*. London: Verso.

New, R. (2000) *Reggio Emilia: Catalyst for Change and Conversation*. University of Illinois Clearinghouse on Elementary and Early Childhood Education.

New, R. (2003) Reggio Emilia: new ways to think about schooling, *Educational Leadership*, 7: 34–37.

Pacini-Ketchabaw, V. and Pence, A. (2007) Innovative approaches in ECE: an international dialogue, *Interaction* (Special Issue), 20(4): 24.

Pence, A.R. (ed.) (2008) Issues in diversity and social equity in early childhood, *Contemporary Issues in Early Childhood* (Special issue), 9(3).

Pence, A.R. and Benner. A. (2000) Child care research in Canada, 1965–1999. In L. Prochner and N. Howe (eds), *Early Childhood Care and Education in Canada*. Vancouver: UBC Press.

Pence, A. and Pacini-Ketchabaw, V. (2008) Discourses on quality care: IQ and the Canadian experience, *Contemporary Issues in Early Childhood*, 9(3): 241–255.

Project Zero (2004) *Making Learning Visible: Children as Individual and Group Learners*. Reggio Children.

Rinaldi, C. (1998) Projected curriculum constructed through documentation – Progettazione: an Interview with Lella Gandini. In C.P. Edwards, L. Gandini and G.E. Forman (eds), *The Hundred Languages of Children: The Reggio Emilia Approach – advanced reflections* (pp. 113–125). Greenwich, CT: Ablex.

Rinaldi, C. (2001) A pedagogy of listening: a perspective of listening from Reggio Emilia, *Children in Europe*, 1: 2–5.

Rinaldi, C. (2005) Documentation and assessment: what is the relationship? In A. Clark, P. Moss and A.T. Kjorholt (eds), *Beyond Listening: Children's Perspectives on Early Childhood Services* (pp. 17–28). Bristol, UK: The Policy Press.

Rinaldi, C. (2006) *In Dialogue with Reggio Emilia: Listening, Researching and Learning*. London: Routledge.

Robinson, K. and Diaz, C.J. (2006) *Diversity and Difference in Early Childhood Education: Issues for Theory and Practice*. Maidenhead: Open University Press.

Rodriguez, C., Pence, A. and Greenwood, M. (2007) Indigenous approaches to early childhood care and education, *Canadian Journal of Native Education*, 30(1).

Schweinhart, L. and Weikart, D. (1999) The advantages of High/Scope: helping children lead successful lives, *Educational Leadership*, 57(1): 76–78.

Shonkoff, J.P. and Phillips, D.A. (2000) *From Neurons to Neighborhoods: The Science of Early Childhood Development*. Washington, DC: National Academy Press.

Shore, R. (1997) *Rethinking the Brain*. New York: Families and Work Institute.

UNICEF (2008) *The Child Care Transition: A League Table of Early Childhood Education and Care in Economically Advanced Countries*. Florence, Italy: UNICEF Innocenti Research Centre.

US Department of Health and Human Services, Administration for Children and Families (2005) *Head Start Impact Study: First Year Findings*. Washington, DC.

Walkerdine, V. (1984) Developmental psychology and the child-centred pedagogy: the insertion of Piaget into early education. In J. Henriques, W. Holloway, C. Urwin, C. Vener and V. Walkerdine (eds), *Changing the Subject: Psychology, Social Regulation and Subjectivity* (pp. 153–202). London: Methuen.

Walkerdine, V. (1985) On the regulation of speaking and silence: subjectivity, class and gender in contemporary schooling. In C. Steedman, C. Urwin and V. Walkerdine (eds), *Language, Gender and Childhood* (pp. 203–260). London: Routledge & Kegan Paul.

Young, M.E. (2002) *From Early Child Development to Human Development*. Washington, DC: World Bank.

PART 2
Critical views in practice

9 When words are scarce, but success depends on them: composing in a Navajo kindergarten

Karen Gallas

Field notes: October 17

I don't know exactly when this happens, but at some point I begin to love the children I teach. That happened this week. Looking at my field notes, it becomes clear that the onset of love seems to coincide with our joining as a community. For me, alone here with no anchors to hold on to, this moment is so precious. I have a place to go where I'm comfortable, where I can be myself and do the things I love, where there are others who are glad to see me each day. Essentially, I am taking the same benefits from this community that my students are: The classroom is a place where we present ourselves to the world freshly, where we are appreciated for what transpires in this place and no other, where we can remove ourselves from the reality of the outside world.

As I look out my window, a lone, young prairie dog is enthusiastically building mounds all across the red dirt that is supposed to be my front yard. Here, the public radio station broadcasts primarily in Navajo, flocks of sheep and goats occasionally wend their way across the playground or the parking lots accompanied only by a herding dog, and the night sky is so big and full of stars that to stare at it is to free fall deeply into space. Here, some families live without water and electricity, young children ride horses and learn to rope calves before they come to school, and butchering a sheep is a regular occurrence. Here, children play surrounded by mountains and mesas, pink walls of rock, and the expanse of high desert filled with sage brush and thousands of wildflowers. They play hard, much harder than any children I've seen in the past, and they play silently, side by side. No one asks what makes the wind, how the rainbows that spring up so profusely occur, why it snows, how the rock became red, where the flowers came from. They don't sing as they play, or tell the 'pretend we are . . .' stories that the children I've known in the past constantly generate. These children don't ask questions. They are children of action, song, and silent imagination.

But I am a child of questions and analysis; my wondering proceeds naturally from astonishment into questions. I am a child of squirrels rather than prairie dogs, of storybooks and ordered gardens. I am a child who grew up swimming in the ocean, who longs for green hills and deep woods. I mark time by tides, seasons, and appointments, by obligations and responsibility. The child I am is the teacher I bring to these children. And the way of life here, the deeply inculcated cultural values and practices around time and space, language, social relations, and metaphysical orientation – all so foreign to me – permeate their work in school. How is it that we are joining?

'How is it that we are joining?' This question came out of a tension and disequilibrium that began in August, when I started a year teaching kindergarten in a Navajo community school. By the third day of school, I realized that after more than thirty years of teaching in rural and urban schools, I was no longer an expert. Instead, I was living and teaching in a cultural environment where, for the first time in my life, I was truly 'other'.

The setting

The small community in which I taught is located on a reservation in the southwestern United States. It has a population base of around 3,000. About two-thirds of the families on the reservation live in family camps scattered across the more remote parts of the reservation where electricity and telephone service are often not available, and the only sources of water are stock wells. The remaining families live within the environs of the school and community offices and have running water, telephone service and electricity in their homes. The unemployment rate in the community typically ranges between 50 and 75 per cent. Thus, the majority of the students in my class that year were living well below the poverty level.

The school served grades K-12, with a 99 per cent Navajo student population. The teachers were predominantly European American, while the teaching assistants were all Navajo. I taught with another part-time teacher and two teaching assistants in a large, beautiful open space with twenty-six students. The room was the best early childhood space I had ever had, equipped with every possible material that a child-centred kindergarten would need. All of the children had attended the Headstart programme on the school campus. In spite of the time spent in that programme, though, I discovered within the first two weeks of the school year that the language challenges for the children were very great. Of my twenty-six students, two spoke fluent English but very little Navajo; two spoke fluent Navajo but very little English. Two additional children spoke fair English but lacked depth in their vocabulary. The rest of the children, totalling twenty, had fluency in neither English nor Navajo. Seven of those children received speech and language services for significant language delays.

Research perspective and conceptual framework

Throughout the year, I used the practices of classroom ethnography to document my work. My data consisted of daily field notes, audiotaped discussions with my students, samples of art and writing, photographs, and memos written to myself around key issues. In spite of this process, it was difficult to reflect on my data from the perspective of my previous work. In addition to the challenges of poverty and language development, much of my data, as well as the experiences I had living in this community, revealed cultural barriers that were affecting my ability to teach and the children's ability to learn. Some of those barriers were the result of the very different cultural ethos we brought to the classroom. Others, however, were more difficult to pin down.

I was no stranger to theories of discourse acquisition and the importance of home language and culture in literacy learning. Neither was I new to the work of teaching in culturally, racially and linguistically diverse classrooms. Yet this setting added multiple dimensions to the teaching challenges that diversity offers. While it was clear to me as the year progressed that something important was gradually occurring, I was unable to offer even a simple explanation of what that something was, and how it had happened. Only when I was training to be a psychotherapist and re-encountered the work of Martin Buber, specifically his philosophy of the 'interhuman' (1965), did I begin to find conceptual structures that helped me make sense of my data.

This chapter, then, will describe the evolution of my teaching practice in this challenging setting. It will consider the value of documenting and reflecting upon the moments in classrooms when teachers and students come to know each other as humans – points of contact when not just minds, but hearts, meet. From this perspective, I will reconceptualize literacy as a lifelong apprenticeship that must be grounded in authentic and respectful relationship. Throughout this chapter, I will use Buber's description of the 'interhuman' to explain what I believe was occurring between myself and my students as we worked together.

The dilemma

> **Field notes: Third day of school**
> The kindergartners are staging a coup, taking over the class each time
> I attempt to 'instruct' them in anything. What it amounts to is a
> bunch of little kids who do not seem to have any use for an adult who
> is attempting to grab their attention.
>   What surrounds this entire phenomenon is an aura of disregard
> for the wishes of adults. For example, consider my Navajo assistant
> teachers. One uses a stern style of discipline: 'Do this or else!' The
> other is more 'anglo,' as she says; she talks in a soft voice and tries
> to persuade. The children ignore them. They ignore me. They are
> bald-faced defiant, and that's the truth. What to do?

In the first week of school, two things became immediately clear. First, I was
unable to maintain control of my class of 5- and 6-year-olds, and second, my
students rarely used spoken language to communicate with their teachers and
each other. The children took readily to the classroom spaces and resources,
and they played and worked harder than any other group of children I had
encountered. What they didn't do while they played, drew, painted and
worked was talk. Words were amazingly scarce, even on the playground. There,
vocalizing consisted mostly of roaring and calls to each other or to me to
watch what they were doing on the play equipment.
    To compound that problem, I quickly realized that, with the exception of
the two children who spoke fluent English, my students and I did not share
a common language. As well, while my teaching assistants spoke English, neither were fluent in Navajo, although one could communicate in basic Navajo.
Our demographics around language mirrored that of the community population as a whole. Most of the children's parents did not speak Navajo fluently;
neither were most of them fluent in English. Thus, the majority of my students
were raised in households where there was no solid first language.
    Compounding this dilemma was the role that silence naturally played in
Navajo culture. In public settings, the Navajo are often silent, and my children's behaviour mirrored this. As well, adult conversations with children are
short and to the point. Soon, I realized that when the children built in the
blocks, they rarely spoke. In the drama centre, they played silently side by
side, dressing up elaborately, setting large meals, but rarely talking. The art
area produced remarkable paintings and constructions, but it was also silent.
Although many of the children drew complex pictures each morning, when
asked for a short comment about their pictures, we could only elicit one-word
responses: 'house', 'hogan', 'rainbows', 'clouds'. Yet, in looking at their art,
watching their outdoor dramas, in considering the elaborate costumes they

assembled and the vast pretend meals they laid out, it was clear that they were silently composing complex texts about their world.

My first dilemma, then, was how to generate the words that would become the texts we might use for our core subjects – how to generate them from the inside out, a commitment to the primacy of children's language and action that is at the foundation of my work in early literacy (Gallas, 1994, 1995, 1998, 2003). In addition, the problem of classroom management remained: while the children were quite respectful of me when I could get their attention, getting their attention was, at first, almost impossible.

At its core, this was the other side of the same problem, simultaneously cultural and linguistic: it was difficult for me as a teacher to elicit any texts from the children that included more than single words, and it was equally difficult for them to understand my 'teacherly' texts and intentions. So what did I do? I began to document what my students were doing, and I also began to self-consciously keep track of what I was thinking, feeling and doing.

And then, in mid-September, something happened:

Field notes: September 19
Today I discovered that if I want these children to come when I call them to join me in a meeting or a lesson, I have to call them with a song or a chant that they know. Then they come running. I learned this the hard way.

This morning, as on every morning since school started, I attempted to gather the children who had been having a short break for snack and relaxation back together in a large group. I tried switching off the lights and making an announcement. I tried walking from group to group and asking them to gather in the meeting area. I tried quietly raising my hand above my head to signal that I'd like them to stop and look at me, something many of their teachers have been working on as a way to gain attention. As usual, none of these techniques worked. Feeling hopeless and out of answers, I pulled a stray chair into the middle of the room. sat down on it, seriously contemplated sitting there silently for the rest of the day, and then, out of the blue, I decided to sing. So I began to sing, 'Little Rabbit Fufu,' if only to amuse myself, and the room went silent, the children turned to look and listen, and then they all walked quietly over to the center of the room sat down and joined in the song.

As the day went on, I tried it again in different forms to see if the behavior was a fluke, or really real. It didn't matter if I sang, chanted, or clapped a pattern. Uniformly, they dropped what they were doing, ran over, and sat down. Apparently, the call has to start with sound and rhythm and music. Then I've got them. How simple, and how

> complex. And even more wonderful is the discovery that once I start the song, I can stop, look and listen, and they will continue the song and the hand motions. It's a marvel!

It was a marvel. If I wanted to gather these children about me for my own purposes, I simply had to sit down in a chair anywhere in the room or the outdoors, and sing. If I sang, they would come. It didn't matter what I sang, they would still come running, sit down around me and join in the song. As an early childhood teacher who knows and sings a lot of songs with my students, this should have been obvious, but what was different was that my prior students had always been responsive to my efforts to gather them together *with my words*; these children, in the early part of the year, were responsive *only* when I sang. So I sang. My new ability to direct and redirect their focus and activity opened up the instructional landscape.

So how are we to interpret this change in the children? Perhaps I had simply stumbled upon a cultural practice; for example, that song and chant in this cultural context was a summons to a gathering. That might be a colourful and, potentially, a culturally aware interpretation of this event. However, in my experience of this community and the ways in which adults related to children, this was not the case. Instead, what had occurred was that in that moment of hopelessness I surrendered, put up the white flag, gave up all aspiration for control and met the children as beings with whom I wanted to share a relationship. As Buber (1958) has written, 'Only when every means has collapsed does the meeting come about' (p. 11). Our true meeting, I believe, began on that day.

Loving them

> The relation to the Thou is direct. No system of ideas, no foreknowledge, and no fancy intervene between I and Thou. The memory itself is transformed, as it plunges out of its isolation into the unity of the whole. No aim, no lust, and no anticipation intervene between I and Thou.
>
> – Buber (1958: 11)

In October the field note entry that opens this chapter was written. After considerable struggle and consternation, and in spite of our immense differences, my students and I were coming to love one another. More importantly, though, what was coming to the surface for me was an understanding that 'loving them' was essential to the process of our *mutual* education. This realization was evolving into a teaching practice grounded in 'the unity of the whole' to which Buber refers. In order to achieve that, I gave up power and let go of objectives. In my field notes I urge myself to stay present in the moments of interaction with the children, to focus on what the children were showing rather than on their deficits in relation to other children.

When I observed that the children had very limited schemata when building with unit blocks, I went in the block corner and built with them. I would paint with them at the easels, compose music with them, think out loud with them through readings of books, write poems, stories and non-fiction texts with them. Essentially, my pedagogical stance shifted from a benevolent authoritative stance to one of a co-learner. This shift also required me to alter my practice as a teacher researcher. Although I continued to collect data, I had no well defined question in mind, as Buber says, 'no foreknowledge . . . no system of ideas . . . no aim'. My first question from the beginning of the school year, 'how do I get them to do something for me?', had been, for the most part, resolved. What I was left with was a desire to keep track of the intensity of our classroom, but without a clear focus. This is not to say that my knowledge of teaching and learning was suppressed, but rather that I let go of preconceptions about who my students were and what they ought to be learning.

Field notes: November 30
I have to write about joy, and song, and laughter, and the lifting of suffering. Today during a simple transition period waiting for the other half of the class to return from gym so we could have a story, Alicia pulled a song from the song box: 'Five Green Speckled Frogs,' an innocuous song that can help children think about number and subtraction. So we sang the song. Five children went in the center. The rest of us were what I call 'the singers,' those who are making it possible for the performance to happen by providing music and voice. We sang the song twice so that all the children could do the movement parts. In the second round of singing I said to the singers, 'let's do it like an opera.' So we sang as if we were all Pavarotti even though none of these children have seen an opera. They knew what I meant because they heard me sing in an exaggerated way: big, tremulous voice, great drama. Then I said, 'how shall we sing it this time?'

'High,' a child said. So we sang the song again in very high, still tremulous voices.

I asked again, 'how shall we sing it this time?'

'Sad.' said another. So this time we were very sorrowful, and the song became hysterically funny as I, and then the other singers, began to dramatically sob between the words, all of us wiping our eyes, the 'frogs' laughing uncontrollably with us. I was weeping from laughing so hard, tears really streaming down my face. As I looked across the circle at Jackie (my teaching assistant), she, also, was laughing and crying. It was a joyful, transformative moment, so precious, one I would never trade for any amount of money.

These notes illustrate the kind of change that was occurring in my relationship with my students and with my work. In other classrooms in which I had taught, this kind of experience would have been primarily instructional. Joviality and fun would certainly have been present, but the primary focus would have been on developing skills in areas that needed remediation. In this case, however, the experience evolved intuitively and intimately, beginning, again, with a song but moving out into a moment of play and genuine contact between beings fully present in that specific moment in time. That moment resulted in a shared text emanating from a deeply embodied place – a place where the words and the texts that we needed grew out of what was felt, rather than what was said. Buber characterizes this process as one of 'drawing forth':

> I am inclined, within the concept of education, to hold the significance of drawing forth to be the decisive one . . . fetching forth out of the child or youth something latent and cultivating it. But what is it that one should fetch forth? . . . No content of an utterance, but the speaking voice; no instructing, but the glance, the movement, the being-there of those teaching when they are inspired by the educational task. Relationship educates provided that it is a genuine educational relationship.
>
> (Buber, 1967: 98)

Composing

In these first examples, and in all of the examples to follow, my sense was that we were composing a body of work that was about literacy and about life. Composing as a definition of behaviour can be understood in various ways. We might say to someone who is tense, upset or discombobulated, 'Compose yourself.' We might talk about how a particular person under pressure was so 'composed'. Each of these meanings suggests that composing has something to do with psyche and identity, with becoming fully who we are, with 'drawing forth'. We also 'compose' in a genre-specific way, as a part of a literacy practice in a specific subject area. We compose stories, essays, poems, musical scores, paintings, lab reports, solutions to maths problems, and even salads. We might also look at a work of art or listen to a piece of music and specifically comment on its composition.

In all of these examples, what stands out for me is the intentional and deeply personal nature of composing. Composing requires deliberate attention to process and product, although, at the same time, composition is something that is ongoing, fluid, and thus does not necessarily require the achievement of a finished piece of work. Composing is a statement about self-determination and autonomy. It takes courage to make something up and stand by it, to present your 'selfness' to a public world. So, in the context of thinking about true literacy across a range of disciplines, I would consider composing to be a broad and essential literacy practice whose origins are found in a desire to make contact with or be in relationship with others.

Apprenticeship

At the same time, composing in our lives does not begin as an isolated human activity. It begins as a relational activity in the intimacy of parent/child interactions. In other words, to a great extent parents or adult caregivers introduce or apprentice children in different ways of composing themselves and composing their world. For example, consider reading in its broadest sense.

The process of learning to 'read' begins with an embrace. It begins with the 'text' of a relationship. That text find its earliest expression in the moments after birth, when a child and parents begin their first efforts at attunement. Parents work to read the infant's cries and movements. The infant learns to follow the parents' eyes, to reflect back in small motions of the hands, eyebrows, eyes and mouth the movements and intentions of the parents as they interact with their baby. These moments of 'reading' begin in the instants after birth and are incrementally expanded as days, weeks and months progress. The texts the baby learns to read become more complex as vision clarifies and her ear adjusts to tone and gesture in the adult, and, similarly, as the adults' ability to 'read' their child improves and expands.

As the baby's attention moves outward to objects, extended family and friends, animals and new environments, each new influence begs to be considered and read as a new text. In that process, the accompanying adult is there to mentor, model and teach how to approach and engage with these new experiences.

Thus, 'reading' the world begins with emotion and affiliation, with contact between humans. The texts we have as our first 'readers', so to speak, are texts of human interaction. Mastery of those texts requires a close affiliation, an apprenticeship, with a teaching other who reads those texts in a spontaneous and honest way. What my students were teaching me, through first their resistance to myself and the other adults, then through their responsiveness when I called them through songs that we had learned together, was that composing and apprenticeship were inseparable, and that they were, at their inception, about drawing forth through relationship based not on my authority as a teacher, but on my ability to work from our common human experience.

The glasses

When I teach, I have learned that I must attach my glasses to my neck with a cord or they will be lost in the depths of the classroom. Every day when I would sit down to read a book with the children or take dictation in their journals, I would dramatically put on my glasses and say, 'Oh my goodness! I can see the words!', or something similar.

One day in mid-winter I came in from my lunch break to find that I had a class full of children, all of whom were wearing glasses on cords made of colourful pipe cleaners. Apparently, a teacher from the Headstart programme had brought bags of pipe cleaners outside at lunch recess, and the kindergartners decided they would make glasses like mine. They wore the glasses for the rest of the day. Off and on throughout the year the glasses would reappear, usually during the afternoon choice time when the children were playing office, reading in the classroom library or writing books.

Here we see my students emulating my role as teacher and reader, perceiving correctly that teacher and reader involved more than the act of teaching and the act of reading. Teacher and reader were personas that I created by virtue of the ways I consciously composed myself and my public texts. They were expressions of my emotional, physical, psychic, cultural, social and cognitive self. For my students, creating and wearing glasses like mine was part of a larger process of trying on the role of reader and teacher. What I am highlighting with this anecdote is the way in which the children brought their sense of who I was to me, demonstrating their intuitive understanding that self *is* text, that text can live outside of words and inside communal action.

Questions

When I started working with these children, I was distressed to find that they did not ask questions at all, although I could see in their drawings, for example, points of wonder and fascination. Based on my understanding of inquiry in science and the ways it is structured as students progress to higher levels of expectation for their performance, I knew that the ability to develop questions that can be systematically studied is critical. The process of eliciting children's questions and then developing science study from them, is, I think, a central part of the elementary teacher's role in science instruction. That is how students begin to see the relationships between their observations of the world, the development of their questions from those observations, and the systematic study of those questions in the science classroom (Gallas, 1995).

So in September I was stumped. How was I going to find the questions when there were so few words? For the next two months I deliberately named and highlighted the moments when I or another adult asked a question. I thought out loud as we worked with science materials, foregrounding my own moments of wonder and surprise, but it appeared that none of my efforts were having an effect, until late October.

Field notes: October 30

Today, a question from Rachelle as she watched me change the filter in the fish tank! 'Teacher, how they can breathe?'

I did a big reaction and said, 'Rachelle, that's a question you just asked! A science question!' She beamed.

Later at recess, the day was gusty with low hanging clouds moving in fast from the north. I looked up and realized how beautiful the clouds were as they swept past each other, a tangle of clouds. As I stood, staring at them, Talia said, 'Teacher, what are you doing?'

I said, 'I'm looking at the clouds. They are moving so fast.' Talia looked up, puzzled, but didn't really look up. She looked out in the distance, not up over her head. I asked, 'Have you ever looked up at the clouds?'

'No,' she said.

I said, 'Well then, look straight up, right above your head.' She craned her neck to see. I said, 'Have you ever laid down on the ground and just watched the clouds?' She shook her head 'no'. I took her over to the sand box, and we lay down on our backs in the sand. Alicia, who had been listening in, followed. I asked her the same question, 'Have you ever looked at the clouds?'

She also said no. So I invited her to lie down with us. She did.

Talia began to talk about the clouds as they rushed overhead. She said, 'Look, there's a dinosaur. It's eating a cloud.' Other children walked over to find out what we were doing lying on the ground. I asked them the same question. They all said, 'no'. They never looked at the clouds, standing up or lying down.

Soon, about six of us were lying on the ground looking at the clouds; other children were standing around craning their necks at the sky above. They didn't talk much, but they were looking. I was talking about what the clouds were doing, asking questions about them, saying what they reminded me of, as was Talia.

Then, Ricky walked over, looked for a bit with us, and she asked a question! 'Teacher, what makes that?', meaning, I think, what makes those clouds there? So, two science questions in one day. We're on a roll!

This day offers a view of how my role as the apprenticing other was unfolding.

Here you see in my actions the immediacy of teaching from the child's point of view, and the spontaneity of the composing process that occurred without prior planning, without preconceptions about outcomes, and within the context of drawing forth from both myself and my students what lay dormant.

That day of two questions was a high point and did not repeat itself very often. I continued to ask questions aloud and point out when questions were asked by the children. Eventually a few questions started to come, and then, finally, one day, as I interacted with a group of children around our snail tank, the questions broke out. In this session we were sitting at a table looking into a large terrarium inhabited by land snails. Baby snails had just hatched and were on the glass sides of the tank. I had noticed them, but the children had not, so in this session I was deliberately drawing their attention to the baby snails. The excerpt below represents about three minutes from a twenty-minute audiotaped discussion (see Gallas, 1995, for a more complete look at Science Talks).

Science Talk – December

David: Ooooh! Baby eggs!

Teacher: Oooh! Wow! We're here to study snails again and David has noticed something. What do you see?

David: Snails?

Robert: Oh yeah, teacher, there's a little egg here.

Joseph: I see a egg!

David: I see a baby egg.

Etta: They're baby snails.

Teacher: There's a whole bunch up here.

Rachelle: Teacher, how they eat the grass? (meaning the lettuce in the tank)

Teacher: How do they eat that? That's a question! Rachelle's got two science questions she's come up with. Fabulous, Rachelle.

Joseph: Teacher, teacher!

David: Where's the babies?

Teacher: What's that you were going to say, David? Well, remember the picture we saw of the snail laying the eggs?

Joseph: Teacher, teacher!

Rachelle: Teacher, teacher, the snails, the snail go under, the snails goes under sand?

Teacher: That's a question, right? Yeah, we saw them down below one day and they were sort of in the dirt. And then I looked the other day and what did I see? All the babies!

Etta: (counting) One, two, three, four, five, six, seven, eight, nine, ten, eleven, twelve

Joseph: Hey Teacher! Com'ere, com'ere!

Teacher: What do you see over there?

Joseph: There's eggs over here!

Teacher: You think those are eggs over there? They look sort of like these, and these look sort of like eggs up here, but you know they could actually be the snails.

Etta: (still counting) sixteen, seventeen, eighteen

Joseph: Teacher, teacher!

Teacher: Joseph, go ahead and talk. You can just talk to us. What are you thinking?

Joseph: How do, how do, uh, um, um, snails break, um, eggs, um, that thing, that one in the middle by that thing (pointing to the chicken egg shells in the tank.)

Teacher: How do they eat the eggs, those egg shells?

Joseph: No, not, uh . . . Yeah!

Teacher: Those big white egg shells? How do they do it?

Joseph: How do they bust it?

Teacher: How do they bust it. And eat it? That's a really good question.

Joseph: And that one that [got] crushed, how did they do that?

Teacher: How do you think? Like pretend you're a snail, and you know how soft they are. Children, Joseph wants to know, the egg shells, how do they eat those egg shells when they're so hard?

Robert: They bust it up with their shell.

Teacher: You think they bust it with their shells, and then they eat it?

Rachelle: Miss Karen, Miss Karen, how they bust that egg?

Teacher: That egg there, the white egg? Yeah, that's what Joseph wants to know. We're asking you. How do you think they do it? How do you think, David? How do you think they eat that egg shell?

Rachelle: We got more questions, huh?

Teacher: Yeah, we've got more. This is the most questions I've ever heard from any kids in this class.

Rachelle: Teacher, where's their mouth?

Teacher: Do you remember on the picture we saw [showing] where their mouth was?
              (No response)

Teacher: Want to bring the picture over? We'll bring the picture, let's have it. And we will look.

Etta: (still counting) twenty-three, twenty-four, twenty-five

Teacher: What do you see, Etta? How many?

Joseph: Teacher, how, how um, how snail c-, how snail c-, uh, lay down on the shell . . .

Etta: Twenty-seven.

Joseph: When they, when they, go in the shell?

Teacher: How do they go in?

Joseph: Um, when they're going and lay on their shells. How they do it?

Teacher: There's another picture over there, Robert. Want to get that? This one shows them laying their eggs in the dirt, huh. And then at the top, it shows the little snails coming out. It's like these little guys.

Robert: Teacher, teacher, how do, how do these born their eggs?

Teacher: How do they born, how do the eggs come out?

Etta: They keep them in their shell.

Teacher: Yeah, they must be in their bodies, you know, in the soft parts. How do they come out?

Etta: We have a lot of snails!

This is how the questions began: halting in construction, but fast and furious, and as the year progressed, the questions continued into everything we did.

Genuine dialogue

> Contact is the primary word of education. It means that the teacher shall face his pupils not as developed brain before unfinished ones, but as being before being, as mature being before developing beings. He must really face them, that means not in a direction working from above to below . . . but in genuine interaction, in exchange of experiences . . . What is needed is not mere seeking for information from below and giving information from above, also not mere questions from here and answers from there, but genuine dialogue.
>
> (Buber, 1958: 102)

I found my actions as a teacher in this kind of event were a subject of scrutiny for some, if not all, of my children. For example, beginning in December, and at different intervals throughout the year, Rachelle would pose one of two questions to me. The first question was 'Teacher, are you a grown-up?' At first, I was puzzled by the question and would answer in the affirmative, that I thought I was a grown-up since I was old. From that would ensue a conversation about how old I was chronologically. Later, in spring, the question changed. Rachelle asked, 'Teacher, are you a kid?' I responded that I certainly felt like a kid, although I was too old to really be one.

This question, I think, is full of meaning, given the ideas I'm working with in this chapter. At first, I found Rachelle's questions quaint and charming. Later, as I considered how my role had evolved in this setting, I saw the questions as attempts to clarify my role in the classroom. I didn't look, talk or behave like the majority of grown-ups or teachers she knew, but I clearly was not a child. Still, there was doubt – I might just be a kid. By the end of the year when Rachelle asked the question again, I said, 'Do you think I'm a kid?'

She shrugged her shoulders and said, 'You act like a kid, but I know you're too big.'

'Teacher, I miss you.'

> Man wishes to be confirmed in his being by man, and wishes to have a pres-ence in the being of the other . . . secretly and bashfully he watches for a Yes which allows him to be and which can come to him only from one human person to another.
>
> (Buber, 1965: 71)

One January morning Elena walked up to greet me, and, as she had done every morning for about four months, rolled up her sleeve slightly to expose a tur-quoise cuff. I pushed my sleeve up slightly to show the one I wore, almost a match to hers, and, as we did every morning, we touched bracelets. She put her arm around me, as she always did, and said, 'Teacher, I miss you.'

I answered, as I always did, 'I miss you, too.'

Maria, who had been drawing in her journal at the table where I was sitting, raised her head, touched my bracelet and said, 'That's Navajo.'

I was surprised at the declaration. In a region where adults wore many different types of silver bracelets from many different tribes, it embraced so much knowledge for a 5-year-old. I said, 'How do you know that?'

She considered for a minute, then said, 'It passes through my heart,' and she returned to her drawing.

We return now, to the question about classroom research that opened this chapter. What might be the value of documenting and reflecting upon the moments in classrooms when teachers and students come to know each other as humans – the points of contact where not just minds, but hearts, meet? We have in this final anecdote two texts composed around the icon of the bracelet. The first text is a morning ritual, uses few words and a small gesture, but expresses a wealth of feeling, affection and association between two individuals from two very different worlds.

During the school year I puzzled over this brief daily exchange. I felt the significance of it, but was unable to articulate its meaning. In the years after I continued to wonder what, in its essence, it signified. Now I understand that without the documentation of this daily ritual my awareness of this moment of 'Yes', and my present understanding of it, would not have been possible: this small gesture enabled me to begin to enter into a heart-space, as it were, with Elena. Through the gesture, Elena and I created a ritual within which to make contact. This contact was not limited to our respective roles as student and teacher, but included our affection for each other as human beings. In truth, we had very little in common that might have helped us understand each other's communications, but under her tutelage I learned that the gesture, three words and our bracelets linked us in a space outside of language and independent of culture.

In contrast to Elena's gesture, the second text, consisting of Maria's five words, 'It passes through my heart', alludes to deep cultural knowledge, a knowledge I worked all year to acquire. Maria's words locate her understanding of culture within her heart, in the centre of her body, not in her mind. Like Elena, her expression is mysterious and metaphorical; it asks me to read the world of our teacher–student relationship differently.

Gestures, songs, the metaphors and questions of 5-year-olds, a moment of stopping to watch clouds in a sandbox – each of these events pulled our different pasts into the present moment and allowed us to reconfigure our future. These are the kinds of moments that Buber (1965) located in the realm of the 'interhuman' – moments when 'each becomes aware of the other and is thus related to him in such a way that he does not regard and use him as his object, but as his partner in a living event' (p. 74). For Buber, those moments open us to the possibility of engaging one another as the 'We'. Within the context of working with diverse cultures, achieving the 'We' does not assume that individual or social identities are lost or sacrificed for community. Rather, Buber (1965) speaks about 'imagining the real' (p. 70) – a gift that results in genuine recognition of the other; 'a bold swinging – demanding the most intensive stirring of one's being – into the life of the other' (1965: 81).

I believe that this process of forging the 'We', is important to all teaching, but when language, race, poverty, trauma and cultural differences between teacher and students present large hurdles to overcome, the process is an imperative. We cannot expect learning to occur if we neglect to build relationships that transcend and transform difference; if we neglect to build learning spaces that transcend and transform, if only for a few hours, poverty and trauma. So many of the moments when we moved forward as a community, both in terms of basic skills and larger literacy understandings, occurred through our co-construction of the 'We'.

Too often, however, our poorest and most marginalized children are denied the 'luxuries' of coming to know deep in their bodies the essential and transformative nature of literacy achieved within a dialogic community. For them, education, rather than being a process of 'drawing forth' their individual and collective potential, becomes a kind of colonizing projection in which those who teach and administer schools seek to shape their students into reproductions of themselves.

Loving them

> Love is responsibility of an I for a Thou.
>
> – Buber (1958: 15)

It is not common in educational discussions to talk about the practice of teaching as a process of coming to love our students. There is no 'love' variable factored into research on best practices in education. Teachers are not generally asked to document the extent to which they do or do not love their students. I now believe, however, that my teaching has to be grounded in a deep and loving regard for my students. Psychologically, it is much easier to abdicate responsibility for student failure by keeping our students and their lives at a distance: blaming family, society, poverty, mental illness for their 'failure to thrive', as it were, in our classrooms. It is also easier to maintain our distance when we use objective structures to shore up our educational system: standards, assessment tools, and mass-produced one-size-fits-many curricula. In promoting the belief that education is primarily about cognitive development and intellectual achievement, we have lost our ability to talk about our hearts. And further, when we objectify our students and look at them within a 'cup half empty' paradigm, the cup will always remain half empty.

My use of the word 'love', when coupled with a sense that we were finding a way to be humanly connected, speaks to a different kind of learning space that incorporates all the parts of our students and ourselves and qualitatively expands our collective lives and achievements. The events described in this chapter suggest that the essential point of contact between myself and my students occurred in what we might call a liminal space where heart and mind were integrated. In this space, texts were created that changed us and helped us grow in our understanding of self, language and culture.

Simultaneously, my students were achieving their academic benchmarks. The words, so elusive at first, finally came. They were not exclusively my words or exclusively their words; they were our words. The texts we needed tumbled out as we composed ourselves. I would maintain, however, that that success would not have been possible without our intuitive desire to really understand and meet each other. For my students and myself, our process of establishing true dialogue and becoming fully embodied in our classroom was one of mutual apprenticeship: even as I was apprenticing the children, they were apprenticing me; and we were all, in the end, composing *ourselves*, building relationships that allowed our individual and collective potentials to blossom.

References

Buber, M. (1958) *I and Thou*. New York: Charles Scribner's Sons.

Buber, M. (1965) *The Knowledge of Man*. New York: Harper & Row.

Buber, M. (1967) *A Believing Humanism: My Testament, 1902–1965*. New York: Simon & Schuster.

Gallas, K. (1994) *The Languages of Learning: How Children Talk, Write, Dance, Draw, and Sing their Understanding of the World*. New York: Teachers College Press.

Gallas, K. (1995) *Talking their Way into Science: Hearing Children's Questions and Theories, Responding with Curricula*. New York: Teachers College Press.

Gallas, K. (1998) *'Sometimes I can be anything': Power, Gender and Identity in a Primary Classroom*. New York: Teachers College Press.

Gallas, K. (2003) *Imagination and Literacy: A Teacher's Search for the Heart of Learning*. New York: Teachers College Press.

10 Childhoods left behind? Official and unofficial basics of child writing

Anne Haas Dyson

> From long sitting, watching, and pondering . . . I have found out the worst enemies to what we call teaching . . . [And] the first is the children's interest in each other. It plays the very devil with orthodox method. If only they'd stop talking to each other, playing with each other, fighting with each other and loving each other. This unseemly and unlawful communication! In self-defense I've got to use the damn thing.
> – Ashton-Warner (1963: 104)

Imagine now a kindergarten classroom, in which lively 5- and 6-year-old children are talking, playing and airing their differences and similarities, if not literally expressing love for, or fighting with, each other. Their dedicated teacher, Mrs Bee, has been trying hard to follow the mandated writing curriculum. That curriculum consists of sets of lessons, developed by the district, to teach kindergartners to engage in the writing process and, thereby, to express their individual selves through 'readable' writing. The children are to be 'independent' in their encoding and to draw on their own 'real' experiences.

Among Mrs Bee's challenges is that bedeviling interest of children in each other. They talk, draw and play much more than they write. And any graphic production is just as likely to be, not 'a' child's, but children's: they appropriate (officially, they unlawfully 'copy') topics and indeed, experiences from each other. Moreover, their 'real' stories, drawn from their 'true' lives, are often made up.

Mrs Bee is teaching at a time when talk and play have become problematic in many early childhood classrooms. Under the influence of state and US federal mandates (for example No Child Left Behind), scripted literacy teaching has become dominant and is viewed as the means for closing racialized and classed achievement 'gaps', despite contrary evidence (see Miller and Almon, 2009).

In this chapter I examine children's composing – especially this apparent 'copying' and 'making up' of 'true' stories – by situating it within the context of their social talk and play. In so doing, I draw on data from two classroom studies, both located in low-income urban neighbourhoods in the United States. One was centred in Mrs Bee's kindergarten, the other in a first grade, Mrs Kay's. Although their classrooms were different in many ways, both Mrs Bee and Mrs Kay taught within schools impacted by societal and political concerns about the achievement of low-income children, disproportionately children of colour; both were under pressure to teach 'basic' skills (for example letters, sounds, spelling, punctuation, grammar) within a writing workshop (or process) model.

Each classroom is itself a 'telling case' (Mitchell, 1984), that is, has its own particular realization of the connection between composing and playful child practices in regulated times. In this chapter, though, Mrs Bee's and Mrs Kay's children collectively help 'tell' about this connection. In the telling, I emphasize their 'unseemly and unlawful communication', particularly the liberties they took with what is mine and 'yours', what is 'true' or not. Situating those liberties within childhood talk and play reveals children's unofficial social worlds – their childhood cultures – and their agency, a quality seldom considered by those anxious to rescue poor children with paced, mandated and often scripted teaching. Below I provide a theoretical backdrop for the child action to come.

Written language and the mediation of childhood cultures

Alicia: (to Ella, who is drawing and writing next to her) Here you [Ella]. Here Denise [another peer]. Here my auntie.
Ella: Where's the bathing suit?
Alicia: I don't have a bathing suit.
Ella: So you're gonna be naked. . . . Don't make me naked. Put some clothes on me. . . .
(to the kindergarten girls drawing and writing around her) Whoever got me in the[ir] picture will come to my birthday. It will be in the summer. It will be in Chicago.
Alicia: O::!

Asked to write about a hoped-for summer pleasure, Alicia, Ella and the other girls at their table all found themselves swimming in the water. And to be so included in someone else's graphic world was valued – worth an invitation to a birthday (even if the invitation itself, or the party, was imagined). What is this sharing of topics, this bargaining for inclusion? What, if anything, does the children's playful interaction have to do with writing development? To answer such questions, recent socio-cultural views of development, child culture, and writing itself will prove helpful.

Children 'grow[ing] into the intellectual life around them'

In the socio-cultural view of learning, children learn through participation in the 'intellectual life around them' (Vygotsky, 1978: 88); that life is organized into human activities or practices, involving certain people, material tools and interactive structures. Children learn through observing those activities, through engaging in them with guiding adults or more skilful others, through listening to stories (real and invented) about how the world works, *and* through their own play (Rogoff, 2003). In this way, children and their peers assume control over what can be a confusing world; they examine the workings of the world around them, create roles, negotiate actions, and face the consequences of their actions as 'pretend' parents and children, superheroes and victims, party givers and invitees, for example. Across cultures, these seem to be children's ways of learning, even though their opportunities to learn, the nature of their interaction with others, the cultural material they play with, and even how that play is viewed by others, all may vary.

Children, then, have some agency in the construction of their own childhood experiences and, thereby, their own learning. They selectively respond to the world around them, based on their dispositions, interests and past experiences (Nelson, 2007). The notion of children's own culture foregrounds this agency and, also, the role that other children play in their learning (Stephens, 1995). By 'children's culture' is meant the communicative and often playful social practices that children form as they respond to the adult-introduced social practices that comprise, and constrain, their everyday experiences in time and space (James et al., 1998; Corsaro, 2005).

What do child cultures have to do with learning to write, in particular?

Mediational tools for childhood cultures

As Vygotsky (1978) noted, it is much easier for adults to teach young children the mechanics of print than to teach them the cultural act of writing. Writing mediates the human desire to symbolize and communicate one's responses to, and experiences in, the world. Indeed, Vygotsky located the beginnings of writing (as the deliberate representation and communication of spoken ideas) in gesture, play and drawing. For example, in play, children rename themselves and objects as other than what they are (for example a mother, baby, kitten); they use their own gestures, movements and voices to symbolize a pretend world. In drawing, young children name their lines, curves and spaces, transforming them into objects, people and actions; indeed, they learn to use speech to plan, monitor and narrate their graphic symbol-making. Thus, their drawings become quite literally a way of writing, that is, a way of graphically rendering and communicating a spoken world.

In the vignette opening this section, Alicia and her peers used drawing as a mediational tool both to represent a desired summer scene – swimming in the local pool – and to negotiate their own relationships. Alicia said to Ella, 'This you'; in so doing she transformed her lines and curves into Ella swimming with her in the pool . . . and, at the very same time, she brought Ella closer to her in the ongoing social world. Ella was pleased to be in Alicia's 'pool' (although she did not want to be naked in it). In response, she offered Alicia – and anyone else who moved to include her in their symbolic world – a place in her birthday party. Moreover, she then included Alicia in her picture *and writing* (to 'I am pw [playing with] alcha [Alicia]').

Written language is another medium, albeit a more abstract one, for negotiating, representing, and constructing a world. Its 'prehistory' is found in, builds on, and is interwoven with, play, drawing, and talk (Vygotsky, 1978). Children will learn the cultural act of writing – of participating in the social and intellectual life around them through written language – if they find that symbolic tool 'relevant to life' (Vygotsky, 1978: 118). And, in school, young children may find symbolic tools relevant if those tools enable them to interact with peers (Dyson, 1989, 2003, 2007).

Teachers provide opportunities and guidance for their young students. And in highly regulated schools, like those in which I observed, they are currently informed by mandated curricula and tests. Sitting side by side, children respond to official activities, and, as in all cultural learning, they observe, listen, seek guidance, and play around with and within recurrent routines and practices. But they are not only attending to and interacting with the teacher; they are also attending to and interacting with each other. Thus, they both conform to their sense of institutional rules and transform them, as both official and unofficial social worlds of expectations and practices evolve. It is within evolving unofficial cultures – these dynamic configurations of child-controlled practices (Sutton-Smith et al., 1995; Corsaro, 2005) – that the 'copying' of interest arises.

Copying behaviour and social actions

When community participants take a discursive turn as speaker or writer, their utterance – that is, their text – borrows from and responds to the texts of others; thus, texts are dialogically linked (Bakhtin, 1981). Learning the way in which literacy practices mediate the negotiation of relationships seems fundamental to learning the cultural act of writing as community participation. And children seem more likely to engage in these dialogic actions with their peers than with their teachers, at least in part because they are closer in status, interest and position in school.

This notion of written texts as linked brings us to children's apparent copying from each other. Such copying is in conflict with writing pedagogies rooted in individualism. School curricula for 'writing basics' stress individual skill mastery (Moats, 2004); those that organize daily writing 'workshops' stress composing as individual expression and the crafting of life experiences (Calkins and Mermelstein, 2003).

Certainly, copying can encompass a range of behaviours and, moreover, can enact diverse social intentions. For example, as an official activity, copying sentence(s) off the board can be a physically oppressive activity, particularly for children with limited writing experience (Dyson, 1985); they may have to twist their head towards the board many times as they slowly draw each letter. And yet, apparent 'copying', as a child-initiated action, may also serve to construct and sustain peer relationships in the unofficial world. For example, deliberately choosing the same topic or wording can be a marker of peer affiliation (cf. James, 1993).

Before examining the unofficial 'copying' practices at play in Mrs Bee's and Mrs Kay's rooms, I briefly describe their distinct classrooms and the procedures for the collection and analysis of data. (A detailed description of the study in Mrs Kay's room is available in Dyson, 2006; the study in Mrs Bee's room is ongoing but teacher and children are discussed in Genishi and Dyson, 2009.)

The data sets: writing 'life stories'

Mrs Bee: Yesterday I told you about . . . when I went snow skiing. And then a lot of you . . . took my story and tried to make it yours. . . . And I saw some of you copying your neighbors' story. . . . You have to have your own story, your own thoughts, your own ideas. . . . I know there are many things that you guys like to do and have already done!

Children then offer their 'own' ideas, including ice skating, another winter sport. Jamal's idea, though, was about a very different sport.

Jamal: I'm gonna write about I went in a horse race.

Mrs Bee: Boys and girls these stories have to be real. . . . (A direction contained in the curricular guide for teachers.)

Amani: In the *TV*::: (explaining how one could be at, if not in, a horse race)

Mrs Bee: It can't be on the TV. It has to be a real story about you. . . . It can't be fake. What do we call fake stories?

Odette: Original.

Mrs Bee: (laughs)

Both Mrs Bee and Mrs Kay were in highly regulated urban schools serving low-income neighbourhoods, and both were following curricular mandates for writing. Still, there were differences between their situations. I describe each setting below and how I studied within them, beginning with Mrs Kay's room in an urban Michigan school whose city was undergoing great financial distress.

Writing in Mrs Kay's first grade

Mrs Kay, who was white, had spent her entire teaching career of over twenty years at her central city school; that school served children with diverse cultural identities, including African American, Mexican American, and white. Mrs Kay had taught through many curricular upheavals. Whatever the curricular demands, she felt that children needed time to make decisions and organize their own activity, as well as to run around and release energy; in addition to the noon recess, she provided time for morning and afternoon recesses, or in-classroom activity choice (for example building with varied construction materials; sculpting with Play Doh; drawing, writing and crafting with paper, scissors, templates and glue). There was ample time for the children to develop recurrent play themes and practices and, as I will illustrate, these could become organizing contexts for official activities, particularly writing.

Unlike Mrs Bee, Mrs Kay had no mandated lesson plans for writing. As was expected in her school, daily she modelled sketching and, then, writing personal narratives; she circulated as children wrote their own 'life stories', and she edited children's products, emphasizing grammar and punctuation skills. Finally, she provided time for each child to read their work.

I had expected that, since this was a first grade, there would be children who were still figuring out the alphabetic system; but, to my surprise, there were not. As it happened, kindergarten was the place where children were to learn their letters and sounds and, if they struggled, they were subject to retention. A state away, in Illinois, Mrs Bee would soon experience a great deal of pressure to get her own kindergartners 'stretching and sounding out words' in writing.

Writing in Mrs Bee's kindergarten

Mrs Bee's children were, with few exceptions, African American and, unlike Mrs Kay's, most knew each other from their relatively small urban neighbourhood. Mrs Bee, who herself was African American, had spent thirty years teaching in what she described as a 'play-based' preschool in a rural area; she had expected that kindergarten would not be so different. But she found it startlingly different, particularly the mandated literacy programmes that expected that kindergartners would learn literacy 'basics' (beyond letters and sounds to writing readable sentences with phonologically sensible, if not conventional, spelling). Although there was time taken for a game of hot potato or an alphabet puzzle, other than the 10–15 minute after-lunch recess (when the weather allowed), academic tasks typically filled the official school day.

Mrs Bee told me that she felt the pressure of the literacy programme, finding it hard initially even to relax enough to sleep at night. In the beginning of the year, most of her children were learning letter names and trying to draw their own names; few were attuned to the alphabetic system. Still, the writing programme was structured in ways similar to Mrs Kay's, although Mrs Bee had a mandated and paced commercial curriculum (that is, it unfolded according to a district-wide schedule). Special emphasis was placed on 'true' personal narratives; and, by the winter months, children were encouraged to draw minimally, if at all, and to sound out their words.

I observed a year in Mrs Kay's room, a year and a half in Mrs Bee's, concentrating on 'writing workshop'. In both rooms, certain children served as anchors for my observations. Those children provided entry into varied friendship groups in the classroom; among them were Alicia and Latrez (both self-described as 'black') in Mrs Bee's room, and Tionna, Lyron (both 'black'), and Ezekial ('Mexican') in Mrs Kay's.

The classrooms were, as just detailed, quite different and, moreover, the children had different degrees of experience with written language. Nonetheless, both classrooms had identifiable, if unofficial, forms of interaction during composing, or what are referred to herein as participation modes (cf. Philips, 1972; Goffman, 1981; Goodwin and Goodwin, 2006). These four modes of interacting were the ways in which children's enacted relationships – their social interactions – were shaping, and shaped by, their ongoing symbol-making. The modes ranged from articulated collegial interest in each other's symbol-making to intense collaborative role play through composing.

To illustrate the varied modes, I draw on data from both classrooms. I highlight what, on the surface, might seem evidence of 'copying your neighbor's story', but, described more thickly (Geertz, 1983), becomes evidence of children's social agency in childhood worlds. The illustrative vignettes are arranged in order of social and textual complexity. That is, the later discussed modes incorporate more deliberate, more extended *textual* interaction. Although such modes appeared primarily in Mrs Kay's room, it is not suggested that the modes are in a set developmental order; children in each room exploited local opportunities for composing. I also make no claim that children do not sometimes simply copy because they need help; they do.

However, I do claim that composing is a mediational tool for varied forms of social participation. When children act on their interest in each other and in what each other are doing, they may learn something more basic than letters, sounds, and sight words (although they may find a reason to concentrate on those particulars); they may learn a sense of mediational agency, that is, a consciousness of how symbolic media are used to participate in and shape the social world. The dialogic processes undergirding this learning may bump up against, or surreptitiously coexist with, the official curriculum.

The unofficial world in formation: participation modes

Copying is wrong, 'under the law', as Alicia peer's Denise said. And yet, social cohesion and coherence are conversationally constructed as people quite literally build their own turns on the words of others. It is this dialogic process, and its diverse social enactments, that underlies the linking of an unofficial child culture and child composing and, also, accounts for some of that unlawful copying. The social enactments illustrated below include collegial, coordinated, complementary and collaborative modes. I begin with the most common, collegial.

Collegial context: being together

Children's talk during writing revealed how cognizant they were of, and interested in, each other's doing. And this articulating of interest is referred to herein as collegial. Some of this talk, that which gave rise to 'copying', involved rounds of storytelling (that is, of telling 'what happened').

From early childhood on, people across cultures tell stories about the remarkable and the unusual, sometimes performing a story with dramatic flair in order to wrap others into the storyteller's social space (Ochs and Capps, 2001; Bauman, 2004). A story thus engenders other's stories; 'I hear you,' listeners may seem to say, 'and something like that happened to me.'

Such collegial sharing accounts for some of the children's spontaneous linking of their products – and their apparent 'copying'. Such linking was common from the beginning of the school year in Mrs Bee's kindergarten. Asked to draw and write a 'real' story, children did not necessarily have 'a' topic but, rather, an evolving conversation and a play with ideas; individual productions linked together and then veered off. This spontaneous linking of stories provided the instructional context for Mrs Bee's first discussions of keeping it real and not copying somebody else's 'real' experiences.

To illustrate, consider the following data excerpt featuring Alicia's peers Latrez, Cici, and their tablemates:

> Mrs Bee has just interrupted the children's composing of a 'true' story to reiterate her expectations, based on the district's adopted writing curriculum:
>
> Mrs Bee: I want you to be sure you're sketching something that's really real about you. I don't want you dreaming up something

about Superman, Batman, and all those folk. Because they're not really real. . . . When those people fly they have strings on them to . . . keep them up in the air. . . . I don't want you people going out of here thinking you can fly, because you can't. . . .

I'll tell you one thing I really like to do, but you can't say it on your paper because it's not your thought; it's mine. You guys are really going to think I'm crazy because I like to water ski, I like to snow ski, I'm a jock. . . .

The children return to their composing. Latrez, however, has a comment for his peers about flying (but not a superhero flying):

Latrez: I seen a balloon when I went on my –
Cici: I seen a air balloon! It was up in the sky.
Latrez: It was the color blue. Yeah, it went all the way in the sky.
Cici: It was over by my day care.
              (raising voice) Mrs Bee, we seen the air balloon!
Della: Me too! I saw the air balloon.

As 'Me too's' arise from the room, Mrs Bee comments:

Mrs Bee: Everybody didn't see an air balloon now. ('I did's can be heard all around.) Only the things you really did see.

At his table, Latrez draws a flying balloon.

Latrez: I'm gonna make a air balloon.
Cici: I seen an air balloon. Red, yellow, different colors!

Now other children are making air balloons. Cici notes that she and Latrez stand out among the crowd:

Cici: You all got one. Me and him got two.
Latrez: I got two air balloons!

Soon, though, one of Latrez's air balloons sprouts petals and becomes a flower and another grows appendages and becomes him flying in the air, propelled by his mother:

Latrez: This how I went up in the sky when I was a baby. My mommy throw me up in the sky. I couldn't come down. I didn't know I couldn't come down. A robot catched me.

In the end, children at Latrez's table had drawn air balloons, in part because they had seen them or, perhaps, wanted to see them. And Latrez, whose products were fluid, moved from a flying air balloon to his own flying through the air, saved by a conveniently located robot. In a similar way, children exchanged varied kinds of stories, including recurring ones of getting bitten by sharks in the lake, the pool or even the bathtub. In this mode, the children did not copy in the official sense; they conversed, and they borrowed from their conversing. (Indeed, as Mrs Bee noted with some frustration in an earlier vignette, some even borrowed from her talk.)

The described collegiality seems similar to that reported by Matthews (1999), based on his studies of young children drawing together; across cultures, children's evolving productions were linked through their conversational topics and rhythms. They seemed attuned to the possibilities and constraints of the page and their peers. Thus, their symbol-making became a 'spatio-temporal theater of symbolic play' (Matthews, 1999: 9–10).

Collegial talk, though, could entail more than an interest in each other's stories. It could, for example, include a kind of supportive 'I gotcha' talk, to quote Alicia's friend Ella – a providing of help, for example, mutual assistance in sounding out a spelling, a content suggestion, or an inquiry about 'sense'. As evident in the brief vignette below, Ella is keen on Alicia's piece; although their topics are different (Ella's is her cat, Alicia's is 'her Tinker Bell'), Ella's suggestions have resulted in shared words and, also, in mutual help with spelling.

Ella: (to Alicia) What are you writing about?
Alicia: Tinker Bell. (reading) 'My Tinker Bell [says but has not written] cute.'
Ella: It's supposed to be 'My Tinker Bell is' whatever color your Tinker Bell is.
Alicia: Her gonna be pink. Don't Tinker Bell have dresses?
Ella: Yes, 'cause I watched the movie.
Denise: Me too. I watched the mo-vie.
Alicia: Ella, no Tinker Bell has no pants on, girl.
Ella: I know that. But they fly. So you might wanta draw fly. And you might wanta do dots.
Denise: Tinker Bell don't have no dots.
Ella: Yeah she do.
Alicia: On their dresses they do. Sometimes on their nails they do. Sometimes they don't.
Ella: 'My cat is white' – (rereading)
Alicia: (rereading) . . . 'My Tinker Bell is' cute. I forgot to write *cute*!
Ella: And you said *pretty* too!
Alicia: How you spell *pretty*?
Ella: 'My cat is' pretty. How you spell *pretty*?
Alicia: P-E
Ella: Pre *ty*, Pretty

And together the girls came up with *prety*.

. . .

Alicia: Oh, you, me, and Denise lost two teeth.

We girls share our work with each other and our words . . . and even the experience of losing teeth.

Coordinated composing: friends doing things together

In the next mode, the children's composing is not linked through their spontaneous, collegial talk but through their deliberate planning.

> 'Hey you guys!' says Tionna, looking up from her journal during writing time. 'We can write about we miss Miss Hache [her class's former student teacher]. . . . Tomorrow we can write about we miss Miss Hache.'
> 'Yeah,' says Mandisa.

Tionna's suggestion of a writing topic was not a spontaneous linking of texts but a deliberate plan to share a topic. Articulated efforts to coordinate composing – through direct suggestions and negotiations – were common in Mrs Kay's room. Indeed, from early in the year, regular companions coordinated both drawing and writing; although the official emphasis was on writing 'life stories', they invented seemingly mundane but shared outings. For example, in September of the school year, Tionna, Lyron and Janette all went to the store together and also rode their bikes to each other's homes according to their texts . . . although they did not even know where each other lived.

Such coordinating of topics – which led to a sharing of words and of spelling challenges – could become a social obligation among friends. In the following example, Lyron asks (to put it mildly) if other children are going to write about a favourite pastime – floor hockey, a kind of hockey where you 'don't need ice skates . . . just regular shoes' but still can play like those professional hockey players appreciated in his northern US state:

Lyron: Janette, write about floor hockey!
Janette: I am. (irritated, as in 'I already said I was')
Lyron: Jon, are you?

Lyron now adds classmates to his own text about who is going to be playing field hockey.

Lyron: I'm writing Janette first. (he has her name tag)
          Jason, your turn. . . . Here you go, Jason.

As Lyron added each name, his voice was full of anticipation, seemingly assuming others' pleasure at being included. In this, he recalled Mrs Bee's Ella, exchanging birthday invitations for representational inclusion. But Lyron had organized for his own inclusion, as he and his peers were writing about a shared after-school activity – floor hockey – and the expected compositions would name names.

Such deliberate coordination was less common in Mrs Bee's room; not only were her children less experienced composers but her teachers' guide was explicit about children being independent. Moreover, because her children needed much help forming letters and encoding messages, Mrs Bee monitored them closely. She was relatively more aware of each child's product and, thus, of any apparent copying of topics or, when topics were assigned (such as 'Thanksgiving plans'), of textual content.

Mrs Bee's children, however, did not seem to understand the blanket admonition against copying. The children's talk suggested that they inter-preted the 'no copying' rule as a matter of who claimed ownership of a topic first, just as they interpreted rights to a valued object, be it a frisbee or an eraser – 'I got it first!' When Jamal announced that he was 'doing swimming' on his paper, the teacher-attuned Alexia said, 'You're copying offa me,' since *she* was writing about going swimming. Her good friend Coretta turned to him and said, 'Have you even *been* swimming before?' In so doing, she linked copy-ing to not being truthful: the children are to draw on their own real lives and not copy somebody else's real life.

Still, even Mrs Bee's children sometimes deliberately coordinated topics and, moreover, could adopt complementary roles in constructing a shared world mediated by texts.

Complementing texts: entering written dialogues

In complementary composing, children shared a topic, but they also separated their roles as social players and, thus, as composers. Their roles, and their mediating texts, became contingent on each other's, and that contingency was shaped by their relationship, the particular practice, and the societal ideologies (for example gender) so embedded. Violations of expectations led to explicit corrections and, sometimes, hurt feelings.

Elena has already illustrated the potential for such a participation mode in Mrs Bee's room; she was pleased with her inclusion in Alicia's swimming production and, in response, included Alicia in her own composing. Such potential was dramatically played out in Mrs Kay's room. For example, her children had an extended, recurrent practice in which they planned pretend get-togethers. Planning these events depended on children being alert to the contingent nature of their writing, that is, to the need to 'build action together' and, thereby, make a coherent if imagined world (Goodwin and Goodwin, 2006: 225).

To illustrate: like his peers Tionna and Lyron, Ezekial was a socially alert player and composer. In contrast, their peer Aaron was not dependable (that is, at first he did not write about a supposedly agreed upon plan); as in other situations, he seemed to miss the social point of the composing – a present togetherness, not a future getting together. For example, since Ezekial and Aaron had agreed that Ezekial was planning to (but would never actually) go to Aaron's house, Ezekial expected that their writing would be linked; but Aaron did not cooperate. Ezekial offered guidance, to no immediate effect. 'Aaron, say [write] "Ezekial is going to bring the college [basketball] game," OK?' (Aaron eventually learned to cooperate, although he complained to me that no one ever actually came to his house.)

The most elaborate complementary composing involved the planning of birthday parties. If one child wrote that various children were coming to his or her party, invitees might write that, yes indeed, they were going to so-and-so's planned (but not actual) party. In fact, a constellation of practices evolved connected to such planning, including practices appropriated from in and out of school (for example making lists of invitees; oral negotiations about who was going to whose house to pick up whom; gathering and exchanging phone numbers). Thus, the unofficial world evolved on the foundation of wanting to be explicitly included in desirable imagined worlds, that is, in play. (For an elaboration of the birthday party practice, see Dyson, 2007.)

The social and textual knowledge revealed by children's contingent world-building coexisted with, but did not inform, the official curricula. In both rooms, there were clear expectations about the kind and nature of texts to be written and the skills thereby practised and demonstrated. The social organization of writing was not questioned (i.e., it was an individual task) nor were genres recognized beyond those officially privileged (no birthday cards, lists, songs . . .); thus, the latter received no instructional attention (for example a genre name, a discussion of features, opportunities for official use). This was true too of composing organized by the most socially and textually complex participation mode: improvisational collaborating.

Improvisational collaborating: jointly enacting worlds

During writing time in Mrs Bee's class, Denise walks over to Jamal and shows him the drawn figure on the back of her composing page:

Denise: This is me, and I'm bigger than you.
Jamal: Nuh uh. . . .
Denise: And that's you. (a smaller figure)
Jamal: Oh, you wanta play? You wanta play? (Jamal turns his writing paper over.) Here – here you go. You got a *big* great head. (turning then to me) That's Denise.

And so the drawn duel continues.

In improvisational collaborating, not only were children's roles contingent on each other (for example party giver, invitee), so too were their very words, which evolved dialogically. Denise and Jamal enacted this participant mode, mediated by drawing and talk. Jamal's 'Oh, you wanta play?' was a rejoinder to Denise's drawn and spoken conversational move: 'That's you.' Improvisational collaboration, though, was strictly a back-of-the-paper kind of participation in Mrs Bee's room. The children could deliberately respond to each other during the daily writing time, but their moves tended to be on the back of a page or erased when done.

In Mrs Kay's room, children did deliberately play collaboratively on paper. The most dramatic illustration was a composing time version of 'The Pine Cone Wars' (for an ethnographic description, see Dyson, 2007).

Initially this play was only a playground chase game, named for the pine cones that teams of children held and sometimes threw as they chased each other about. The wars travelled into the classroom as a kind of playful drawing duel between Lyron and Manny during composing time. The improvisational nature of the boys' collaboration is clear in the following sample vignette, as is the central role of drawing and talk as mediational tools:

> Manny and Lyron, seated kitty corner from each other, are doing their respective 'quick sketches' (which takes them most of the 45 minute writing period). They each have their own journals, they each are drawing, but they are clearly playing together:
>
> Lyron: Manny, your men and my men are fighting with their swords.
> Manny: Well I still got men up here on Earth. Lyron, look it! . . . Look how many people that are from Earth.
> Lyron: Manny, here's me and you on the bridge fighting, on my bridge. . . . I kicked you off the bridge.
> . . . [omitted data]
> Here's where one of your guys jumped one – one of my guys . . .
> Elly: (a tablemate who has been listening) Lyron, you better watch out and you better not cry because looky what he [Manny] has coming.

Writing was not particularly relevant to the children's activity, and after spending the writing period warning each other of what sort of doom was about to befall them, each player wrote some variant of 'So-and-so and I will have a war. I will win. He will lose.' Their texts were complementary, but they were written quickly without any apparent dialogue.

Apparently inspired by Lyron and Manny, composing-time battles soon spread throughout the class, as teams of children took on other children in their daily productions. At Manny and Lyron's table, Tionna was the sole girl who decided to play war; initially, though, she planned to play with her friend Mandisa, who sat at another table. However, her decision to play upset her friend Lyron; he objected because girls 'don't even know about war'. Tionna took offence ('Yes we do'), and soon a gendered war erupted. And in that war, writing became a more central mediational tool. The gendered war had, after all, erupted in verbal conflict; thus, it became a kind of verbal one-upmanship. For example, Manny wrote in part:

> The gerls will lorste [lose] . . . We [boys] have two big casle. They have ten little tents.

But Tionna wrote:

> We are tofe girls we stol there money . . . Thay oldy have one tent we have a lot of Cacle.

The children's loud, gendered war play unnerved Mrs Kay. Their play with what could be deemed violence was displayed in writing, not lost in talk or located off-centre-stage in a picture. Mrs Kay banned war; it became once again only a playground game among friends.

Mrs Kay's action was not unreasonable, but the point here is that, in this curricular situation, questions about child texts that focused on characters' motives, plot resolutions, or children's own varied views about war as a topic were not part of official 'basics'. Moreover, the social organization of the children's writing – their collaborative production – also was unremarkable within the writing curriculum.

However, children's deliberate enactment of composing as a dialogic process seems basic to understanding written language as a human tool for social participation. Indeed, children's capacity for responsiveness could potentially fuel composing curricula in contemporary times.

On writing and childhoods

> They teach each other all their work . . . arguing with, correcting, abusing or smiling at each other. And between them all the time is this togetherness, so that learning is so mixed up with relationship that it becomes part of it. What an unsung creative medium is relationship.
> – Ashton-Warner (1963: 104)

In this chapter, I have troubled the dominant approach to child composing in these regulated times – one that sees learning to compose as acquiring skills for independent self-expression. In contrast, herein, learning to compose is 'all mixed up with relationship' and, more particularly, with participation in the making of children's own childhoods. As Bakhtin (1981) argued, one expresses oneself in the course of responding to, and participating in, the social world even as that world is being constructed through talk.

Too often, writing's foundational 'basics' are thought of as a set of skills (for example writing one's letters, learning one's sound/symbol connections). But the *basics* of writing are not found in these skills, however important. They are found in mobilizing and adapting one's symbolic and cultural possibilities for responding to the communicative situation at hand.

So, I have aimed to illustrate how children have used shared practices to make their entry into school writing 'relevant' to their lives together as children (Vygotsky, 1978: 118). To do so, I have taken instances of what could be deemed 'copying', in other words, a failure to independently mine one's own true experiences for self-expression. But apparent 'copying' could be the manifestation of enacted social relations; among these modes of participation were those deemed collegial, coordinated, complementary, or even collaborative.

Whether it was made manifest on the back of a sheet of paper or captured in upfront writing, the child social activity presented herein has demonstrated how children's 'unlawful' interest in each other may lead them to 'copy', 'make up' and jointly create a world mediated through texts. Indeed, children's interest in being responsive to each other could lead to sustained composing, itself mediating the playful enactment of an imagined world.

The point here is not to discount the responsibility of policy makers and teachers to plan for, guide and assess student learning. Nor is it to dismiss the importance of children learning such basic information as letters and sounds. But it is to suggest that children's engagement in the complex communicative act of writing is not energized or organized by letters and sounds but by their own social agency and desire to participate. State and federal policies, driven at least in part by No Child Left Behind legislation, have helped push paced, scripted literacy education for young children. But they have left behind children's social agency and their construction of their own social worlds – the very worlds that make writing worth learning.

As official writing instruction becomes more regulated and more tied to narrowly defined, taught and tested skills, children's playful talk and imagination, as well as their multimodal composing, become irrelevant, distracting, even 'the worst enemies' to teaching. But scholars who look to the nature of literacy practices in contemporary times underscore the importance of what Jenkins (2006) refers to as 'participatory cultures' – which term seems a reasonable description of what was happening to at least some extent in the classrooms discussed in this chapter.

Jenkins (2006: 6) argues that participatory cultures shift 'the focus of literacy from one of individual expression to community involvement'. Emphasizing older children, he suggests that 'new literacies [for example blogging, pod casting] almost all involve social skills developed through collaboration and networking' in a playful, artistic context. These skills, he explains, build on traditional literacy ones. But, I would suggest, young children too can construct participatory cultures even as they learn those traditional skills, or so I would hope.

Indeed, I have been privileged to observe skilful teachers with the professional and curricular space to both organize activities to guide children into literacy use *and* allow children ample space to organize their own use. Teachers may even explicitly discuss with children the nature of collegial relations and possible ways of organizing composing (for example collaboration, coordination; Dyson, 1993, 1997). Teachers who have public forums for sharing and discussing children's work can also explore the complexities of the larger classroom community and the ways in which stories reverberate differently in that community because of, for example, gender or cultural identity.

Children's intense interest in each other, often manifest in their talking and playing, is not the enemy to good teaching. It is the lively fuel that, channelled by both official and unofficial practices, may energize children's capacity to write and rewrite their own worlds.

References

Ashton-Warner, S. (1963) *Teacher*. New York: Simon & Schuster.

Bakhtin, M. (1981) Discourse in the novel. In C. Emerson and M. Holquist (eds), *The Dialogic Imagination: Four Essays by M. Bakhtin* (pp. 254–422). Austin: University of Texas Press.

Bauman, R. (2004) *A World of Others' Words: Cross-cultural Perspectives on Intertextuality*. Malden, MA: Blackwell.

Calkins, L. and Mermelstein, L. (2003) *Launching the Writing Workshop*. Portsmouth, NH: Heinemann.

Corsaro, W. (2005) *The Sociology of Childhood*, 2nd edition. Thousand Oaks, CA: Pine Forge Press.

Dyson, A. Haas (1985) Three emergent writers and the school curriculum: copying and other myths, *Elementary School Journal*, 85(4): 497–512.

Dyson, A. Haas (1989) *Multiple Worlds of Child Writers: Friends Learning to Write*. New York: Teachers College Press.

Dyson, A. Haas (1993) *Social Worlds of Children Learning to Write in an Urban Primary School*. New York: Teachers College Press.

Dyson, A. Haas (1997) *Writing Superheroes: Contemporary Childhood, Popular Culture, and Classroom Literacy*. New York: Teachers College Press.

Dyson, A. Haas (2003) *The Brothers and Sisters Learn to Write: Popular Literacies in Childhood and School Cultures*. New York: Teachers College Press.

Dyson, A. Haas (2006) On saying it right (write): 'fix-its' in the foundations of learning to write, *Research in the Teaching of English*, 41: 8–44.

Dyson, A. Haas (2007) School literacy and the development of a child culture:

written remnants of the 'gusto of life'. In D. Thiessen and A. Cook-Sather (eds), *International Handbook of Student Experience in Elementary and Secondary School* (pp. 115–142). Dordrecht, The Netherlands: Kluwer Academic Publishers.

Geertz, C. (1983) *Local Knowledge*. New York: Basic Books.

Genishi, C. and Dyson, A. Haas (2009) *Children, Language, and Literacy: Diverse Learners in Diverse Times*. New York: Teachers College Press & The National Association for the Education of Young Children.

Goffman, E. (1981) *Forms of Talk*. Philadelphia: University of Pennsylvania Press.

Goodwin, C. and Goodwin, M.H. (2006) Participation. In A. Duranti (ed.), *A Companion to Linguistic Anthropology* (pp. 222–244). Malden, MA: Blackwell.

James, A. (1993) *Childhood Identities: Self and Social Relationships in the Experience of the Child*. Edinburgh: Edinburgh University Press.

James, A., Jenks, C. and Prout, A. (1998) *Theorizing Childhood*. New York: Teachers College Press.

Jenkins, H. (2006) *Confronting the Challenges of Participatory Culture: Media Education for the 21st Century*. Chicago: MacArthur Foundation.

Matthews, J. (1999) *The Art of Childhood and Adolescence: The Construction of Meaning*. London: Falmer Press.

Miller, E. and Almon, J. (2009) *Crisis in the Kindergarten: Why Children Need to Play in School*. College Park Maryland: Alliance for Childhood.

Mitchell, J.C. (1984) Case studies. In R.F. Ellen (ed.), *Ethnographic Research: A Guide to General Conduct* (pp. 237–241). San Diego, CA: Academic Press.

Moats, L. (2004) *Language Essentials for Teachers of Reading and Spelling*. Longmont, CO: Sopris West Educational Services.

Nelson, K. (2007) *Young Minds in Social Worlds: Experience, Meaning, and Memory*. Cambridge, MA: Harvard University Press.

Ochs, E. and Capps, L. (2001) *Living Narrative: Creating Lives in Everyday Storytelling*. Cambridge, MA: Harvard University Press.

Philips, S. (1972) Participant structures and communicative competence: warm springs children in community and classroom. In C.B. Cazden, V.P. John and D. Hymes (eds), *The Functions of Language in the Classroom* (pp. 370–394). New York: Teachers College Press.

Rogoff, B. (2003) *The Cultural Nature of Human Development*. New York: Oxford University Press.

Stephens, S. (1995) Introduction: Children and the politics of culture in 'late capitalism'. In S. Stephens (ed.), *Children and the Politics of Culture* (pp. 3–50). Princeton, NJ: Princeton University Press.

Sutton-Smith, B., Mechling, J., Johnson, T.W. and McMahon, F.R. (eds) (1995) *Children's Folklore: A Source Book*. New York: Garland Publishing.

Vygotsky, L.S. (1978) *Mind in Society*. Cambridge, MA: Harvard University Press.

11 'Improper' children

Liz Jones, Rachel Holmes, Christina MacRae and Maggie MacLure

Introduction

This chapter draws on research that is derived from a project whose principal aim was to investigate how children earn negative reputations such as being considered to be 'naughty'.[1] In particular it highlights how certain behaviours on the part of young people (4–6 years of age) become untenable to practitioners because they instil a form ontological insecurity in terms of their own performances (Butler, 1997). By framing the data within notions of abjection (Douglas, 1966; Kristeva, 1982), we mark out how pedagogical mechanisms, including those ways in which 'the child' is conceptualized, become momentarily insecure, creating cognitive dissonance and leaving a severe sense of helplessness where everything that is of comfort in terms of what it means to be a teacher, disintegrates. In this space of abjection, meaning collapses and the 'clean and proper' becomes soiled, and is manifested in/as 'improper' children.

As a starting point we offer a brief résumé of the context in which the research was undertaken in order to provide context. We then move to present examples of data that attempt to capture what it might mean to be a 'proper' child within the context of early schooling. Our analysis at this point details some of the discursive practices which work at both summoning the 'proper' child and giving her substance, since without these insights it is difficult to appreciate what works at constituting the 'improper' child. Attention is then focused on some of the tensions, stresses and strains that swirl between 'improper' children and adults. It is across and within these pressures, anxieties and apprehensions that we have found it productive to engage with Mary Douglas's work on taboo, impurity and defilement and with Julia Kristeva's notions concerning abjection. The chapter concludes by considering a number of complex/tricky 'so what' questions for further thinking and discussion.

Situating the chapter

This chapter emerges from an ethnographic research project which investigated the processes by which children become viewed as 'a problem' in their school lives. The research centred on children who were in their first eighteen months of schooling. Hence we observed the children in their very initial stages of formal schooling when they were aged 4–5 years and we continued to track them as they moved from the first/reception classroom to Year 1 where UK children are 6 years of age. During the eighteen-month time span, a researcher spent a day a week in the classroom of four different schools in one of the large conurbations in the north of England. One was a Roman Catholic school in an area of the city with high levels of poverty. Another was located in a relatively affluent suburban district where the school population was mainly white. The third was in the heart of the city centre where over thirty different family languages were spoken by the children in the group; and the fourth was also a city school in an area of deprivation with children who were mainly of white heritage. Besides observing and tracking actions within the classroom, time was also spent watching and noting children's interactions in the playground, lunch queues and other settings within the schools in order to understand how children act and are perceived by others when outside the classroom. The data we draw on for this chapter are our written observations from the visits.

As previously stated, a key focus for our study was problematic behaviour as it emerged within and was shaped by the culture of the classroom. The research started from the premise that securing a successful reputation as a 'good' pupil, or acquiring a negative one as a 'problem' is never the sole responsibility of the individual child. In school contexts, children must not only act appropriately, but must be recognized as having done so. Reputation is therefore a public matter. A post-structuralist approach has been adopted when analysing the data. Such an approach conceptualizes subjectivity as an outcome of discursive practices that constitute and make sense of the world (Britzman, 1990; Gee, 1990; Brown and Jones, 2002; MacLure, 2003). Indeed, across the four sites it was possible to identify a number of discourses that within early years have gained considerable momentum and which would be immediately recognizable to those conversant with the field. These included: child development and developmentally appropriate practice (DAP) (Bredekamp, 1987), play-based curriculum and humanist individuality.

Performing as a proper child

> . . . nothing seems more ineffable, more incommunicable, more inimitable, and therefore more precious than the values given body, made body by the

> transubstantiation achieved by hidden persuasion of an implicit pedagogy, capable of instilling a whole cosmology, an ethic, a metaphysic, a political philosophy through injunctions as insignificant as 'stand up straight' or 'don't hold your knife in your left hand' . . . The whole trick of pedagogic reason lies precisely in the way it extorts the essential while seeming to demand the insignificant.
>
> – Bourdieu (1977: 94–95)

Schooling demands that children behave in ways that are regarded as normal, and what counts as normal is dictated by the discourses of the 'regular' classroom environment (Stormont-Spurgin, 1997). Both gaining access to and maintaining one's 'proper' place (Graham, 2006) within the regular classroom demands that children 'perform' their identities (Butler, 1997) within the discursive frames that regulate standardized or customary forms of participation (Popkewitz, 2004). Being a 'proper' child is not a straightforward matter for many young people, even though the rules and requirements are rehearsed many times a day, displayed on walls, endorsed in assemblies,[2] regulated by reward systems and so on. This is partly because *interpretive work* is required in order to understand what 'being good/proper' involves. Children need to learn what they are expected to do, or to refrain from doing, in order for their behaviour to be assigned to the category of 'good', or any of the various related categories that are used to regulate behaviour. These we noted would include 'sitting beautifully'; 'properly'; 'nicely'; 'good listening'; 'being sensible'; not being 'silly'; putting 'hands up' and waiting to be chosen to speak while the teacher is speaking.

Some of the requirements imposed upon children were reasonably easy to trace back to particular behaviours (though not necessarily easy to comply with), such as putting hands up; but others needed quite sophisticated 'categorization work' (Baker, 2000). In one scenario for example, the following observational notes were made:

> Olivia is sitting with her legs outstretched and is asked by Ms K to 'Sit properly in the classroom, Olivia, please.' (Chesterfield, 18 January 2007).

In this context, Olivia was required to examine her own posture and relate this to her knowledge of the rules for correct sitting in order to know she has offended and what she needs to do to 'sit properly':

Being 'sensible' – a common term that was used in each of the four schools – may even be open to interpretation, as may be the range of behaviours that will be judged not to be sensible. In the following example, Ellie must inspect her own past behaviour and future intentions, and identify the nature of Ms F's dissatisfaction with her, in order to know what she has done to warrant the call to 'behave more sensibly':

Field note
Ms F starts a whole-group activity on the carpet.
Ms F: Ellie, come and sit by me.
Ellie: Why?
Because you'll behave more sensibly, that's why.
(Chesterfield, 20 April 2007)

Part of the problem with such interpretive requirements is that the evaluations are made *retrospectively*: children must read 'back' from the adult's assessment to the behaviour which has provoked it. At Chesterfield, weekly 'certificate assemblies' celebrated a wide range of behaviours and competences. For instance certificates were awarded:

Field note
For always listening and being kind and helpful;
For always listening and working hard;
For fantastic joining in on the carpet;
For working really hard with his letter sounds;
For settling in so well (two new girls)
(Dronsfield, 18 September 2007)

Interpretive work is needed if children are to identify what they have done in the past week that counted as 'fantastic joining in on the carpet', or 'being kind and helpful'. And even when evaluations are made immediately after a particular action, children still need to do self-inspection to know what is specifically being referenced when they are commended for 'sitting beautifully' or for 'good listening'. Occasionally, children did not seem entirely sure what they had done in order to 'earn' an evaluation as good:

Field note
Christopher comes up to the researcher and says 'I've got a certificate'
Researcher: Why?
Christopher: For being good
Researcher: What did you do that was good?
Christopher: I was playing nicely
Researcher: What were you playing with?
Christopher: I don't know
(Chesterfield, 29 September 2006)

The space between evaluations and the behaviours to which they retro-spectively refer may be large enough for the evaluation to be *withdrawn*. For instance, Brent's teacher was angry with him (and his mother) when he came to school in wet clothes. As the class sat on the carpet before assembly, Ms M picked up a (blank) certificate:

> **Field note**
> 'This certificate was for you Brent. It was for good listening. I can't give it to you now can I, 'cause you didn't listen to me yesterday when I told you not to get soaked again.' She tells the Teaching Assistant[3] in front of the assembled children that Brent's mum had been with him and hadn't done anything about it.
> (Martinsfield, 6 July 2007)

Brent's offending behaviour (coming to school 'soaked') is retrospectively identified as a breach of the 'good listening' for which he was prospectively to be commended, although he was not aware of the impending commendation until the point at which it was withdrawn. Evaluations and behaviour may exist in a strange 'future pluperfect' timescale in which the import of child-ren's own actions will have been deferred, or even altered, by unforeseen events and unpredicted interpretations by others.

We identified that certain objects operated as materializations of power in the four project classrooms, aimed at rendering the children's bodies as docile. For example, carpeted areas where children would be gathered together were key sites for this regulation of the active body. The act of sitting on the carpet carried with it a set of implications where the contours of the child's body had to satisfy the requirement of 'sitting up straight, with arms folded and legs crossed'. Thus, matter such as carpeting becomes felt in the broadest sense – emotionally, physically and psychologically. The engage-ments that occur when a child's body connects with the material trouble the boundaries that are ordinarily erected between stuff that is inert and that which is 'natural'. Intra-actions (Barad, 2008) between the material and the body worked to subdue children's bodies and contribute towards the ebb and flow of agency. Children were sent to 'stand by the door' in one school when they had failed to comply with the requirements for sitting 'properly' (as regu-lated) on the carpet. However, these significant locales were also sites of resist-ance. For instance, while the intra-action between the 'spot' by the door and the child initially evoked obvious discomfort, the power of this spot had a limited life and was clearly affected by time. Children found other material items, such as the nearby Velcro name stickers, with which to distract them-selves, and thus changed the discursive status of the act of 'standing by the door'. Somerville (2004) notes: 'just as we can theorize that language is always already there, we can also theorize that body/matter is always already there, and the body can intervene in discourse just as discourse can intervene into the body' (p. 51).

Breaching boundaries

As noted above, interesting boundaries and complex relations could lie between inert objects and the constitution of the proper child, yet these boundaries were also open to various interferences. Such interferences were more marked when the margins that separated adult and child relations were trifled with. Take as an example the following extract of data where the children are sitting together on the carpeted area listening to a story about a postman who is struggling to deliver the mail on a particularly windy day. The teacher asks: *'Who likes to get a letter through the door?'*, whereupon Chloe responds, *'As long as you don't have to pay some money.' The teacher laughs* (field note, Dronsfield, 11 January 2007).

We laugh because something strikes us as funny. But there are moments when laughter is used as a cover. It conceals other emotions which while hard to explicate precisely, nod towards feelings of anxiety, nervousness and apprehension. Laughter in this instance is a symptom of an inner discomfort where what gives us comfort is destabilized. Given the occasion, we can hazard a guess that the expected response to the question: 'Who likes to get a letter through the door?' would be (should have been) unequivocally positive. The teacher's laughter can be understood as a response to finding something both funny and simultaneously rather 'peculiar'. In this case Chloe breaches what is 'properly' known about or associated with young people. It is because she has a knowingness that is un-childlike that she breaches a boundary, so while not a 'danger', in that the matter can be laughed off, she nevertheless threatens the social order (Butler, 1999). The familiar performance that is normally enacted at carpet time has been (in)significantly altered, and in so doing the line that lies between adult and child has momentarily faltered.

Similarly, the next example details similar infringements of 'the line':

> **Field note**
> In the art area, Ms S is trying to wind up a stick of glue. 'Why don't you wind it that way?' suggests Daniel to Ms S. 'Instead of telling me what to do, why don't you concentrate on your own work. Turn around and get on,' she replies.
>
> (Limefield, 7 March 2007)

Daniel, while showing initiative and clearly wanting to help, has nevertheless stepped out of a boundary or crossed a line. In this instance it seems that by making a suggestion, one moreover which could be understood as being kind and helpful, he has nevertheless destabilized Ms S. She appears displeased and it seems that it is this that prompts her to both ignore his suggestion while simultaneously implying he has erred. Her admonishment to 'turn around and get on' could be understood as a timely reminder to 'turn' in terms of 'revert': where he should turn back again to being a child – one moreover that does not tell adults what to do. Following Douglas (1966), we can perceive both Chloe and Daniel as unsettling 'patterns' and 'systems of ordering'. Douglas notes:

> from all possible materials, a limited selection has been made and from all possible relations a limited set has been used. So disorder by implication is unlimited, no pattern has been realised in it, but its potential for patterning is indefinite. This is why, though we seek to create order, we do not simply condemn disorder. We recognise that it is destructive to existing patterns; also that it has potentiality. It symbolises both danger and power.
>
> (Douglas, 1966: 94)

We would suggest that both Chloe and Daniel have gone against what is customarily sanctioned within early years education, of who the child can 'be'. Their utterances jar against those boundaries or framing mechanisms in which we situate children so as to 'know' them. The examples briefly allude to other possibilities, in which we could frame the children as examples of not being innocent; rather they have grasped some of the economic realities in which they find themselves situated. Nor do we normally credit them with having knowledge that stands outside that which we developmentally assign to them. Hence, the reiterative practice of adults asking children questions to which the adult already knows the answer. In the example of Daniel, we momentarily glimpse a child who understands both the problem and its solution and in so doing momentarily positions himself within the power/knowledge nexus where the adult is rendered as 'other'. It is possible we think to perceive of both instances as quick flashes of something akin to taboo, where children, by using their wits, make claims to subjectivities which in the adults' minds they are not yet eligible, ready or, indeed, have no right, to inhabit. They are in this sense 'dangerous'. Chloe's witticism and Daniel's suggestion tamper with those systems that circulate around what it means 'to be' an adult and a child within an early years classroom. Both the laugh and the admonishment of the adult can be understood as 'a crisis' where the ground for 'knowing' who one is, is threatened.

While Douglas's anthropological studies prompted her to examine the ways in which boundaries invoked social order, Kristeva's interest in boundaries followed a psychoanalytical perspective. She offers us an alternative way of perceiving both Chloe and Daniel, where they can be understood as being neither subject nor object within the (adults') terms in which they are situated. Thus, in speaking as he does, Daniel is seen as being out of order whereas Chloe is seen as being un-childlike. Both momentarily refuse the subjectivities that adults would prefer them to have and in so doing they are no longer known objects within the adult's gaze. They constitute a crisis because they are between two categories where they are neither subject nor object, and thus within Kristeva's terms are 'beset by abjection' (1982: 1). They have 'fallen' from what within the scope of the adult, is 'possible', 'tolerable' or 'thinkable' (Kristeva, 1982: 1). It is in the inability to 'see' the child as either subject or object that the self (the practitioner) who needs the other (child) in order 'to be', flounders, and it is in this floundering that abjection takes its place. Within Kristeva's psychoanalytical theories the laugh and the admonishment can be seen emerging from the unconscious so that 'it draws [the practitioner] toward the place where (traditional) meaning collapses' (1982: 2).

We found also that there were curious bonds, unions and attachments between imaginative worlds and children's positions/positioning within these. In the example that follows it is apparent that there are some anxieties about how children re-enacted the story of Goldilocks and the three bears:

Field note

Teacher:	There is something I would like you remember about the Goldilocks' house
Becky chips in:	Be sensible and play properly
Teacher:	Yes, but you also need to talk to each other about who's being who and what words you will use to tell the story.

(Limefield, 21 November 2007)

Within the child's response we can catch some of the rhetoric surrounding the rules and customary conventions of play, in that it should be both 'sensible and proper'. But it also illustrates some of the anxieties and pressures that teachers are under when, on the one hand, they might well have a commitment to children's 'free play' yet on the other they have to work within curriculum guidelines, where it is stipulated that children should be able to demonstrate various skills, including the ability to recall well known fairytales/stories. While we might understand and perceive the teacher's promptings as relatively benign and sensible advice, it nevertheless foregrounds the ways in which the children must make an appeal to an external authority when deciding 'who will be who' and 'what words will be used'. It is within such moments that it becomes possible to see the injunctions of the 'hidden persuasion of an implicit pedagogy' (Bourdieu, 1977: 95) at work. So, while the teacher is not attempting to 'instil a whole cosmology', she is nevertheless trying to tie imaginative play to a particular set of parameters.

Interestingly, we had another encounter with *Goldilocks* in a different location.[4] At Chesterfield school the class teacher had gathered the children together onto the carpeted area so that, as a group, they could retell the story by acting it out. The teacher began by choosing six children who 'would be the woods'. These children were encouraged to stand up and to wave their arms about 'like branches'. Ms H then asked of the remaining seated children: '*Who would like to be Goldilocks?*' Samuel, an African Caribbean boy was the first to put his hand up. Ms H responded to him by saying: '*No Samuel. You can't be Goldilocks . . . for obvious reasons*' (field note, Chesterfield, 23 November 2007).

While we can be critical of Ms H's response on a number of fronts, and where, as a consequence, we could produce a typology of good/bad practice, we think that it is more fruitful to return to notions of taboo and abjection. By aligning Ms H's practice against these ideas we want to foreground how she found herself within what we have come to think of as an 'intolerable' space. So while, on the one hand, the (im)possible is allowed, in that children can be trees, on the other hand, a black boy cannot be Goldilocks.

As a first step we need to refer to certain polarities in order to make evident just what sorts of work that these perform on Ms H. We think that it is because Samuel is willing to perform as 'other' to him/self, that is, as white, blond and a girl, that he violently interrupts the smooth place (Deleuze and Guattari, 2002) that Ms H constructs in her mind's eye of what it means 'to be' within the classroom. For Deleuze and Guattari, 'the smooth' is associated with 'close vision-haptic space' where 'the whole and the parts give the eye that beholds them a function that is haptic rather than optical' (2002: 43). And while 'haptic' conventionally refers or relates to the sense of touch, following Deleuze and Guattari, we feel it can also be used in the sense of touching a nerve where the sorts of play that Samuel was proposing on the stratified body of 'the child' was simply untenable. To depart from or even tamper with signifiers, including those of 'white', 'blond' and 'girl', is clearly one 'line of flight' (Deleuze and Guattari, 1988: 506) that Ms H cannot permit herself, or indeed Samuel – *for obvious reasons* – to take. In volunteering to take on this (im)possible part it is as if the young boy pushes or violently ejects her from what is 'obvious' to the horror of incomprehension or abjection. Put a little differently, to let Samuel be Goldilocks would be like letting something healthy – maybe even life itself – become infected, and, as we know, infections can lead to death.

While we have included data that focus on the interplay between adults and children, the next extract focuses just on children.

> Outside in the home corner, children are role playing – bulldogs, puppy dogs and cats. There is a mum who is looking after the animals. Joshua, Olivia and Tyler are animals, all eating everyone else's food. 'That's the last of the dog food,' said Joshua. He takes a teapot and

says to Olivia, 'I'm pouring boiling water all over you.' Olivia responds, 'I'm telling my cousin, my BIG cousin of you.' Joshua stops pouring. 'I'm telling him,' says Olivia.

(Chesterfield, 12 March 2007)

Despite the absence of a teacher there are, we think, moments within the data that cast interesting shadows across much that is assumed and privileged within early years pedagogical practices. Take as an example the way that the children-as-animals are eating 'everyone else's food'. While this could be considered a form of sharing, it prompted us to wonder whether it was the kind of sharing that we – including three of us (Jones, Holmes and MacRae, who were all previously early years' teachers) – are accustomed to promoting within early years education. Here it is the discourse of liberal humanism that is central to practice (Walkerdine and Lucey, 1989), where, as a consequence, utterances such as *'It's so lovely seeing so many of you playing fairly in the house, especially you Ricky. You're playing properly . . .'* (field notes, Martinsfield, 14 October 2007), and others of this ilk, were relatively commonplace across the four sites. Joshua's threat to pour boiling water over Olivia serves to jolt us into a problematic space where our adult and teacher-like anxiety about violence and disrespect (and the felt imperative to stamp it out) comes up against our recognition that this is a play situation with pretend boiling water, regulated by children who want our interventions. Yet again, this does not prevent the pretence from also being a real threat, as Olivia clearly feels when she replies that she is going to get her 'BIG cousin' to sort Joshua out. One possible reading of Olivia's engagement with Joshua's 'excitable speech' (Butler, 1997) is that she herself resolves the situation, by abruptly terminating the status of the encounter as 'play' and returning it to a 'real' world of power and rivalry. But of course we do not know, and never will know, whether the big cousin was 'real' or another member of the imaginary family of dogs and humans conjured up by the children. The piece prompts questions that we will never be able to address with any certainty, but they nevertheless bring us face to face with those borders within which the integrity of identity is maintained. Joshua, when uttering, 'That's the last of the dog food', seems to locate himself within a place where order, including a lack of dog food, seems to matter. Unless these things are noted, dogs will go hungry. But in the next breath he seems to have crossed to some other location. The teapot, boiling water and his threat unhinge him from his previous persona and contribute towards making him a threat or what Kristeva terms 'an impossible' subject. Olivia, in order to safeguard herself from the ambiguity that Joshua threatens – where one minute he's knowable, the next a threat – summons the big cousin. It is the possibility of the violence that lurks within this figure that quells the potential violence lying within the pretend boiling water. The big cousin acts therefore 'as repression', which Kristeva visualizes as the 'constant watchman' who is necessary in order to maintain distinctions between a knowable Joshua and his untenable other.

Infringements of the body

Not too surprisingly, in each of the four classrooms there were rules that safeguarded against physical infringements. On a number of occasions we observed a relative laxity around these. Boys' 'rough and tumble' play did not seem particularly to alarm adults even when it was quite ferocious. Perhaps this is because it sits comfortably within prevalent discourses around what it means to be a (young) boy. However, there were moments when teachers had to impose penalties around physical play that was deemed to be beyond the pale. Robert, for instance, had to forgo a week of outdoor playtime when he inadvertently kicked Charley in the genitals. His teacher, in trying to think of a punishment that might bring home to Robert just how dangerous such kicking could be, chose 'missing outdoor play' because 'he [Robert] really loves it'. During the week-long punishment Robert was required to spend the time sitting on a chair reading just outside of the teachers' staff-room.

There were rare instances of children attacking members of staff, but when it did occur schools attempted to harness the support of the child's family to establish an understanding about the school's expectations. In this way it was hoped that both school and home could share the responsibility for regulating the child's behaviour so that it conformed to the school's outlook. Carter exemplified such a practice. He had arrived in the reception class from the preschool nursery/kindergarten class with a reputation for being 'very difficult'. Such difficulties included resisting adults when he would not do as he was told. So, for instance, when other children were helping by tidying up toys and equipment, special measures had to be taken by staff to cajole him into being 'helpful'. His recalcitrant behaviour became untenable to the adults when he resorted to lashing out physically. Strategic steps were taken that included staggering Carter's time at school as well as assigning him a support worker. Her role was to work with Carter, particularly when a potential 'crisis' seemed imminent, to keep the violent behaviour at bay, while simultaneously offering him alternative ways of behaving. Despite there being several lengthy periods when Carter could successfully function as a 'proper' pupil, he was eventually excluded from his school when – for the second time – he hit Ms F, his class teacher, in the face. Towards the end of the project there was an opportunity to talk to Ms F. She was asked what it was like to be hit in the face by Carter. She recalled feeling 'really shocked . . . the last time I think anyone hit me in the face was when I was a child myself and another child hit me. I can remember just wanting to run away. I probably did run away.'

Being smacked in the face is horrible and certainly we are not seeking to condone or excuse such behaviour. We do, however, want to use the 'ruins of an experience' (Britzman, 2003: 23) as the grounds for thinking about what happened. We have previously mentioned a child (Robert) who, albeit inadvertently, struck out at another child, and as a result had to miss outdoor play sessions. His bodily separation from the social was temporary mainly because it did not in any serious way threaten the boundaries that maintain the social order. If you like, his actions could be seen as manifestations of what common sense would have us construe as 'boys being boys'. But in Carter's case, his hand against a teacher's face evokes what Kristeva describes as the 'horror of abjection'. Carter has defiled in a most profound way the borders, binaries and distinctions that work at separating out 'teacher' from 'child'. His smack, unlike Robert's kick, cannot be tolerated because it threatens the symbolic space that has to be maintained between Ms F and Carter. Such a space is crammed with a host of rituals and taboos that circulate around teacher/child relations and which have to be maintained in order to keep the threat of the abject at bay. In smacking Ms F, Carter breaches all that gives Ms F substance and security. As she herself notes, the smack 'shocked'. This shock can be likened to what might be described as an ontological shudder in which normal sense, including one's sense of oneself, is fractured. In short, the child's relationship to the teacher and the teacher's relationship to the child is transformed. As a child, Ms F might have fled, but in this instance she has to stand her ground. Carter, however, has to 'go' because he constitutes the abject. He is the 'Other that both engenders [Ms F's] identity' and simultaneously 'challenges the integrity of it by confronting it with its own unstable border' (Cook, 2003: 2). In other words, Ms F has a necessary dependence on Carter in order to recognize herself. It is only by dispelling Carter by putting him outside that she can secure and protect her teacher identity from the threat of dissolution. The smack momentarily 'disappears' Ms F so that she is fleetingly a child again. If she 'really' had been a child then there might have been some possibilities to rethink Carter where a discursive frame – perhaps one not too dissimilar to the one circumscribing Robert and Charley's fighting – could have been brought into play. As it is, his smack threatens the very core of Ms F's being and as such is profoundly unbearable where there is no exit other than the reiterative, exhausted route of exclusion.

Concluding remarks

By working within the anthropological frames of Mary Douglas and the psychoanalytical theories of Julie Kristeva we have opened up some 'chinks' that could be possible starting points for discussions with teachers out of which different behaviours might emerge. One point of departure could centre on teacher/child interactions. Previously we have tried to illustrate how, at times, children threaten adults in ways that are not straightforward and hence are difficult to explain in normal, rational or common-sense ways. It is because such children confound us that we sometimes retreat to corrosive practices where we insist they conform to a mythical or stereotypical notion of what constitutes the child. In setting aside such myths, including that of the 'innocent' child, we might recognize that some young people have wisdom and experiences considerably in advance of either the innocent child or indeed the normative one that lingers within the trajectory of developmental psychology. Such recognition is the precursor for establishing different relations or interactions between adults and young people.

The practitioners that we observed across the eighteen-month period worked extraordinarily hard in trying to act in the children's best interests. However, such interests, we would argue, are tied to political imperatives to produce normalized subjects where practitioners are effectively placed in the role of 'colonizer' (Cannella and Bailey, 1999). In answer to the question 'how might things be different?', we recognize that any *major* changes in terms of pedagogical styles and behaviour are nigh on impossible because such innovations would have to be linked to, and occur within, powerful discursive and institutional forces. We would also have to offer solutions that were 'clear cut'. However, such an endeavour would ultimately fail because part of the problem that we are excavating is that the production of identity and behaviour in classrooms is regulated/constricted by both the structure and stricture of what Derrida (1998) referred to as a *double bind*. That is we are confronting a dilemma that within the terms of conventional logic would require us to settle for one thing over another. Carter (and his family), in order to 'settle', are required to holistically embrace the discursive frame that school offers. For it is only by being 'certain' about Carter that those adults with whom he interacts gain their own necessary 'ontological security' about what constitutes 'the child'. Oscillations from this are a cause for summoning the 'watchman of repression', or, in this instance, exclusion. Thus, another step in considering how things might be different, would be to return to the 'politics of knowing and being known' (Lather, 1991: 83), a step which would have to be taken in the knowledge that it would not increase either our certainty or our authority about, for instance, 'best practice', but might prompt different questions leading to different imaginings, including those associated with childhood.

Notes

1. The research that underpins this chapter was supported by funding from the UK Economic and Social Research Council ('Becoming a Problem: How and Why Children Acquire a Reputation as Naughty in the Earliest Years at School', RES-062-23-0105).

2. Assemblies take place on a regular basis in English schools. It is a time when the whole school is gathered together in a large hall so as to participate in activities such as collective worship and/or rewarding children. Rewards might include certificates, stickers or in some instances prizes such as a set of coloured pencils.

3. Teaching Assistants are practitioners who, while taking on many of the duties associated with teaching nevertheless do not have teaching status and all that that implies in terms of remuneration, cultural capital and so on. They are directed in their activities, and while they might contribute towards the planning of teaching programmes they do not have direct responsibilities for them.

4. It was not unusual to find the same stories being used in each of the four schools at similar points in time. This is because all four locations have to work within the foundation stage curriculum guidance set out by the Department for Education and Skills (2007).

References

Baker, C. (2000) Locating culture in action: membership categorisation in texts and talk. In A. Lee and C. Poyton (eds), *Culture and Text: Discourse and Methodology in Social Research and Cultural Studies*. Lanham, MD: Rowman & Littlefield.

Barad, K. (2008) Posthumanist performativity: towards an understanding of how matter comes to matter. In S. Alaimo and S. Hekman (eds), *Material Feminisms* (pp. 120–156). Bloomington, IN: Indiana University Press.

Bourdieu, P. (1977) *Outline of a Theory of Practice*. Cambridge: Cambridge University Press.

Bredekamp, S. (ed.) (1987) *Developmentally Appropriate Practice in Early Childhood Programs Serving Children from Birth through Age 8*. Washington, DC: National Association for the Education of Young Children.

Britzman, D. (1990) The terrible problem of knowing thyself: toward a post-structural account of teacher identity, *Journal of Curriculum Theorizing*, 9(3): 23–46.

Britzman, D. (2003) *Practice Makes Practice*. New York: State University of New York Press.

Brown, T. and Jones, L. (2002) *Action Research and Postmodernism: Congruence and Critique*. Buckingham: Open University Press.

Butler, J. (1997) *Excitable Speech: A Politics of the Performative*. New York: Routledge.

Butler, J. (1999) *Gender Trouble: Feminism and the Subversion of Identity*, 2nd edition. London: Routledge.

Cannella, G.S. and Bailey, C. (1999) Postmodern research in early childhood education. In S. Reifel (ed.), *Advances in Early Childhood and Day Care*. Oxford: Elsevier/JAI Press.

Cook, K. (2003) Lustmord in Weimar Germany: the abject boundaries of feminine bodies of representations of sexualised murder, *Essays in Philosophy*, 4(1): 1–10. http://www.humboldt.edu/~essays/cooklin.html

Deleuze, G. and Guattari, F. (1988) *A Thousand Plateaus: Capitalism and Schizophrenia*, trans. B. Massumi. London: Athlone.

Deleuze, G. and Guattari, F. (2002) *A Thousand Plateaus: Capitalism and Schizophrenia*, trans. B. Massumi. London: Continuum.

Department for Education and Skills (2007) *Practice Guidance for the Early Years Foundation Stage*. London: HMSO.

Derrida, J. (1998) *Limited Inc*. Evanston, IL: Northwestern University Press.

Douglas, M. (1966) *Purity and Danger*. London: Routledge & Kegan Paul.

Gee, J.P. (1990) *Social Linguistics and Literacies: Ideology in Discourses*. London: Falmer Press.

Graham, L. (2006) Speaking of 'disorderly' objects: a poetics of pedagogical discourse. Paper presented to the American Educational Research Association Annual Conference, San Francisco, 6–11 April.

Kristeva, J. (1982) *Powers of Horror: An Essay on Abjection*, trans. L.S. Roudiez. New York: Columbia University Press.

Lather, P. (1991) *Getting Smart*. London: Routledge.

MacLure, M. (2003) *Discourse in Educational and Social Research*. Buckingham: Open University Press.

Popkewitz, T.S. (2004) The reason of reason: cosmopolitanism and the government of schooling. In B.M. Baker and K.E. Heyning (eds), *Dangerous Coagulations: The Use of Foucault in the Study of Education*. New York: Peter Lang.

Somerville, M. (2004) Tracing bodylines: the body in feminist poststructural research, *International Journal of Qualitative Studies in Education*, 17(1): 47–63.

Stormont-Spurgin, M. (1997) I lost my homework: strategies for improving organization in students with ADHD, *Intervention in School and Clinic*, 32(5): 270–274.

Walkerdine, V. and Lucey, H. (1989) *Democracy in the Kitchen: Regulating Mothers and Socialising Daughters*. London: Virago.

12 'Like a wild thing': analysing the 'deviant competence' of girls in home–preschool communications

Michele Leiminer

This chapter interrogates a particular parent–teacher–child conversation in order to highlight their role not only as an important site of interactions but also as a space in which the participants negotiate, make meaning and respond to each other in a multiplicity of complex ways. Here, I use conversation analysis and adopt a feminist post-structuralist position to reconsider the ways in which girls are located in early childhood education discourses and how they competently navigate their way through these discourses.

Utilizing a feminist post-structuralist position to reconsider and reimagine the sociological positions of ethnomethodology and conversation analysis makes possible the seeing of a new competence that girls engage in during home–preschool communications: managing the competing gender discourses of their mothers and their preschool teacher, and publicly performing the management of a non-unitary 'I'. A non-unitary 'I' refers to the post-structuralist position that individual subjects 'are not stable, unified or fixed, but rather are shifting subjects, who are dynamic, contradictory and changing' (Robinson, 2006: 141). As such, there are multiple, often contradictory, 'I's' or selves. As parent–teacher–child conversations are joint constructions of these participants, parents and teachers, as adults, powerfully mobilize certain gender discourses. Children who actively participate in parent–teacher conversations are given the work of managing these often competing discourses; difficult work indeed. In this chapter I analyse data from a larger study of children's participation in parent–teacher conversations (predominantly mothers) in preschool settings (the year before formal schooling commences). In this study, 252 home–preschool conversations were audio-recorded in three sites. Of these conversations, 110 involved the participation of children in the home–preschool talk. Children's presence and participation in parent–teacher conversations ranged from being an overhearing audience being spoken for and about, to participating as 'more than a child'. The data analysed in this chapter consists of transcripts of audio-recorded conversations between one child, Jennifer, her mother and the preschool teacher at Poinciana Preschool. Jennifer participates as 'more than a child', displaying the 'deviant competence' of managing the conflicting and competing gender discourses of her mother and the preschool teacher. This was her invisible, competent work in home–preschool communications.

In this chapter I explore the complex intertwining of gender, age and children's interactional competence. Specifically, I analyse how Jennifer, a girl of 5 years of age with a gender history different from a preschool version of the social world, can be brought into view as a competent, although 'deviantly competent' participant. Jennifer, with the help of her mother, did not conform to the conservative gender expectations of the preschool she attended. She proudly told her news of riding her bike like a 'wild thing', and her mother openly and publicly supported her reporting these desires to the teacher. In these ways she was able, with her mother's help, to resist traditional gender expectations and to take up 'non-normalising discourses of gender' (Robinson, 2006: 145).

The research literature around girls and 'pre'schooling and schooling provides examples of the pervasiveness of traditional gender relations, but also of girls who actively resist conservative, traditional gender expectations. For example, Cook-Gumperz (2002), in investigating the play of children 3–5 years of age, found that the traditional gender order was remarkably resilient and intact, although a number of oppositional, resistant stances were taken up by girls, most often through fantasy play. Davies (1998) reports a number of incidents that were observed in videotaped episodes of play in primary school playgrounds. She found that there was a shifting, fleeting quality to power in these complex social worlds of children. Girls acted in powerful ways but it was often very difficult for teachers to see these acts as powerful when they simultaneously characterized girls as oppressed. In addition, women's and girls' sexuality was often used in the school context to maintain them in subordinate positions. This was achieved by way of an almost undetected desire on the part of teachers to regulate girls to subscribe to 'morally correct characteristics' of sexuality, and in so doing circumventing their power. While the teachers in Davies's 1998 study were consciously striving to implement gender equity practices in their school within a post-structuralist framework, overall Davies noted that there was a lack of desire on the part of most teachers to facilitate change (1998: 146).

According to Robinson (2006: 145–146), 'children's transgressions from what is generally perceived to be appropriate masculinity and femininity are most likely to be punished in various ways rather than encouraged'. The adults in children's lives, often teachers and parents, can be punishers or liberators of children's gender performances. In the following vignette and analysis I will examine how one girl, Jennifer, manages a transgressive gender performance.

While highly acceptable to her mother, this performance meets with substantial resistance from the preschool teacher. The analysis will demonstrate how Jennifer very competently handles this interactional problem.

I explore the 'competent interactional and discourse work' that Jennifer is able to do in talk between her mother, Margaret, and the preschool teacher, Mrs Allen. Gender is a strong focus in this chapter for there is a noticeable disjunction between the preschool and home versions of 'girlhood' and childhood. Jennifer's mother and the preschool teacher struggle throughout the talk as to whose proposed version of the world should be taken up. This struggle also defines the parameters of Jennifer's possible participation in the event. She is presented with very little space to participate.

Theoretical position

Within the new social studies of childhood and sociology of childhood (James et al., 1997) the notion of children's social competence has become an emergent paradigm (Prout and James, 1990), being labelled the 'competence paradigm' (Hutchby and Moran-Ellis, 1998: 5). Its political project has been to

> establish, theoretically and, to a lesser extent, empirically, the status of children as competent social agents and of childhood as a constructed arena of action both enabling and constraining the exercise of agency . . .
>
> (Hutchby and Moran-Ellis, 1998: 6)

Taking for granted that children are competent social actors (Alanen, 1998), I seek, in this chapter, to challenge the 'ideological singularity of the child' (Thorne, 1987: 101). In addition, I approach the topic as both an explicative and a critical study whereby I utilize feminist post-structuralism to 'reconstruct' a version of the ethnomethodological tools of category analysis (Baker, 2000) and conversation analysis (Leiminer and Baker, 2000). Together with feminist/post-structuralism (Davies, 1998, 2000) they provide powerful lenses to examine children's participation and competence. While I am interested in adult–child relations and relations of power as played out in home–school communications, I wanted to explore these relations from particular children's positionings as gendered and classed beings rather than becomings (Speier, 1976; Waksler, 1986, 1999; Qvortrup, 1995), and not from the singularized 'child' (Davies, 1982; Thorne, 1987). In so doing I use as an example an analysis on particular children's participation in talk with their mothers, fathers and teachers. By looking in a very detailed manner at transcripts of recorded parent–teacher–child conversations, two layers of analysis become possible: the interactional strategies and techniques used by children in talk with adults, and an analysis of particular children's and adults' take-up of certain discourses-as-resources to propose certain school and home versions of the social world. The close analysis of participants' use of categories allows for an in-depth understanding of the building blocks of discourses-in-use to see how children's actions and possibilities for agency are constrained. It also allows for a degree of evaluation as to the implications of closer relations between home and school, for children with particular backgrounds and histories.

In terms of a politics of change, the analysis shows in close detail how subjection operates, how fine-grained, and taken-for-granted it is. As such, it is possible to understand that each seemingly minor transgressive action a child takes is an action of immense difficulty, importance and competence. This analysis speaks powerfully to how difficult change to more equitable practices is in these contexts. Adults, through the coercive nature of discourses that speak through them in relation to children (Davies, 1989: 2), define the parameters of participation for children. They are responsible for the socialization and education of children, and they patrol gender, class and stage of life borders. For any possibility of change we need to look to adults (in ascendant/unmarked positions such as teachers) as those who are in the best position to create/allow for additional subject positions that can be made available for children to take up.

I view children's and women's lives intertwined in very powerful ways. As feminist researchers have noted, there are strong parallels between women's studies and childhood studies (Firestone, 1971; Thorne, 1987; Alanen, 1992; Oakley, 1994). Just as women's work was largely invisible, so too is children's. At this point in time it seems that work needs to be done that highlights the competence of children, thus making it visible. For just as it was the case with women, it is not that children are not doing valuable and competent work, it is just that it is not recognized as such.

'Aligning with the home': Jennifer's competence in talk at the preschool

The mother–teacher–child conversation

After listening to, and transcribing, a number of parent–teacher conversations from preschool settings, one phenomenon I have found is that children are frequently deliverers of news between home and preschool, and from preschool to home. As tellers of the news in these parent–teacher conversations, children are being apprenticed in how to speak with adults. These news 'tellings' are mostly adult initiated and take the form of: 'tell mum x' or 'tell Mrs Allen y'. In other words, the children are being instructed in *what* might be newsworthy for a child to tell an adult carer, and, as we see below, children are also 'assisted' by adults in shaping the form of the telling.

I was initially drawn to analysing the particular conversation presented here because I noticed that Jennifer appeared to spontaneously initiate talk in the form of a news telling with the preschool teacher, by attempting to tell her the news from home (or at least from outside preschool). This was in contrast to other instances of children telling the news that were adult initiated. I noticed how Jennifer gained the floor and managed to stay in the conversation with the help of her mother and, to a certain extent, the teacher. I wanted to analyse how she 'gained the floor' and how she was able to participate in the talk. How was she constrained and/or enabled to participate in the talk and tell her news, and how did she manage these different mother and teacher versions of the social world?

The conversation occurred on the morning of 17 June between Jennifer (child), Margaret (Jennifer's mother) and Mrs Allen, the preschool teacher. It took place at the front door of the preschool at the beginning of the day, as Jennifer arrived at preschool with her mother. All participants' names have been changed and I was also present to hear the conversation. The participants in the conversation are:

C: Child (Jennifer)
M: Mother of Jennifer (Margaret)
PT: Preschool teacher (Mrs Allen)
R: Researcher (Michele)

Tarrant is a friend of Jennifer's who also attends the preschool

An explanation of the transcript notation can be found in the appendix to this chapter.

```
 1  C:   did you did you know how Tarrant hurt his arm
 2       (0.6)
 3  PT:  when
 4  C:   he hurt it (0.2) because he fell off his bike
 5  PT:  oh (.) so is he coming today
 6  M:   have you got some [other
 7  C:                     [yes
 8  M:   bike news for Mrs (.) Allen
 9  C:   yes (.) I have a brand new bike
10  PT:  but it's not your birthday is it ((high pitched))
11  C:   no I I
12  PT:  don't you have to wait for a birthday
13  C:   no but (.) I had NO BIKE↑ AT↑ ALL↑ ((high pitched))
14  PT:  so you thought you'd better get one
15       (0.4)
16  C:   yes
```

17   PT [to chase Tarrant down the hill]
18   C: [so I have] a brand new purple one with <u>hearts</u>
19   PT: <u>HEARTS</u>
20   R: ha
21   (0.2)
22   PT: does it have <u>trainer wheels</u> (0.2) or are you off trainer [wheels
23   C: [it has train
          (.) it has <u>training wheels</u> and I ride
24   (1.0)
25   M: like a <u>wild</u> thing don't you
26   C: mm hm mm mm
27   M: it's just great we just got it yesterday
28   PT: how wonderful

Jennifer initiates the conversation with Mrs Allen, directing a question at her, 'Did did you know how Tarrant hurt his arm'. Both the topic and structure of Jennifer's turn are very important for her gaining the floor, in two very different ways. First, of particular note is that Jennifer has staged her entry into the conversation by presenting herself as a deliverer of news about another child, in this case a boy from the preschool classroom whom Mrs Allen is particularly interested in. She could have attempted entry by presenting her own news of her new bike, but she chose otherwise. Certainly, from the teacher's uptake of her news, and Jennifer's gaining of the floor, her strategy of presenting a topic that is newsworthy to the teacher to gain entry and speaking space has worked.

Jennifer has also structured her turn in a special way that gains her entry into the conversation. This strategy which children use for gaining entry into adult talk was analysed by Harvey Sacks (1974, 1995), who noted that children as young as 3 years old initiate talk with adults by using a particular type of question. For example, 'you know what mummy' or 'you know something daddy' – a question that is answered with a further question. These utterances are powerful ones for children, according to Sacks (1974, 1995), for two reasons. First, asking a question expects an answer in reply. As such, questions are effective ways of opening up conversations, or gaining the floor. Second, because the answer is a further question, the child is then obliged to speak and answer the adult's question. The child can then talk about the topic they wanted to talk about. The format is explained below:

Question	C:	you know what, mummy?
Question	M:	what?
Answer	C:	((child talks about what they want to talk about))
Next turn	M:	((adult regains initiation))

However, this questioning device also has the effect of restoring the adult as next speaker, and therefore the adult is back in control of the conversation. By using this device, children demonstrate their knowledge of their restricted rights to talk. According to Sacks (1974: 231): '[children] have restricted rights which consist of a right to begin, to make a first statement, and not much more. Thereafter, they proceed only if requested to'.

In line 1 we see Jennifer's attempt to apply this entry device, with her question, 'did did you know how Tarrant hurt his <u>arm</u>'. In this, a preschool context, Jennifer has changed the form of the opening turn described by Sacks. Instead of an open 'you know what mummy', designed by a child for their mother, she has used 'did did you know how Tarrant hurt his arm'. In the construction of her turn she names a preschool child, Tarrant. By naming a preschool child, Mrs Allen, as preschool teacher is more deeply implicated in the talk, for according to an early childhood version of preschool teacher, Mrs Allen should be interested in her students, and their attendance (Ritchie, 2003). This helps to guarantee a reply from Mrs Allen. But it is not just 'any' boy she has named, it is Tarrant. Mrs Allen has a particularly strong relationship with Tarrant's mother, Margot, who has requested before that Mrs Allen take special care of him. Margot and Jennifer's mother are also close friends. So Jennifer has placed an additional sweetener in her question, virtually guaranteeing a response. These extra details add to the newsworthiness of her topic and her ability to gain the floor in this context. Establishing newsworthiness is an important dimension in news telling (Baker and Perrott, 1988). Jennifer displays the knowledge that any topic for conversation that she might wish to raise with the preschool teacher must be newsworthy to her. She uses a variant of the questioning device, containing sufficient news, to gain the attention of Mrs Allen, and the floor.

Therefore, in contrast to the 'what' question Sacks (1974) describes, Jennifer uses a 'how' question instead. In the preschool context, the requirement for Jennifer to establish newsworthiness has meant the inclusion of additional information in her question. While Jennifer may have structured her question in such a way as to possibly set the teacher up to respond with 'how', allowing her to then tell her 'bike news', what actually happens is the teacher assesses the topic. This is in contrast to the case of 'you know what mummy', whereby no topic is pre-specified, and the adult responds with 'what'. A result is that the teacher is able to choose not to pursue the topic in the way Jennifer might have expected, with a reply of 'how'.

1 C: did you did you know how Tarrant hurt his <u>arm</u>
2   (0.6)
3 PT: when
4 C: he <u>hurt it</u> (0.2) because he fell off his <u>bike</u>
5 PT: oh (.) so is he coming today

The preschool teacher accomplishes this by replying with 'when', not the preferred question, 'how'. In this way the teacher attempts to restrict the topic Jennifer can talk about, away from possible 'bike news' to Tarrant's injury. Irrespective of this topic change initiated by the preschool teacher, in line 4 Jennifer pursues the completion of the device as she initially directed it. It is as if she is responding to the 'how' question the teacher could have supplied when she says, 'he hurt it (0.2) because he fell off his bike'.

In line 5, the preschool teacher is restored as speaker, continues as questioner, and takes control of the trajectory of the conversation. This time Mrs Allen changes the topic to whether Tarrant, Jennifer's friend who also attends preschool, will be attending today. At this point, Jennifer's attempt to introduce her bike news via Tarrant's bike injury has failed. Although Jennifer has succeeded in introducing news about Tarrant to the preschool teacher, the specifics of *how* Tarrant hurt his arm is less newsworthy to the teacher than whether Tarrant is coming to school or not. Jennifer's lesson in what counts as news in preschool has commenced.

The talk continues:

```
5   PT:  oh (.) so is he coming today
6   M:   have you got some [other
7   C:                     [yes
8   M:   bike news for Mrs (.) Allen
9   C:   yes (.) I have a brand new bike
```

Jennifer's answering of the teacher's question is delayed until line 7 because her mother, Margaret, in line 6, interrupts the existing topic of talk with the preschool teacher to make space for Jennifer to regain the floor and to tell her additional bike news, 'have you got some other bike news for Mrs Allen'. With this action, Margaret powerfully constructs a space for Jennifer to speak about her news from home with the preschool teacher. In this way, Margaret positions her daughter as 'someone who can speak for herself' with the preschool teacher, should a space be made available. Her proposed version of the social world is one in which girls/daughters are able to tell the news of home to school.

The version of the social world that Jennifer's mother proposes is one in which mothers deem what is important home news, and daughters are the deliverers of this news of importance from the home to the school. More specifically, daughters/girls should be able to tell news about themselves and their personal actions to the teacher. In contrast, the preschool teacher's proposed version of the social world is one in which home news is relevant only when it is important to the school. According to her version, teachers should teach families what is school-worthy (cf. Keogh, 1996), and not the other way around. In this case, a girl telling news of riding her new bike is not school-worthy, given the lack of uptake by the teacher that follows.

In terms of the sequencing of the conversation, and Jennifer's positioning as 'child', line 6 is very interesting. Hutchby and Wooffitt (1998) note that a next speaker can self-select, but usually only at a possible turn completion point. In line 6, we see Jennifer's mother self-select as next speaker, but with no legitimate grounds to do so. It may be that Margaret takes it that she has moral grounds as a mother to take this action, thereby positioning Jennifer as child/daughter. Margaret is able to insert herself into an incomplete question–answer pair, courtesy of the restricted conversational rights of children (Sacks, 1974; Speier, 1976). She is able to claim what Speier (1976) calls 'a right of local control over the conversation' (p. 101). As Speier (1976) states:

> I wish to point out, following Sacks' lead, that children have restricted conversational rights. The manner in which they can participate in conversations with adults is internally controlled by an asymmetrical distribution of speakers' rights, wherein adults claim rights of local control over conversation with children, and children are obliged to allow them that control. children's failure to do so can be met with the sanctioning power of adult speakers.
>
> (Speier, 1976: 101)

That Jennifer and Mrs Allen orient to this mother (adult) right is evidenced by how smoothly this adult intrusion proceeds. This is the first of two mother (adult) initiations that Jennifer handles almost seamlessly. This competence would suggest she has had a certain amount of practice in managing adult initiations. Margaret's claim of local control over the conversation is also noteworthy, in that it positions Jennifer as 'daughter' (female child) in talk with her, while at the same time she positions Jennifer as 'more than a child' in her expectation of Jennifer as an active and competent participant in talk with the teacher.

The interdependence of participants lays a foundation for the types of work possible by children in adult talk. Mothers, fathers and preschool staff can negotiate and provide a space of possibility for children to participate within. For Jennifer, her mother alone seeks this space for her as 'more than a child/girl', but only for Jennifer's interactions with the preschool teacher. As a consequence, only a space of minimal possibility is created. What is at stake for Jennifer as a result of this narrow, mother (adult)-defined space, is the limitation of the type of, and extent to which, additional types of competence can possibly be, and are, attributable to Jennifer.

Given the limitations of this space of minimal possibility, Jennifer manages to do the work of aligning with her mother, complete with contradictions, very well indeed. This work requires her to closely monitor the conversation, choosing the appropriate status of herself as child/girl, and interacting as such. In talk with the preschool teacher, Jennifer performs as 'more than a child/girl', but must move from this position to do 'compliant daughter/incompetent child' with her mother. In her participation, Jennifer very clearly illustrates the particular competence of aligning with her mother and 'doing childhood'.

In section three, Jennifer's mother's introduction to tell the bike news allows Jennifer in line 9 to answer her mother and announce the news, 'I have a brand new bike'. This is displayed by the preschool teacher, in line 10, and again in line 12 when she uses the story's announcement to heckle and question that Jennifer should have a new bike when it is not her birthday.

```
 9   C:  yes (.) I have a brand new bike
10   PT: but it's not your birthday is it ((high pitched))
11   C:  no I I
12   PT: don't you have to wait for a birthday
13   C:  no but (.) I had NO BIKE↑ AT↑ ALL↑ (((high pitched))
```

The preschool teacher's version of the social world presented is one whereby bikes are special occasion presents, such as birthdays, and inappropriate for an everyday gift. This might imply that a child who receives a special occasion present at any time is receiving too much, or 'spoilt'. In line 13 Jennifer disagrees with the preschool teacher's version of when bikes can be given as presents, suggesting that because she had no bike at all, it was okay to receive the bike as a present *now*.

```
13   C:  no but (.) I had NO BIKE↑ AT↑ ALL↑ (((high pitched))
14   PT: so you thought you'd better get one
15       (0.4)
16   C:  yes
```

The preschool teacher continues in a mocking/jesting manner in line 14, 'so you thought you'd better get one'. Although presented in a mocking manner, this is an interesting categorization of Jennifer by the preschool teacher, for it positions her as 'one who would expect that her actions get results', in this case a bike. She is presented by Mrs Allen as one who expects to be an active and competent agent in her social world, at least at home. With the preschool teacher's use of 'you', Jennifer the child is presented as a decision maker, not her mother. In line 16, Jennifer agrees, 'yes'.

```
17   PT  [to chase Tarrant down the hill]
18   C:  [so I have] a brand new purple one with hearts
19   PT: HEARTS
20   R:  ha
21       (0.2)
```

The teacher continues mocking in line 17, perhaps attempting to retrieve her previous topic of Tarrant by specifically referring to him again, 'to chase Tarrant down the hill'. In this turn, Mrs Allen's jesting is achieved by her introduction of Jennifer as an active child, chasing Tarrant on her bike. Her use of this non-feminine storyline constructs a character for Jennifer, as 'one who rides down boys', and, as such, is not feminine. MacNaughton (1995: 34) explores the concept of storylines and power, suggesting that, 'by definition active childhood and passive femininity exist at the intersection of competing discourses. For girls, therefore, their position as children must remain shaky and partial, continually played across by their position as feminine'.

18	C:	[so I have] a brand new purple one with <u>hearts</u>
19	PT:	<u>HEARTS</u>
20	R:	ha
21		(0.2)

In contrast, Jennifer presents herself in line 18 as owning a 'feminine' bike, one with hearts. This utterance is started simultaneously with the preschool teacher's in line 17, 'so I have a brand new purple one with hearts'. Jennifer's proposed version of the social world is one whereby a girl can be feminine and ride bikes.

Jennifer's assertion in line 18 is not a reply to the preschool teacher's question in line 17, but instead is a powerful move whereby she gains control of the topic, speaking over the teacher to maintain control (although fleetingly). She moves the talk back to her bike and what it looks like. The teacher is then in a responding position to Jennifer for only the second time in the conversation. The teacher responds in line 19, with 'HEARTS', said relatively loudly and in an amused manner, confirming the newsworthiness of the bike's decoration. I laugh then, which may be taken as displaying an alignment (Jefferson, 1979) with the teacher's position.

22	PT:	does it have <u>trainer wheels</u> (0.2) or are you off trainer [wheels
23	C:	[it has train (.) it has <u>training wheels</u> and I ride
24		(1.0)

In line 22 the teacher regains control of the direction of the conversation, this time with a limited response question, an either/or question of pedagogical character, 'does it have trainer wheels or are you off trainer wheels'. This type of question restricts the range of responses available to Jennifer. It may also be seen as an attempt to constrain a very competent conversational participant (see Leiminer and Baker, 2000). Partially, the teacher's strategy works. Jennifer provides an answer that is restricted to one of the alternatives supplied by the teacher, 'it has training wheels'.

The preschool teacher's question about training wheels introduces a possible lack of competence in Jennifer's version of herself as active girl child. Jennifer agrees that her bike does have training wheels, but she states that 'she rides', once again establishing herself as a competent, active girl, and gaining further control of the talk. She does not take this further however.

```
25   M:  like a wild thing don't you
26   C:  mm hm mm mm
27   M:  it's just great we just got it yesterday
28   PT: how wonderful
```

Instead, a one second pause allows her mother to self-select and continue for her daughter, taking control of the conversation in line 25, continuing to tell the news for her. Margaret remedies any notion that her daughter may be lacking in bike-riding competence, suggesting that her daughter rides 'like a wild thing'. This is the second mother (adult) initiation that Jennifer has handled almost seamlessly. Margaret directs a question at Jennifer, 'like a wild thing don't you'. Margaret's categorization of Jennifer as a 'wild thing' supports the proposed version of Jennifer as 'active child and girl' to which she subscribes, and to which Jennifer aligns. Margaret's strategy once again positions Jennifer as respondent in the talk, and as 'child' in line 26, but this time it is to her mother, and not the teacher. Jennifer very actively and strongly agrees with her mother's description, and her version of the social world. In line 27 Jennifer's mother concludes the story, emphasizing her version of the social world that the bike is 'just great', and as such, so too therefore, is the active, girl child. She emphasizes the mother–daughter, even perhaps a family, alliance with her use of 'we', 'it's just great we got it yesterday'. Margaret certainly wants this news to be told in a particular way, emphasizing her daughter as active and competent.

Mrs Allen does not strongly agree with Margaret's proposal, replying with, 'how wonderful'. The use of 'how wonderful' does very important work for the preschool teacher. It is a positive assessment, but is ambiguous in that it could be an assessment of the first or second topic in the turn, 'it's just great we got it yesterday'. That is, it could be taken as 'how wonderful for you that you just got the bike yesterday', or agreeing 'how wonderful the bike is'. It allows both the mother and the preschool teacher to maintain their divergent versions of the social world. It also brings closure to the conversation.

Conclusion

In this chapter I analysed Jennifer's participation and competence in a mother–teacher conversation that occurred at her preschool. I examined in detail the specific interpretive competences (conversational sequencing and category work) that Jennifer was able to display in this conversation. Jennifer's participation and competence were contingent upon the space constructed by the participants in the talk. She participated in the context of divergent mother and teacher versions of the social world. In the data examined in this chapter there were no alignments between mother and teacher versions. In this conversation there was also an ongoing struggle between the home and the preschool for the power to define whose version of the world would define the talk. The power to direct the conversation moved between the preschool teacher and Margaret, and Jennifer, her daughter.

Mrs Allen's version of the social world proposes that children's desires should not be indulged excessively, and that girls do not engage in the activities of an active childhood (MacNaughton, 1995). Jennifer's mother's version of the social world is one in which girls should be active and wild, and children's desires should be indulged if possible. The versions of childhood and girlhood that Jennifer's mother and the preschool teacher utilize are so divergent that Jennifer's possibilities for participation are curtailed.

Jennifer has to decide how to participate in this context of highly contradictory and contested positions, with her mother strongly pursuing a particular version of the social world, speaking from an economically advantaged and quite powerful position, especially when contrasted with the other preschool mothers. Her strategy was to align with, support and present her mother's version of the social world, which she did very competently.

Children's parents can provide a consistent version of their child as boy or girl/child throughout the talk. They can position them as more than a child/boy or girl. In contrast, in this chapter Jennifer had to manage her mother's contradictory versions of girl/child. In talk with the preschool teacher Jennifer had to perform her mother's version of active, wild girl/child; however, in talk with her mother she had to revert to a version of compliant daughter/ 'incompetent' child. She managed to move between these two versions seamlessly. In so doing she demonstrated the ability to competently manage different and contradictory versions of self on the one occasion. She very competently managed the public performance of a non-unitary 'I'. This, I argue is her 'deviant competence'.

The analysis of mother–teacher–child talk highlights contradictions. Most clearly, it was possible to see how the space Margaret created for her daughter's participation with Mrs Allen allowed Jennifer to display her competence of aligning with her mother's version of the social world. This allowed Jennifer to present a version of active girl to the preschool teacher, in certain moments of talk. However, the analysis also demonstrated how Margaret restricted the participation of her daughter to that of 'incompetent child' in the same conversation. So although Jennifer's talk and actions with Mrs Allen actively contributed to a redefining of 'the competent preschool girl', in the same conversation they contributed to a consolidation of 'the compliant daughter/incompetent child'. In this way, in collaboration with her mother, she affected the participation of the preschool teacher. She also contributed to a broadening of the discourse of girlhood. In her talk and actions with her mother she contributed to limiting the discourse of girlhood. Therefore, at times Jennifer's work contributed towards an erasure of the binaries girl–boy and competent–incompetent, but at other moments her work helped to sediment them, especially the binary adult–child.

Here, I explored the complexities of Jennifer's competence in participating in home–preschool communications. The analysis demonstrated how Jennifer, a child with a gender history different from a preschool version of girlhood, very competently participated, but how her competence was not recognized by the preschool teacher. I outlined the narrow range of competence recognized by the preschool teacher's version of the social world, and provided evidence for a much more complex array of competence that children demonstrate. Rather than always utilizing a preschool version of the social world to view and assess children's actions and competence, if teachers can broaden the categories they utilize to view children's actions, more of their actions will come into view as being competent.

This research takes seriously the notion of children's social competence, documenting multiple versions of children's interactional competence in home–preschool communications. In doing so, it addresses the issue of how and to what extent teachers, and schooling, recognize and value a range of children's interactional competence. I problematize the concept of children's competence as displayed in their participation in parent–teacher conversations at preschool. Utilizing 'a' preschool teacher's version of the social world informed largely by discourses of developmental psychology, traditional gender relations, explicit age or 'stage of life' categories and middle-class orientations to education makes visible only a very narrow range of children's competence. Viewing children's actions from different positions, or using different categories to analyse them, allows for a wider range of competence to be recognized.

The complexity of the work that children are required to do is heavily influenced by the extent to which home and preschool versions of the social world collide or synchronize. The more asymmetrical these versions are, the more difficult the interactional task is for the child. Therefore it can be seen that different children are engaging in work of differing complexity. The more marginalized a child's history, the more difficult is the interactional work they are asked to engage in. Therefore, for a child with marginalized history, the interactional work they are required to do is extremely difficult. Compounding this already difficult task is that the competences these children do display are not visible or recognizable when utilizing only a preschool version of the social world to make sense of children's actions. In this way, disadvantage is further entrenched.

I propose that a competent–incompetent binary seems unable to usefully engage with the complexity of children's competence in parent–teacher conversations. Rather, competence is a rich and complex phenomenon dependent on each viewer's assessment to make it relevant. The selection of a particular category to assess a particular occasion makes relevant only certain actions as competent; others remain invisible or incompetent. The implications for practitioners are centred around broadening the range of category knowledge they bring to a reading. This can make visible to practitioners the competent, complex and difficult work that children with gender, class and stage of life histories different from a preschool version of the social world are required to do when a preschool version of the social world alone is utilized.

Adopting an ethnomethodological perspective and searching for the 'good sense' of children's actions allows me to bring into view the previously invisible competence of children's work in parent–teacher conversations. I analysed children's specific interpretive competences in terms of the conversational sequencing work they do, as well as their use of categories. Their competence often extends further, to managing the public performance of a non-unitary 'I', and managing conflicting discourses of the home and school, as Jennifer displayed. This is the invisible micro-political work of 'little children' (Denzin, 1971) and their 'deviant competences' in home–preschool communications.

Acknowledgement

Thank you to all participants who agreed to participate in the study and have their conversations audio-recorded.

References

Alanen, L. (1992) *Modern Childhood: Exploring the 'Child Question' in Sociology*. Jyväskylä, Finland: University of Jyväskylä.
Alanen, L. (1998) Children and the family order: constraints and competences. In

I. Hutchby and J. Moran-Ellis (eds), *Children and Social Competence: Arenas of Action* (pp. 29–45). London: Falmer Press.

Baker, C.D. (2000) Locating culture in action: memberships categorisation in texts and talk. In A. Lee and C. Poyton (eds), *Culture and Text: Discourse and Methodology in Social Research and Cultural Studies* (pp. 99–113). Sydney: Allen & Unwin.

Baker, C.D. and Perrott, C. (1988) The news session in infants and primary school classrooms. *British Journal of Sociology of Education*, 9(1): 19–38.

Cook-Gumperz, Jenny (2002) Girls' oppositional stances: the interactional accomplishment of gender in nursery school and family life. In B. Baron (ed.), *Gender in Interaction: Perspectives on Femininity and Masculinity in Ethnography and Discourse*. Philadelphia: John Benjamins.

Davies, B. (1982) *Life in the Classroom and Playground: The Accounts of Primary School Children*. London: Routledge.

Davies, B. (1989) *Frogs and Snails and Feminist Tales: Preschool Children and Gender*. Sydney: Allen & Unwin.

Davies, B. (1998) The politics of category membership in early childhood settings. In N. Yelland (ed.), *Gender in Early Childhood Years* (pp. 131–148). London: Routledge.

Davies, B. (2000) *A Body of Writing 1990–1999*. New York: Altamira.

Denzin, N. (1971) The work of little children, *New Society*, 12–14.

Firestone, S. (1971) *The Dialectic of Sex: The Case for Feminist Revolution*. London: Jonathan Cape.

Hutchby, I. and Moran-Ellis, J. (1998) Situating children's social competence. In I. Hutchby and J. Moran-Ellis (eds), *Children and Social Competence: Arenas of Action* (pp. 7–26). London: Falmer Press.

Hutchby, I. and Wooffitt, R. (1998) *Conversation Analysis: Principles, Practices and Applications*. Cambridge: Polity Press.

James, A., Jenks, C. and Prout, A. (1997) *Theorising Childhood*. Cambridge: Polity Press.

Jefferson, G. (1979) A technique for inviting laughter and its subsequent acceptance/declination. In G. Psathas (ed.), *Everyday Language: Studies in Ethnomethodology* (pp. 79–96). New York: Irvington.

Keogh, J. (1996) Governmentality in parent–teacher communications, *Language and Education*, 10(2/3): 119–131.

Leiminer, M.J. and Baker, C.D. (2000) A child's say in parent–teacher talk at the preschool: doing conversation analytic research in early childhood settings, *Contemporary Issues in Early Childhood*, 1(2): 135–152.

MacNaughton, G. (1995) *Rethinking Gender in Early Childhood Education*. St Leonards: Allen & Unwin.

Oakley, A. (1994) Women and children first and last: parallels and differences between children's and women's studies. In B. Mayall (ed.), *Children's Childhoods: Observed and Experienced* (pp. 13–32). London: Falmer Press.

Psathas, G. (1995) *Conversation Analysis: The Study of Talk-in-Interaction*. Thousand Oaks, CA: Sage.

Qvortrup, J. (1995) Childhood and modern society: a paradoxical relationship. In J. Brannen and M. O'Brien (eds), *Childhood and Parenthood*. London: Falmer Press.

Ritchie, S. (2003) Community-oriented classroom practices. In C. Howes (ed.), *Teaching 4 to 8 year olds: Literacy, Math, Multiculturalism and Classroom Community* (pp. 25–46). Baltimore, MD: Paul H. Brookes.

Robinson, J. (2006) *Diversity and Difference in Early Childhood Education: Issues for Theory and Practice*. Maidenhead: Open University Press.

Sacks, H. (1974) On the analyzability of stories by children. In R. Turner (ed.), *Ethnomethodology: Selected readings* (pp. 216–232). London: Penguin.

Sacks, H. (1995) *Lectures on Conversation*, vols 1 and 2, ed. G. Jefferson. Oxford: Blackwell.

Speier, M. (1976) The child as conversationalist: some cultural contact features of conversational interactions between adults and children. In M. Hammersley and P. Woods (eds), *The Process of Schooling* (pp. 98–103). London: Routledge & Kegan Paul.

Thorne, B. (1987) Re-visioning women and social change: where are the children? *Gender and Society*, 1(1): 85–109.

Waksler, F.C. (1986) Studying children: phenomenological insights, *Human Studies*, 9: 71–82.

Waksler, F.C. (1999) Children as interactional partners for adults: some preliminary considerations. Paper presented at the Eastern Sociological Society, Boston, MA, March.

Appendix

Transcript notation

The symbols used in the transcripts have been selected from those developed by Gail Jefferson, as reported in Psathas (1995). The following are the features used in these transcripts:

()	word(s) spoken but not audible
(was)	best guess for word(s) spoken
((high pitched))	transcriber's description
voice	normal speaking voice
VOICE	volume is extremely loud
wild	emphasis
do:on't	sound extended
[	two speakers' turns overlap at this point
=	no interval between turns

(2.0)   pause timed in seconds

Punctuation marks describe characteristics of speech production. They do not refer to grammatical units:

?   a question mark indicates a rising intonation

13 At home with the future: influences on young children's early experiences with digital technologies

Joanna McPake and Lydia Plowman

Early years curricula encourage practitioners to build on children's home experiences. Research into the kinds of activities that young children engage in at home and considerations of how to link these to their experiences in preschool settings can therefore make an important contribution to practice. This chapter, which draws on studies investigating young children's home experiences with digital technologies, seeks to identify some of the key factors that influence the nature and extent of these experiences. Although *digital divides* – reflecting classic social divisions of economic status, gender and ethnicity – have been extensively explored in order to understand the causes of inequalities in access to digital technologies, our research concluded that parental attitudes towards these technologies are more influential than economic disadvantage in determining young children's experiences.

To explore this issue in greater detail, we have drawn on the concept of *prolepsis*, a key influence on parents' interactions with their children deriving from the projection of their memories of their own idealized past into the children's futures (Cole, 1996). Parents' assumptions, values and expectations are influenced by their past experiences, enacted in the present, and are then carried by their children into the future as they move from home to formal education. We argue that prolepsis has powerful explanatory force for understanding the kinds of decisions parents make about activities such as the extent to which children engage in technological play.

It is now widely recognized that children's learning begins in the home, and early years practitioners around the world are encouraged to recognize this and to build on children's home experiences. So, for example, Scotland's *Curriculum for Excellence* states that:

> Parents are the first and most influential educators of their children. It is important that staff across all early years settings recognise the

interests and experiences children bring from home and use these as a starting point to extend learning.

(Scottish Executive, 2007: 22)

In order to do this, practitioners need to understand more about the kinds of activities likely to be available to young children at home. Much of the research in this field has focused on early language and literacy experiences, but there is growing interest now in children's early experiences with digital technologies. Such technologies, which include not only computers, mobile phones and games consoles, but also many toys, musical instruments and domestic appliances, are now widely available in the home and increasingly accessible to young children. Many have the potential to support early learning, both to support traditional aspects of education in the early years, particularly for literacy and numeracy, as well as to increase young children's familiarity with contemporary social practices. Digital technologies have had a significant impact on the ways in which we communicate with others, on shopping, on leisure activities and on ways of working – and young children learn about these from observing their parents, siblings, friends and neighbours, and by joining in themselves. Thus, given the pace of technological change, children's early experiences at home and in the community are likely to be radically different from those of a few years ago and will continue to evolve quite rapidly.

The research

This chapter draws on two research studies conducted by the authors in the first decade of the twenty-first century, exploring the home experiences of young children – aged between 3 and 5 years of age – with digital technologies. The broad aim of both studies was to answer the following questions:

- What do young children do with digital technologies at home?
- How varied are their experiences?
- Do these experiences support or enhance early learning?

The first study, 'Already at a Disadvantage? ICT in the Home and Children's Preparation for Primary School' (McPake et al., 2005), investigated the impact of socio-economic disadvantage on preschool children's developing competences with digital technologies, focusing on children's technological experiences in the home in the year before they began formal education, and investigating concepts of advantage and disadvantage in this context. The study also addressed teachers' perceptions of children's ICT competences on entry to school. The research took place over six months and involved:

- a survey of the views of parents of children aged 3 to 5 years, who were attending eight nurseries in central Scotland;
- case studies of sixteen children, aged 3 to 5 years, from families selected following the survey; eight of these families were defined as 'disadvantaged' and eight as 'more advantaged';
- interviews with staff from four of the primary schools which the case study children were likely to attend in due course.

The second study, 'Entering e-Society: Young Children's Development of e-Literacies' (McPake et al., 2007), focused more specifically on early digital literacy (the competences needed to make effective and creative use of digital technologies), by:

- defining and describing early digital literacy;
- exploring the relationship between young children's development of print and digital literacy;
- identifying key factors responsible for digital divides between children who have the opportunity to develop high levels of digital literacy, compared with those who do not;
- considering the implications for children as they start primary school.

The research occurred in three stages:

Stage 1: established a broad picture, via a survey of 346 parents of young children in central and western Scotland.
Stage 2: investigated issues in greater depth through 24 case studies, based on five rounds of visits to families over an 18-month period.
Stage 3: explored preschool and early primary education professional perspectives through an expert forum.

In broad terms these two studies found that most young children had many opportunities to experience a wide range of digital technologies, including telephones, computers, electronic musical instruments, MP3, CD and cassette players, televisions, video and DVD players, still and video cameras, games consoles, and domestic appliances. As a result, by the time they were ready to start school most had established early digital literacy (basic operational, social and cultural competences), and used this to support the development of early print literacy, numeracy, information-gathering and problem-solving skills. (See also Plowman et al., forthcoming b and c, for further discussion of the project findings.)

Economic disadvantage and digital technologies in homes

In both of these studies, a key focus was on the variation of children's experiences from one family to another, and on the question of whether children whose technological experiences were more limited might be at a disadvantage once they started primary school. We selected young children from 'more advantaged' and 'less advantaged' families and explored how their experiences with digital technologies might differ. We defined the two groups principally on the basis of parental income, although we recognized that other factors (such as disability, location (rural or urban) or social isolation) might also contribute.

In both studies, there were differences between the more advantaged and the less advantaged families in terms of the kinds of technologies available in the home. Advantaged families were more likely to have expensive and up-to-date technological items, but this did not always mean that children in these families had greater access to digital technologies. Children in less advantaged families typically also lived in 'high-tech' homes, though the technologies might be older and have been purchased second-hand or indeed be of uncertain provenance. These parents were often more relaxed about children using and exploring technology at home precisely because it was less valuable and less sophisticated than was the case in some of the more advantaged families. In those homes, expensive equipment, purchased for adult use or for work purposes, was frequently not made available to children.

One example from our case studies shows how limited resources need not prevent children from learning to use a range of technological items, particularly when parents are convinced that the early acquisition of technological skills will have long-term benefits.

Kirsty: making the most of limited resources

Kirsty Bennet was a 4-year-old girl living with her mother and her 9-month-old brother Hamish. Ms Bennet was a lone mother who stayed at home to look after the children and therefore had very little income. The family owned a TV, a video camera and a mobile phone with a digital camera and an internet connection (used daily to check their bank balance), and technological toys which included a dance mat, hand-held electronic games and a *LeapPad* (a console for interactive books which are read aloud using a 'magic' pen).

The family often went to the library, both to read books and for Kirsty to play with some of the electronic toys there to help children learn to read. They did not have a computer, but visited Ms Bennet's mother on a regular basis to use hers.

Ms Bennet and her mother were both very competent computer users, having undertaken a number of courses in the past. Ms Bennet continued to update her skills with the intention of finding office work when Hamish started school.

Kirsty was a competent user of all the technologies available to her, operating the TV controls independently and accessing games via the interactive features. She was an enthusiastic user of the *LeapPad* and could access children's websites on her grandmother's computer. She particularly liked finding online drawing and painting games.

Ms Bennet encouraged Kirsty to learn to use the computer, and the other technologies they had at home, because she felt strongly that these things would be important for Kirsty in the future and that she would be at a disadvantage if she did not learn how to use them.[1]

'Entering e-Society' extended 'Already at a Disadvantage?' by investigating parents' attitudes towards their children's technological experiences, and compared the views of more and less affluent parents. Towards the end of the study we asked the nineteen parents still involved in the research (eight less advantaged and eleven more advantaged) to comment on a set of statements, based on the range of views expressed in interviews in earlier stages of the research.

We found very few differences between the two groups. Most parents were enthusiastic about technologies in the home, and comfortable with their use. For example, almost all (18 of the 19 parents) felt that their children's use of technological items was right for their age, and that playing computer games was harmless fun. Most (16 parents) made use of the technologies they had in the house without planning deliberately to teach their children how to use them. When asked whether children might be missing out on more important things if they played with technological toys and games, the majority (16 parents) saw this as a question of balance:

> It depends. As long as they're doing other things and that's not all they're doing. Alex loves football and goes to training twice a week and loves to play outside. If he has a chance to go out and play he will forget about the computer – football definitely takes precedence.[2]

On these points, there was general agreement. Other issues produced more varied responses: just over half (11 parents) agreed that they were not very confident about their own abilities to help their children learn to use technologies:

> I would like to know more about the computer. [. . .] I could help Liam

with the basics but he will far surpass me. I can teach my children sums and things I learned at school, but as far as technology goes I'm very limited.

These views were often linked to the belief that children 'pick up' technological skills 'naturally' and do not require any formal teaching. Liam's mother believed that he would soon 'surpass' her, and indeed that his 6-year-old sister had already done so (see Plowman et al., 2008).

Parents were also divided on the importance of their children learning to use technologies at this stage. Just over half (11 parents) thought that they would be at a disadvantage if they did not:

> I don't know how young they have to be to learn [to use digital technologies] but I do think they need to learn young these days. Certainly in schools because it's so competitive now and everyone uses technologies, and they'll need to be smarter than me!

However, about one-third (7 parents) were unconcerned:

> I think they are too young now, and they will pick it up later anyway.

Similarly, just under half (9 parents) thought that investing in technological items would pay off when their children went to school:

> Especially computers – both to help with school projects and general computer knowledge. If they go into school with some background, it will help them. They need the help from home as well as school.

This was one topic where less advantaged parents felt more strongly than those who were more advantaged. Three-quarters of the less advantaged parents (6 of the 8 in this category) were in favour of investing in technologies, while around two-thirds of the more advantaged (7 out of 11) were ambivalent:

> Will early investment in technology pay off when children start school? Possibly, but not necessarily. I know some friends whose kids don't use computers at all and by the time they get to a certain age they'll all be at the same stage anyway.

Another area of difference between the two groups related to the belief that using certain kinds of technology could damage their children's health and development. Overall, around half (10 parents) thought this was the case. Around two-thirds of the more advantaged parents (7 out of 11) expressed concern:

> I know there's a lot of talk about mobile phones, and I don't know if that's right or wrong, but I would never encourage them to use mobile phones. They've asked but I've said no because I don't think it's necessary for them to use them.

However, a similar proportion of the less advantaged parents (5 out of 8) said that they were not worried about this.

> You hear this kind of thing [about mobile phones] but I don't believe it.

Our analysis of parents' attitudes towards their children's experiences of digital technologies thus indicates that most parents – regardless of economic background – were in favour of children exploring and learning to use the different technological items available to them. Some parents, particularly the more advantaged, were ambivalent about the long-term benefits of these experiences and had some concerns about possible effects on children's health. Thus, our case studies showed that explaining the digital divide on the basis of economic advantage or disadvantage is a complex matter. Children from less advantaged families may not live in homes with the latest technologies, but they may have greater access to more basic equipment. Their parents may be more convinced of the benefits of early opportunities to learn to use these technologies, and less concerned about potential risks, than the parents of children from more advantaged families.

Parental perspectives on children's experiences with digital technologies at home

Although we concluded that economic disadvantage was not the most important factor influencing young children's experiences with digital technologies, our case studies clearly demonstrated that some children had greater opportunities than others to use a range of technological toys and other tools. By the time they were about to start school, some were more technically competent and more aware of the range of potential uses of different technologies than others. If economic advantage or disadvantage was not the most obvious explanatory factor, what else might account for these differences?

More detailed analysis of our case study data showed that parents' views on the potential benefits (or dangers) of early exposure to technologies were a powerful predictor of the extent of the opportunities young children might have to explore or play with different technological items. These perspectives were influenced by a number of factors, particularly parents' technological expertise, itself a product of their own experiences of using different kinds of technology, and views on the importance of digital technologies in the future, whether for educational, work or leisure purposes.

The importance of these various factors is illustrated by the experiences of two of our case study children, Grace and Catriona. They both came from more advantaged families, remarkably similar in terms of demographic characteristics but very different in terms of parental attitudes towards digital technologies. As a result, the children's early experiences of learning to use technologies differed.

Grace and Catriona: the impact of parental attitudes

Grace and Catriona were both 4 years old at the start of the study. They both had 6-year-old brothers, and their parents had similar professional backgrounds. Their fathers had skilled jobs requiring specialist technical competences: Catriona's father, Mr Stewart, was a marine pilot whereas Grace's father, Mr Baxter, was responsible for the production of a local newspaper. Mrs Baxter was a childminder and Mrs Stewart was involved in home care for the elderly. Both the Baxters and the Stewarts had early experiences of learning to use computers.

However, the Baxters had negative views of their early technological experiences, describing these as boring and irrelevant. Mrs Baxter was concerned that video games make children aggressive and that having internet access at home would encourage her husband to take up online gambling or become otherwise 'addicted to the internet'. She did not encourage her children to learn how to use currently available technologies because she believed that any skills that the children acquired now would quickly become obsolete. In contrast, the Stewarts were confident and enthusiastic users of home technologies, and used the internet for shopping and banking. They had positive views of technology in the future, expecting that many more labour- and time-saving devices would become available, and believing that children should take every opportunity to develop the technological skills which would enable them to take advantage of these features.

Grace's and Catriona's own abilities to use digital technologies appeared to be related to their parents' attitudes and experiences. Grace had very limited skills: at the beginning of the project, in contrast to almost all the other children participating in the study, she could not use the TV controls, and she owned virtually no technological items, other than toy versions of a laptop and a CD player. Her favourite activities were playing with Barbie dolls, dressing up, playing outdoors and swimming. Mrs Baxter did not encourage any technological activity and described Grace as uninterested in these things. At the same age, Catriona was fully competent with TV controls and the mobile phone and played computer games with her older brother. Her favourite activities included playing with dolls, painting, watching TV and playing computer games. By the end of our visits, she could also find favourite websites on the internet, enjoyed the dance mat, had decreed *LeapPads* and *VTech* toys to be too babyish for her, and could take pictures with the digital camera. Mrs Stewart was pleased that she was 'not frightened' of technology. Catriona's favourite activity continued to be painting and drawing, which she did both in the traditional manner and on the computer.

These and other examples from our case studies showed that parents' technological experiences, both earlier in life and at the time of the research, and their aspirations for their children's futures, were more influential than family income on the access which children were given to technologies in the home and the opportunities they had to learn to use them. We turn now to consider the implications of this in greater detail.

Prolepsis: understanding the influence of parental experience and aspirations

Cole (1996) argues that one of the key influences on parents' interactions with their children is *prolepsis*, a term deriving from a Greek verb meaning 'to anticipate'. In this context, prolepsis refers to the ways in which children's social and cultural development is determined by cultural and historical constraints which pre-date their existence, and Cole (1996: 184–187) provides several examples from different parts of the world. Referring to a study conducted in the UK in the 1950s, he noted that gender stereotyping was commonplace from birth, so that parents commented that girl babies would not be able to play rugby, and that they would be a source of concern to their fathers as adolescents. Future gender differences feature prominently in other cultures' responses to new babies, too. For example, in the Zinacanteco culture of south-central Mexico, baby boys and baby girls were given symbolic objects representing the kinds of work they would be expected to do in later life.

A significant feature of this behaviour is that parents (and other adults in the community) project into the children's future lives their own view of what it is like to be an adult and, in these accounts, what differentiates men and women in their community, on the basis of present experience. Typically, they do not expect the future to be very different from the way things are now. Equally significant is the notion that in order that their children become the kinds of adults which their community expects to produce, parents turn to their own childhoods (now in the past) in order to identify the processes which made them the adults they are today and which, they assume, will be similarly effective for their own children. Thus, as Cole remarks, 'they "reach into" the cultural past, project it into the future and then "carry" that conceptual future "back" into the present to create the sociocultural environment of the newcomer' (1996: 186).

In our studies, prolepsis is at work in terms both of parents' (and other adults') long-term views of their children's future, and of how their own experiences in the past have influenced the way in which they think about this future. We have seen from the cases of Grace and Catriona how their parents' early experiences with technologies influenced the extent to which the children had access to technologies and were encouraged to use them; and also how these decisions are explained by their parents both in relation to their own past experiences and in relation to the kinds of technological futures their children will encounter.

Sometimes parents may seek to avoid aspects of their own past lives which they saw as leading to problems later on. Grace's parents had negative experiences with technology in the past and were unconvinced of the need to prepare for a more technologized future because their experiences suggested that the technologies of the future would bear no resemblance to those currently in use. Moreover, they saw technologies as a threat to the kind of childhood they wished their children to have. Technological play could lead to aggression and addiction, and would interfere with, or limit, the amount of time available for the kinds of activities they saw as more appropriate: in Grace's case, playing with dolls and physical exercise. In these choices, we can intuit two aspects of Grace's future which her parents were keen to ensure: one based on traditional gender expectations of girls as caregivers, and one perhaps influenced by modern concerns about the effects of children's lack of physical fitness. Technological play can be seen by parents as inimical to developments of this kind. Digital technologies, particularly video games, are seen to be aimed more at boys than at girls and to cater for boys' predilection for action and aggression rather than girls' traditional interest in nurturing and social roles. Technological play is also seen as taking up time that children might otherwise have spent playing outdoors.

In contrast, Catriona's parents, with positive experiences of technology in their own past, projected a future for their children in which technology would play an increasingly important role and where it would be important for Catriona *not to be frightened* of using technology, both for work and in other aspects of everyday life. Unlike the Baxters, they did not see technology as getting in the way of traditional activities such as playing with dolls, creative play or exercise, but rather as offering alternative ways of pursuing these interests. More significantly, perhaps, they encouraged Catriona to learn with technology, encouraging her to play with technological toys such as the *LeapPad* or the *VTech* console. In this way, they both reflected their own past experiences where digital technologies had played a positive role in their studies, and projected a future for Catriona where this would be increasingly significant.

Among the case study families, the Baxters and the Stewarts were unusual in that both sets of parents had had quite extensive experience of digital technologies, as students and then in work contexts. This is likely to become the norm for parents of young children in a few years' time but, at the time of the research, this was not so for most of the parents. They had grown up in the 1970s and 1980s, before digital technologies became widely available in the home, and many had only recently begun to use computers, mobile phones and other such items. Consequently, many were tentative about their own competence and were surprised by the apparent ease with which their own children mastered the technologies available to them. Plowman et al. (2008) explore why parents believe that their children 'just pick up' technological skills, failing to recognize that they in fact model and support their children's learning in various ways.

Disturbing prolepsis

Where parents encounter childhood practices which they themselves had no opportunity to experience, the operation of prolepsis is disturbed. Although many of the parents intuited that digital technologies would play an increasingly important role in their children's future lives, they could not refer back to their own childhood experiences as a way of understanding how best to prepare their children for such futures. As technology had no place in their own childhoods, parents felt ambivalent about its role in their children's lives and saw it as potentially threatening.

Alex: prolepsis interrupted

Alex was a 4-year-old boy living with his parents, Mr and Mrs Simmonds, and his older sisters Laura (age 12) and Shelley (age 10). Mr Simmonds worked from home as a music teacher and Mrs Simmonds had recently returned to full-time work for the Council in the area where they lived, in the west of Scotland. Their earnings placed them in the 'average' bracket, neither 'disadvantaged' nor 'more advantaged'.

Their home was defined by us as 'high tech'. There were two TVs and two computers in the home. One computer, in Mr Simmonds's studio, had broadband, while the other in Laura's bedroom, did not have internet access. Both parents and Alex's older sisters had mobile phones and digital still and video cameras. Mr Simmonds had an electronic drum system which he used for teaching and playing. The family had a PlayStation and a GameBoy. Alex had remote controlled cars and received electronic educational games for Christmas, including a *LeapFrog* Phonics Writing Desk.

Alex was competent with most of the technologies available to him at home. He could use all three remote controls to change channels on both TVs, play games on the interactive TV setting and use the DVD player. He enjoyed playing free demo games on Sky Interactive, and after coming home from nursery would typically go straight to this or to the computer to play games on children's websites. He knew how to open Internet Explorer, then his own collection of favourite sites, and then select *CBeebies* or *Yahooligans* (two websites targeting preschool children). He would play these games happily for long periods of time and was keen to show his mother how to play. He was competent with the PlayStation when it was in operation and could not understand why his mother was not able to use it. He could use the electronic drum set, putting on the headphones and using the controls to change tempo, etc. He 'knows what he's doing', according to his mother, although he was not supposed to play by himself. He could take photos with the digital still camera and review these on the camera.

Mrs Simmonds did not learn to use technologies while at school and had not had any opportunities to acquire even basic operational skills in her first job. As a result, she felt disadvantaged when she was looking for a new job and competing with younger people who were more technologically competent. In her next job, in a bank, she finally had the chance to learn to use Word and email. Now working at the Council office she was learning new skills as the need arose. Mr Simmonds had recently bought a computer and had taken an introductory course to get over his fear of using it because he needed certain music applications for his work. At the time of the study, he had taught himself to use email, the internet and Media Player, wrote music on the computer, and downloaded music for students.

Alex's parents did not know how he had learned to use the various technologies available in the home. Mrs Simmonds was quite surprised and proud when Alex opened an application on the computer for the first time and found what he was looking for himself. She thought that he learned to use these technologies on his own, by trial and error. But both parents also had a general feeling of being overwhelmed, unsure what he would be like when he was older. They wondered whether he would go on to a career in computers, but at the same time were worried that he spent too much time on these kinds of activities. They had concerns about his coming across inappropriate content on TV or on the computer, and also that technology-based play could be detrimental to social development. They often told him to stop watching TV or playing computer games, encouraging him instead to play outside.

The work of Cole and other cultural-historical researchers implies that prolepsis is a universal feature of human life (as demonstrated by examples from a wide range of 'traditional' and 'modern' societies around the world) and one of the key mechanisms by which culture is embedded in human development. He makes clear that prolepsis requires at least the impression of cultural continuity from one generation to the next but there have been few studies exploring what happens when prolepsis is disturbed or interrupted as a result of major societal changes.

Parents recognize that the advent and near ubiquity of digital technologies has significantly changed the nature of childhood, and that it is difficult to be confident about appropriate ways to ensure the best possible futures for their children. In most cases, they cannot rely on their own past experiences as a guide. Some of our case study parents had come to uneasy compromises, such as that reached by Alex's parents, allowing their children access to technologies, concerned that not doing so might blight their future prospects. At the same time they worried that this could limit features they valued from their own childhoods (particularly playing outdoors and playing with other children), features that they felt also had an important role to play in enabling their children to grow up to be the adults they hoped they would become.

Research on the early experiences of children growing up in culturally diverse societies such as the UK and the United States (for example Gregory et al., 2004; Long et al., 2007; Kenner et al., 2007) addresses some of these issues. In culturally diverse societies, prolepsis becomes more challenging because parents' (and other adults') past experiences of growing up, in many cases in another country with very different social and cultural traditions, may not provide a clear guide for their children's futures. Their studies of children of Puerto Rican origin in the United States and children of Bangladeshi origin in the UK (among others) show that certain cultural traditions associated with the country of origin (for example religious practices or storytelling) retain a key role in enabling children to develop identities as 'Puerto Ricans' or 'Bangladeshis' despite living in another country where other identities (as 'Americans' or 'Britons') are likely to become increasingly salient.

The studies found that both grandparents and siblings had important roles to play in proleptic activities, such as storytelling or role-play games. In these, younger children learned not only about the traditions of the culture of origin which families hoped the children would continue to practise, but also about their possible future roles in British or American society. A key finding was that young children were not passive recipients of these various futures but, rather, played an active role in their reconstruction or enactment. Kenner et al. (2007) use the term *synergy* to define this relationship, summing up in this way their observations of grandparents and grandchildren learning together in the context of both traditional and technological activities:

> Grandparents treated children as competent co-constructors of the event, giving them plenty of time to act and only offering guidance when this was evidently needed. At the same time, the warmth and closeness of the relationship reassured children that guidance was

continually available. Meanwhile, children also provided support for adult learning, particularly when using the computer together. They expressed mutual care and sensitivity for their grandparents as learners.

(Kenner et al., 2007: 239)

We see this development in the thinking about the operation of prolepsis as an important way of countering any notion that young children are entirely at the mercy of external forces in terms of the kinds of experiences they have with digital technologies. Although economic disadvantage may make a material difference, and although parents' own experiences and expectations have a powerful role to play in determining the nature and extent of children's activities in the early years, the children themselves are not passive recipients. Rather, they play an active part in transforming these opportunities into experiences which are meaningful to them. Their choices can influence their parents' lives in the same way as their parents' choices guide theirs. Where parents saw opportunities for their own learning in their children's interest and growing expertise, the value of these shared activities was valuable and transformative.

Colin: learning together

Colin was 3 years old at the start of our study. He lived with his mother, Ms Knox, and his 5-year-old sister Emma. Ms Knox worked part-time shifts looking after adults with learning difficulties. The family's income level placed them in the 'disadvantaged' bracket.

The family home was defined as 'high tech'. There were five TVs and one computer, with CD and DVD player/writer, printer, scanner, photocopier, Instant Messenger, and broadband internet access. Ms Knox had bought it, and a digital camera, about a year before the study began. It was their first computer and they were all learning together. The children had a *Leapster* and a *LeapPad* that both Colin and Emma liked to use, and a dance mat. Both children had CD players, as well as an electronic violin and many battery-operated and remote-controlled toys and games.

By the age of 3 years, Colin had developed basic operational skills such as switching the TV on and off himself. He could play games on the *CBeebies* site by himself or with his sister, and they competed for turns to use the *Leapster* and the *LeapPad*. Colin loved taking photographs with the digital camera and looking at his collection of photographs on the computer, although he would ask Emma for help to download them from the camera.

Ms Knox had not used computers at school or on the vocational courses she had taken since then, but the purchase of the computer had made a great difference to her own technological competence and to the children's. They embarked on learning to use it together, initially with help from a more experienced relative, and the computer and the camera now played an important part in family life. Ms Knox and the children communicated regularly with relatives in Australia via the webcam and email. Although Colin could not read or write, he would add emoticons to email messages and liked to send and receive photographs. During the study, the Knox family went on an extended family holiday to Australia to visit these relatives, and as a result the opportunities for electronic contact were even more highly valued after the trip.

The computer had pride of place in the living room and was in constant use, for games, for information seeking, for viewing photographs and for communication. Ms Knox expressed the view that her children were more technologically competent than she was: 'I'm not very good at these things – Colin is better than I am!' Yet when Colin asked for help with a game he was playing, she sat down and worked out with him how to resolve the problem. She explained that she had once been frightened of technology but was now a convert. When Colin was ready to set out on his career she wanted him to have greater opportunities than she had had: 'For lots of things, including job opportunities, new technologies will be important in Colin's life. There will be more opportunities for him to find out what he wants to do.'

For Ms Knox, digital technologies offered the promise of a better life, not only in terms of work opportunities, but also – in contrast to the views of some of the other parents – as a way of combating social isolation, through communications with distant friends and relatives. Moreover, the family was developing a shared bond through their mutual enthusiasm for the opportunities offered, and Ms Knox saw these as extending her own educational horizons as well as those of the children. She had few qualms about involving her children in technological activities at a young age because she saw these as enhancing rather than limiting their experiences.

Conclusions: children's technological futures

The lives that children born in the first decade of the twenty-first century will lead are likely to be very different from those of their parents. Digital technologies are transforming the way people work, shop, study and play so rapidly that it is difficult to anticipate what these activities will be like in twenty years' time, when the children in our case studies will be completing their studies, beginning work and starting their own families. How can parents best prepare children for adult life in an unpredictable future?

Our research has shown that most parents believe that competence with digital technologies will be important and that an early start is likely to be advantageous. But the opportunities they make available to children are influenced by their attitudes to technology, fruit of their own past experiences, and by the kinds of futures they envisage for their children. This means that when children enter early years education, their technological competence can vary quite substantially (Plowman et al., forthcoming a). Practitioners seeking to develop this competence need to recognize the reasons for this variation and to reflect on how to respond: this variation is the result not just of families' economic status but also of their attitudes and aspirations for their children. Many parents are unsure of the value – or the dangers – of introducing their children to technological activities at a young age, and practitioners, as they seek to understand children's early experiences, may find that parents look to them for reassurance and encouragement. The task of the practitioner is therefore not simply to assess the child's competence and build on this but also to take into account parental perspectives and how these are likely to have influenced the child's own view of technologies, now and in their future.

Acknowledgements

The authors gratefully acknowledge receipt of grants from Becta for 'Already at a Disadvantage?' and from the ESRC (Economic and Social Research Council) for 'Entering e-Society' (RES-341-25-0034). Christine Stephen was a co-investigator on the projects described here.

Notes

1. All of the vignettes presented in this chapter are based on case study field notes made during the course of 'Entering e-Society'. All names are pseudonyms.
2. Comments reported here were spontaneously generated as a result of the statement task.

References

Cole, M. (1996) *Cultural Psychology: A Once and Future Discipline*. Cambridge, MA: Harvard University Press.

Gregory, E., Long, S. and Volk, D. (eds) (2004) *Many Pathways to Literacy: Young Children Learning with Siblings, Grandparents, Peers and Communities*. London: Routledge.

Kenner, C., Ruby, M., Jessel, J., Gregory, E. and Arju, T. (2007) Intergenerational learning between children and grandparents in east London, *Journal of Early Childhood Research*, 5: 219–243.

Long, S., Volk, D., Romero-Little, M. and Gregory, E. (2007) Invisible mediators of literacy: learning in multicultural communities. In Y. Goodman and P. Martens (eds), *Critical Issues in Early Literacy*. London: Routledge.

McPake, J., Stephen, C., Plowman, L., Sime, D. and Downey, S. (2005) *Already at a Disadvantage? ICT in the Home and Children's Preparation for Primary School*. Coventry: Becta. www.ioe.stir.ac.uk/research/projects/interplay/docs/already_at_a_disadvantage.pdf (accessed 4 July 2009).

McPake, J., Stephen, C. and Plowman, L. (2007) *Entering e-Society: Young Children's Development of e-Literacies. Summary of Findings*. Stirling: Stirling Institute of Education. http://www.ioe.stir.ac.uk/research/projects/esociety/publications.php (accessed 4 July 2009).

Plowman, L., McPake, J. and Stephen, C. (2008) Just picking it up? Young children learning with technology at home, *Cambridge Journal of Education*, 38(3): 303–319.

Plowman, L., Stephen, C. and McPake, J. (forthcoming a) *Growing Up with Technology: Young Children Learning in a Digital World*. London: Routledge.

Plowman, L., McPake, J. and Stephen, C. (forthcoming b) The technologisation of childhood? Young children and technology in the home, *Children and Society*.

Plowman, L., Stephen, C. and McPake, J. (forthcoming c) Supporting young children's learning with technology at home and in pre-school, *Research Papers in Education*.

Scottish Executive (2007) *A Curriculum for Excellence. Building the Curriculum 2: Active Learning in the Early Years*. Edinburgh: Scottish Executive. http://www.ltscotland.org.uk/curriculumforexcellence/publications/Buildingthecurriculum2/index.asp (accessed 4 July 2009).

14 When robots tell a story about culture . . . and children tell a story about learning

Marina Umaschi Bers

C.P. Snow, in his classic book *The Two Cultures*, describes two different ways of thinking and knowing (i.e. epistemologies) used in the sciences and the humanities (Snow, 1959). This observation is echoed by Bruner's distinction between the logico-paradigmatic way of knowing, traditionally held by scientists, and the narrative mode of knowing of humanists (Bruner, 1986). Although the 'two cultures' metaphor is limited as people hardly fit into binary stereotypes (Brockman, 1996; Brown and Clewell, 1998), the epistemo-logical divide still permeates society.

Schooling often has the responsibility to introduce and expose children to a variety of ways of knowing. However, there is frequently a 'division of labour' between those who enjoy and are good in science, mathematics, engineering and technology (SMET) and those who enjoy and are good at reading, writing and the social sciences. Early on, students label themselves (or are labelled) as belonging to one or the other group (Swan, 1995; Frierson, 1996). This results in a great majority of students, mostly women and minorities, ruling out SMET in their career paths (Alper, 1993; Hammrich, 1997; Erinosho, 1999; Pulis, 2000). In consequence the United States, among other countries, struggles to diversify the engineering workplace (Holden, 1989) and involve women and minorities in scientific careers (Kubanek and Waller, 1995; Bae and Smith, 1997; Thom, 2001).

Early childhood education provides a wonderful opportunity to address this challenge. In the early years, most educational settings expose all chil-dren to both narrative and logico-paradigmatic ways of knowing. Compared to other segments of the educational experience, early childhood has an advantage when attempting to integrate these two realms of knowledge (Badra and Palleschi, 1993). There is consensus in the field about the importance of emergent and integrated curriculum that derives from the child's own interests.

In contemporary times, epistemological pluralism, or the ability to build knowledge in diverse ways (Turkle and Papert, 1992) can be facilitated by the use of new technologies that allow young children to become 'little story-tellers' and 'little engineers' (Bers, 2008b). In this context, the use of robots and robotic kits that extend the tradition of early childhood 'manipulatives' and add on a technological component are powerful tools to engage young children in designing, building and programming interactive projects (Bers, 2008b).

This chapter starts by presenting the theoretical, pedagogical and technological frameworks for working with robotics and young children. Most specifically, the chapter focuses on integrating robotics with cultural narratives and presents two learning experiences. In the first one, educators encounter technologically rich design by first developing a robotics curriculum that integrates social sciences with SMET, and then adapting it to their classrooms. In the second experience, parents and young children engage in the construction of robotic projects to represent an aspect of their family's cultural heritage.

Both learning experiences integrate robotics with cultural narratives. Similarly, both highlight the possibilities of new technologies to bridge the divide between the different epistemologies or ways of knowing. The chapter closes by proposing that a technologically rich design-based approach to learning that integrates the narrative and the logico-paradigmatic ways of knowing might act as a catalyst for engagement with SMET ideas for those who are traditionally marginalized from it. Simultaneously, it might encourage those who feel more aligned with SMET to enrich their experiences with a more social or humanistic aspect that embraces narrative perspectives.

Foundations

A design-based approach to learning that encourages the use of new technologies is based upon the design process used in engineering and software development (Bers, 2008a). It engages learners in several steps:

1   Identifying a problem (it can be personally meaningful or a real-world need)
2   Doing background research or needs analysis
3   developing possible solutions
4   Implementing working prototypes
5   Testing and evaluating the prototypes
6   Communicating findings
7   Redesigning the solutions based on the information gathered. This iterative design cycle repeats itself in the creation of technological artefacts.

By providing contexts in which young children can experience the process of design, the children are able to acquire knowledge, skills and habits of mind that apply to both ends of the spectrum of the epistemological divide: the sciences and the humanities (Davis, 1998). For example, the iterative design cycle can be used in building a robotic toy car as well as for writing an essay or creating a storytelling character (Bers and Cassell, 1998; Bers et al., 1998). Although there are differences in the language used, for example we might talk about debugging software, fixing a broken artefact or editing a story, the core idea of designing and revising in a systematic way based on feedback, is found in all of these activities.

Design-based projects can also provide ways for children to make personal connections with new areas of knowledge and skills, and to engage in problem solving, seeking multiple strategies, decision making and collaboration as they approach new problems (Schleifer, 1997; Rogers et al., 2001). The constructionist theory of learning (Papert, 1980) pays particular attention to the role of new technologies in supporting children to become designers. Constructionism has its roots in Piaget's theory of constructivism. However, whereas Piaget's theory was developed to explain how knowledge is constructed in our minds, Papert pays particular attention to the role of constructions in the world (concrete) as a support for those in the mind (abstract) and is a pioneer in proposing computers as powerful tools to create and facilitate design projects.

Constructionism has two fundamental ideas that inform educational practice: (1) powerful educational technologies engage children in design-based activities that are epistemologically relevant, personally meaningful, and have resulting products that can be shared with a community; and (2) the importance of manipulative objects that have computational power, such as robotic construction kits, for supporting the generation of concrete ways of thinking and learning about abstract phenomena (Bers et al., 2002).

Constructionism shares with other educational approaches, such as 'learning by designing' (Kolodner et al., 1998), 'knowledge as design' (Perkins, 1986), 'design education' (Ritchie, 1995), and 'design experiments' (Brown, 1992), the tenet that design-based activities are good ways for students to engage in learning by applying concepts, skills and strategies to solve authentic problems that are relevant and personally meaningful (Resnick et al., 1996a). While in early childhood education there is a strong tradition of engaging children in making objects, machines and tangible models with low-tech materials, constructionism has paid particular attention to newer technologies, in particular robotics.

Robotics: tools for design-based learning

Most new technologies that propose a design-based approach to learning belong to the family of constructionist tools (Resnick et al., 1996b). For example, the Lego Mindstorms robotics kit, which is used by all of the projects described later in this chapter, provides opportunities for design involving both programming and building activities, thus promoting both technological fluency and engineering design skills. Lego Mindstorms is a commercially available construction kit composed of a tiny computer embedded in a specialized Lego brick, called RCX, which can be programmed to take data from the environment through its sensors, process information, power motors and control light sources to turn on and off (see Figure 14.1).

The robot can be programmed or 'taught to move' using a graphical language, ROBOLAB, with tiered levels of programming that allows users to drag and drop graphical blocks of code that represent commands (i.e. left and right turns, reverse direction, motor speed, motor power) to produce behaviours for a robotic construction (Portsmore, 1999). Users can drag the icons together into a stack, in a similar way to assembling physical Lego bricks, and arrange them in logical order to produce new behaviours for a robotic construction

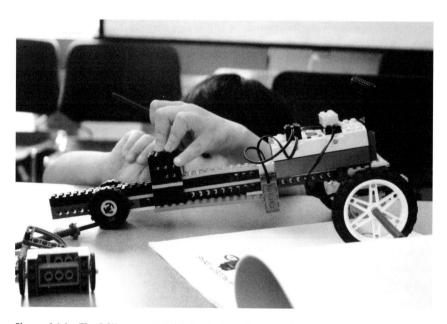

Figure 14.1   The RCX programmable brick with wheels, motors and sensors.

(see Figure 14.2). Lego Mindstorms and ROBOLAB have successfully been used in early childhood education (Resnick, 1998; Bers and Urrea, 2000; Rogers et al., 2001; Beals and Bers, 2006; Bers, 2008a).

Three major factors make this technology particularly appealing for design-based activities that engage both ways of knowing described by Bruner (1986). First, the physicality of the robotic construction kit supports the integration of art materials. Second, the ubiquity of the technology, so that once the robot is designed, built and programmed, it can exhibit its interactive behaviours anywhere.

Learning stories

This section presents two different approaches to use robotics that attempt to bridge the gap between the two 'cultures' and the two 'ways of knowing', the narrative and the logico-paradigmatic. In the first experience, educators encounter the concept of technologically rich design by first experiencing the development of a curriculum that integrates social sciences with SMET via the use of robotics, and then adapting it to take to their own students. In the second experience, parents and young children engaged in the construction of robotic projects to represent an aspect of their family's cultural heritage.

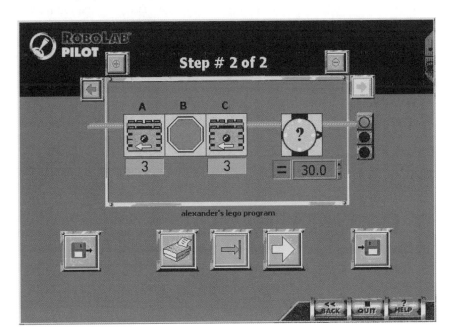

Figure 14.2 The ROBOLAB programming environment.

Both learning experiences integrate robotics with cultural narratives. Both highlight the possibilities of new technologies to bridge the divide between both epistemologies.

Educators exploring the Aztec culture: chinampas and the agricultural system

The first learning story tells of early childhood educators who developed a curriculum unit that integrates the social science frameworks, most specifically the Aztec civilization, with the science and technology state frameworks in Massachusetts, which focus on 'materials, tools, and machines [that] extend our ability to solve problems and invent ... and engineering design [that] requires creative thinking and strategies to solve practical problems generated by needs and wants' (Massachusetts Departments of Education, 2006: 86). Teachers first experienced the curriculum themselves and then adapted it to work with their students. In this chapter, I will focus on the educator's learning experience. This is important as teachers need to feel competent and confident regarding the use of robotics, otherwise the likelihood of projects such as this to succeed is reduced.

As a first step, teachers were introduced to the Lego Mindstorms robotic kit and the ROBOLAB programming language. Most of them were familiar with Lego but had not worked with robotics before. They understood how to work with the traditional blocks but the addition of gears, sensors, the RCX and programming was challenging. They were introduced to the 'culture' aspects of their project through a short video entitled *Mystery Quest: Alien Adventures into Lost Worlds* (National Geographic Television, 1998) and were asked to discuss two questions: What is an archeologist? What is culture?

The educators were assigned to work in 'archeological teams' to explore the Aztec culture. They used classroom resources such as pre-selected texts, computers – internet searches, encyclopedia software – and they chose an Aztec artefact (object, place or process) that they found to be most characteristic of the civilization. They kept a design journal to brainstorm ideas about how to reproduce the artefact with the robotic kit and to reflect on their learning processes. Finally, each archeological team presented its work.

Some archeological teams chose the Aztec's religious ceremonies, the Aztec calendar, the Aztec waste management, and transportation systems. In this chapter I report the experience of the team who chose the Aztec's agricultural system. One of the participating teachers reports in her design journal:

> We learned that the Aztecs built their empire on swamp lands, clearly not an ideal place for development. In order to build or farm, the Aztecs first had to create solid ground. Using a technique of laying down layers of mud and logs to build the land up above water, they

were able to create land for the city's development. The farming landmasses were called 'chinampa's and they could be dragged around by wooden boats at the early stages and brought to a farming site where they would root.

Chinampas was a good choice for a design project. From an engineering perspective, the system itself seemed fairly easy to build, although it had a variety of moving parts. From a social sciences or humanities perspective, it would demonstrate the challenges faced by the Aztecs in their need to have solid land upon which to develop their culture.

Once the team chose the Aztec agriculture system, the members looked at the aspects of a chinampa field which they thought could be transformed into 'moving parts' with robotics. The reflective design journal shows the iterative nature of this design process:

> Our first idea was to make a boat that could travel through the Chinampas. It would show how people traveled around the fields to tend the crops and how the Chinampa fields could be set up in an orderly fashion. Our next idea was to make a Chinampa to 'sway' in the water. While we were not sure that Chinampas actually swayed, it would illustrate the period of time where Chinampas are not solid grown yet. It was also possible that the Chinampas could move due to tidal changes, boats moving through the fields, or people walking on top of them. We decided to make a Chinampa field that was a mixture of art and Lego. It would include one or two boats that could travel through the field. At least one of them would be dragging an early Chinampa. We would also include one or two swaying Chinampas surrounded by stable Chinampas growing a variety of crops. One stable Chinampa would have an Aztec house. We also wanted to include a 3D aspect, which would show a cross section of the different levels of root growth in a maturing Chinampa. It would show an immature Chinampa where no or few roots were visible, a medium Chinampa where the roots were beginning to be substantial, and a mature Chinampa where the roots had anchored into the ground beneath the swamp.

One of the teachers, with no previous engineering or technological experience, relates her iterative process of design while building the boat that would navigate the Chinampa.

> After experimenting with a few designs, I decided that the motor and necessary gearing was too bulky . . . My next idea was to use a belt that could be attached to the motor through gears, and the boat could sit

on top of it. Then, when the motor rotated, the belt would rotate, and the boat would move . . . I used a medium sized, flat Lego piece to stabilize each end. The end without the motor had a large gear, connected to the chain, and supported over the Lego floor by a bar. The end with the motor had some additional gears to slow down the rotation of the motor. Next, I wrote the program that governed the motor. When one of the touch sensors was held down, the motor would move in one direction. When the other touch sensor was held down, the motor would move in the other direction.

A second teacher, who built a floating chinampa, wrote about her design process.

Our idea was to have a moving Lego piece that would represent an un-secure chinampa. The chinampa would tilt back and forth in time to the rhythmic movements of surrounding water. The first step was to determine what tool I would use to simulate the movement of the chinampa. When I realized that I could control the specific distance that the motor rotated through the amount of time that it moved, I decided to create the tilting chinampa through a system of gears. This was an unsuccessful prototype because the gears did not turn properly with a flat surface positioned on top. I realized that I needed to raise the chinampa above the gears. I made a support system that attached to one long rotating bar. This support system successfully held up a flat LEGO piece that represented the bird's eye view of a chinampa. The support system would bounce back and forth of two side walls that along with the computer program controlled the chinampa's movement. The trickiest part for me was developing the program for the chinampa's movement. I had the most trouble wiring my pieces and understanding the order of the programming blocks . . . I found that if I gave the Chinampa a break by stopping the program for a couple seconds the Chinampa fared much better.

In their design journals, both of these educators show their learning process through trial and error. They brought to their final design the use of art materials, with which they were already familiar, and incorporated recyclable materials to make the simpler and non-moving parts, such as rectangular sponges with brown boards for non-moving chinampas, green stickers for grass, pipe cleaners for tree and wooden manipulatives for other building structures (see Figure 14.3).

After the experience, before setting out to work with their young children in a modified version of this project, one of the novice teachers reflected on her learning experience.

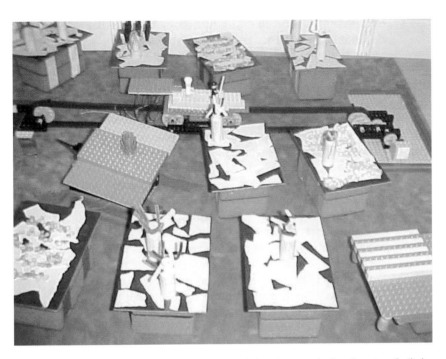

Figure 14.3 A working interactive prototype of the Aztec agricultural system built by educators.

Having never previously worked with robotics before, I was incredibly proud and surprised at my abilities with the technology. I really enjoyed having a final project to show. My time spent just simply playing with the manipulative did not go wasted. It was definitely the main reason that I was able to design and create what I did. Before I spent time just playing with the manipulative, I felt like I was over-whelmed by how to get gears to turn and rods to connect. Just playing with the pieces helped me to understand how pieces could connect and work together. The most challenging piece of this project was creating a design for what I wanted to build. I didn't feel as though I'd had enough experience with the manipulative to be able to design what I had on paper, although I felt that once I started building, I would surely know where to go from there. We used the technique of changing and analyzing as we built the systems. This was a very effect-ive technique for me because I didn't feel skilled enough to guess where steps would go wrong and not work. After I'd finished working on the floating chinampa, I realized that I could've done a more pro-ficient job. Instead of building a system of levels and rods, I could've used a couple pieces that Mindstorms had already been designed to do what I'd done with a bunch of smaller pieces. I was pleased that I discovered different ways of looking at building technology, and that there really wasn't just one way to do it.

This teacher is reflecting on her growing technological fluency gained through the iterative design process, but most importantly she is also discovering a new sense of confidence in her own learning potential. A different teacher, with more knowledge of robotics who had participated in previous robotic experiences, wrote:

The process we used for this project was very different from how I worked in groups in the past. Traditionally, people split up and work on aspects that they feel they can do best. But we tried to do each part together giving everyone the experience of being both the learner and the teacher. At times it was frustrating because it seemed inefficient, but overall I think we all learned more from the project than we would have if we just split up the tasks . . . I felt that this experience was telling as to how students coming from multiple learning backgrounds might contribute to the project.

After participating in this experience, the teachers went on to work with students and adapted the overall idea of the project to fit their individual groups. They kept the core idea which was to integrate both social sciences and SMET into a single project. For example, some of them adapted activities suggested in the Massachusetts Science and Technology/Engineering Curriculum frameworks for older children, such as Local Wonders. This activity engages students in constructing prototypes of a significant structure or building in their community and investigating the related engineering concepts as well as the building's socio-historical impact. Other teachers focused on students' design, implementation and programming of technological systems as a window into exploring the worldviews of cultures traditionally studied in the social science curriculum. For example, while one teacher worked with a team of children studying ancient Rome and developed and tested an early form of a Roman catapult, another worked on China and experimented with ways to build walls that could not be knocked down.

Families exploring their culture through robotic project

The second learning story introduces Project InterActions, a research programme that explores the different types of interactions that can occur in a learning environment where parents and their young children come together to learn about robotics and explore their cultural heritage (Bers, 2007).

Following the design experiments research methodology (Brown et al., 1989; Cobb et al., 2003; Barab and Squire, 2004; Fishman et al., 2004), as part of this project six different studies were conducted over a period of three years. Each study consisted of family workshops that met for two and a half hours during the weekend for a period of five weeks. A total of 132 learners participated in all the design experiments studies.

Previous research has looked at the many interactions that exist when parents and young children come together to program and build meaningful robotic projects that represent a shared family value or cultural heritage (Bers et al., 2004; Beals and Bers, 2006; Bers, 2007). For example, families created final robotic projects such as the 'Easter Bunny', a cardboard bunny mounted on a robotic car that would carry a basket with chocolate eggs; the 'Go-Lem, a Matzoh-Seeking Robot' that goes forward, lights up, and plays the Passover melody 'Dayenu' at the push of a button; a birthday cake that sings an Armenian children's song, to reflect the mother's cultural heritage, with flashing lights as candles; a flashing Christmas tree, and a manger for Jesus with a hovering moving angel. The idea of integrating the use of technology with cultural heritage stems from the desire to help all children, and not only those who already have a technical mindset, to develop technological fluency (Bers and Urrea, 2000). The narratives behind the different cultures have the power to engage both the 'little storytellers' and the 'little engineers' (Bers, 2008b).

During one of the workshops, 6-year-old Gary and his dad decided to build a Christmas tree that would light up, sway, and play music. The pair started by collecting small, coloured, translucent Lego pieces and placing them in their Lego tree. As Gary began to experiment with the lighting system on his tree, he ran into a problem: the tree was colourful but did not light up. So Gary set out to explore how to fix the problem by finding new pieces, such as bright white lights that could be powered by the RCX. However, these new pieces did not provide any colour to the tree. Gary was not willing to sacrifice colour for brightness, so he asked his dad for help. They talked about creating a system in which the lights on the Christmas tree will turn on in a serial order, beginning from left to right, so it would display an interesting pattern.

Gary is an active 6-year-old who is beginning to encounter the principles of design-based learning by first identifying a problem (colourfulness versus brightness) and testing different options. Gary decides that only one wire needs to be connected to the RCX. The other wires could be used to connect each light to the next so that when the program is turned on, the power flows through the wires sequentially. At first, Gary does not know how to connect the wires. He often puts them in backwards while he talks to his dad: *'I'm not sure which way I put it [the connecting wire] in, but I'll try and see.'* To see if he is right, Gary turns on the program. He knows that if the light turns on, he attached the wire correctly and if it doesn't, he has to go back and reverse the wire(s). This understanding clearly demonstrates his developing sense of trial and error and the iterative nature of the design cycle. Once all the lights are working, Gary again becomes concerned with the aesthetics of his project. He sets out to make all the lights on the tree symmetrical in placement and colour. In doing this, Gary decides that he wants to add more lights.

To keep everything symmetrical, he puts the new lights on top of the existing lights (same colour). He now faces the task of connecting these new lights. Despite his father's comment that there might be too many wires on the tree, he continues working on it. In his eagerness, he does not use the same method of trial and error to check his work, but decides to just connect them all at once and try it out at the end. Gary turns the power on and, to his dismay, only the first few lights work.

Gary begins a ten-minute effort to try to reconnect the wires, this time in a systematic way. After each attempt, he turns on the power to see if he was successful. When he is not, he tries again. The multitude of wires, thirteen in total, is very confusing, and Gary turns to his father for help. Gary's dad helps him check each wire, looking first to see if any of them are reversed. When they don't find any problems in the wiring, his father explains to him that they need to take the lights off one by one, starting from right to left, and then turn on the power to see if they can determine where 'the system breaks down'. In this way, the father models the process of debugging or systematic trial and error. Eventually, Gary's dad withdraws and lets Gary take over. The problem wire has been identified and fixed. By the end of the session, Gary's Christmas tree is shining brightly and he proudly shares his accomplishments (see Figure 14.4).

Gary's father took a supporting stance and let Gary experiment with the technology, make mistakes and fix them. Although he did not have formal background in education, his natural instinct was to let his child play with the materials and to support him in trying out his own ideas, even if some of them were time consuming and probably doomed to failure. However, when needed, he introduced the concept of systematic debugging, as opposed to just unsystematic trial and error.

Gary and his dad decided quickly to build a Christmas tree; not much conversation about culture happened between them. However, for other parent–child dyads, choosing a culturally relevant theme posed multiple challenges. For example, a father–daughter dyad spent a long time discussing what things were important to them and decided that spending time together was an important value for them. So they chose to make a project that reflected one important aspect of spending time together: the bedtime story. They chose their favourite character from a book the father would read in the evenings to the daughter. They created 'Uncle Feather' that flaps its wings, turns and drives forward and backwards (see Figure 14.5).

Figure 14.4 A Christmas tree with blinking lights.

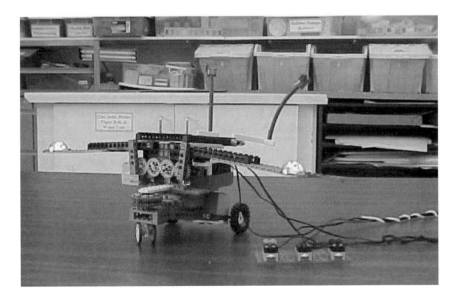

Figure 14.5 Uncle Feather.

This dyad had to negotiate the daughter's intent to make a 'perfect' bird with their limited technical capabilities. As they had agreed on making the bird move back and forth, the daughter found large green grass plates and combined them with long black girders and called them wings. Next, she wanted the bird to fly. After several exchanges in which the father explained that he could not make that happen, they agreed on having the bird flap its wings. This posed many technical challenges and the father set out to work on his own. In his journal he wrote:

> I was very interested in using the differential [gears] and using a third motor to control the steering . . . We used the software at home and used a pair of tasks to control the steering, the flaps and the direction. We made use of techniques we had learned earlier to combine three touch sensors as digital inputs and three long wires to make it a remote control bird.

This project quickly became technologically sophisticated and the 6-year-old daughter was not able to understand most of its workings. However, when requested, she proudly showed her bird and explained how her daddy made it for her. Although her role in making Uncle Feather was very different from the one played by Gary in making his Christmas tree, both of these young children engaged, together with their parents, in problem solving and different aspects of the design process. As both of them grow, hopefully this first experience with robotics will contribute to their curiosity for learning about SMET. Regardless of their fathers' approach to working with them (supporting them versus taking over), both men became special role models for approaching technical challenges.

Figure 14.6 shows a different kind of project in which a father and his daughter had a hard time coming up with a project idea. After much conversation, they realized that keeping the house in order was an important family value. So they decided to create a machine that could help the child organize her room. The 6-year-old who worked on this project reflected:

> The hardest part was to put it together. I learned that you cannot just go and say 'I'm going to build a robot'. You actually have to think about what you are going to do and you have to build it piece by piece.

While this project was not complex in terms of its technical implementation, the father and child spent a long time choosing a project that was important for them as a family and talking about family values. For them, the meaning of culture was not associated with a particular tradition, religion or heritage, but to their daily rituals, such as cleaning up.

Figure 14.6 The picker-upper.

In order to engage families in thinking about culture and integrate it into their robots, Project InterActions exposed them to cultural narratives through picture books and cultural objects from different traditions. We did not teach about culture but rather we provided an open environment and let parents and children talk to each other. Our hope was that they would engage in conversations that they would not have otherwise. For example, the mother of a 5-year-old told researchers:

> Because [my daughter] comes from more than one cultural tradition, the notion of culture in our family is complex, and this project provided us with an opportunity to discuss culture in our family . . . It raised thought-provoking questions for her such as what is culture? Why are there different languages? How are grandma and grandpa Armenian if they don't live in Armenia? and so on . . . During dinner she asked her dad, 'What is a Muslim?' This is the first time she has taken any interest in culture and understandings of it.

In the same way as families approached culture differently, they also took on different working styles – during the workshop we noticed a variety of interaction styles between parents and children, some more effective than others (Beals and Bers, 2006). For example, some parents initiated and directed their work together, some put the child in charge, and some parent–child dyads seem to enjoy taking turns being in charge. It was not easy for all of the parent–child dyads to become comfortable with each other in new roles as both teachers and learners. In most of the cases, it was the parents, and not the children, who had the most difficulty adjusting to this. It often initiated anxiety for a parent when they were required to learn something new and, at the same time, support and scaffold their child. This was true regardless of the previous level of confidence that parents had with technology.

For most parents, Project InterActions was an opportunity to spend time with their children doing something together: '*My son and I never play with LEGO together. This is the first time. I am learning too. I have never done anything like this.*' The same was true for the children, who enjoyed the chance to have their parent's devoted attention. A 4-year-old boy said: '*I am not sure what I want to make today but I am going to think about it and figure it out. I think that this class is fun. I like working with my dad. It's the best thing.*'

It was difficult for parents to understand that the process of learning was as important as, or even more important than, the final product, the working robot. Some of the parents were worried about getting it right, and in some cases their attitude was getting in the way of their working together with their children. Thus, as the conveners, we gave all participating adults a handout containing suggestions that reflected the learning philosophy of the workshop:

- This is a pilot research project. We are all exploring together.
- Families have different ways of working together. Find a way that works for you and your child.
- Learning new things is hard . . . sometimes it is harder for adults than for children.
- Learning about technology can be very frustrating and anxiety provoking.
- Are you passing your own anxieties to your child?
- Don't worry, nobody gets it right the first time or even the tenth time. In fact, there is no 'right' way.
- Adults and children can learn in very different ways.
- We are not expecting families to have perfectly working projects.
- Play with the materials and the ideas. You don't have to get it right.
- Success is measured very differently for children and for adults.
- Ask questions (to your child, to us, to other families).
- Talk to each other, look at each other's projects, copy the things that you like . . . you are not cheating.
- We learn by doing and by making mistakes.
- Have fun and relax! This is a time to spend together with your child.

Most of the parents reported that the single thing they enjoyed most during the workshop was working together with their children. One mother with a strong IT background shared how happy she was that her child had learned to 'deconstruct an action into a sequence of steps' and therefore was able to talk with her about programming. This new connection with her son was very important to her since she was used to expressing herself through programming. '*This [workshop] has gotten us started, and I think we will continue together [programming] at home.*' Other parents also expressed how rewarding it was for them to see their children showing '*keen interest in working on a project from an original idea to accomplishing their goals by solving problems and proudly presenting and demonstrating their projects to us*'.

Other parents felt that their children's presence in the workshop was critical for their own learning, as stated in the final project website by one of the fathers:

> The hardest thing was to develop designs that we could then create to make what we wanted. We just never were able to pull the construction off. And while I was disappointed and ready to give up, Paul [the son] never wanted to quit. I learned that he has a great perspective on projects like this and knows that with the right time, parts, and design, we eventually were able to create our project.

Conclusions

This chapter has suggested that robotics can be a powerful activity for engaging young learners in a technologically rich design-based experience. It also suggests that, while there are many ways of working with design projects and robotics, most of which involve the use of competitions and challenges aimed at solving problems, an approach that integrates the use of cultural narratives with the development of technological fluency can be successful at providing a bridge between two different epistemologies or ways of knowing: the narrative (mostly used in the social sciences) and the logico-scientific (mostly used in SMET disciplines).

Here, I have chosen to share two different kinds of learning stories: experiences done by early childhood teachers and experiences done by young children and their parents. Both of these cases are different in their approach to 'culture' work. While the activities with teachers focused on the social sciences state frameworks traditionally aimed at older grades, the work with parents focused on the family's culture, through the multiple windows they thought about shared meaning by a group of people who hold common values and beliefs. However, both groups took the design process used in engineering and software development, and the steps involved in systematic design, debugging and implementation, from an idea to a working robot. And both used culture as the context for becoming technologically fluent.

The core message of this chapter is that by creating learning contexts for young children that incorporate powerful machines, such as robotics, these experiences constitute natural digital extensions of traditional early learning manipulatives, which have long been posited as essential for early learning. Further, they are active learners who are producers of new knowledge rather than consumers of what already exists. Early childhood is a time of fluidity and experimentation between roles and epistemological styles. While most ways of using technological tools such as robotics, focus on 'little engineers' who will grow into 'big engineers', the ideas inherent in this chapter advocate the importance of respecting and inviting different ways of knowing and motivations while working with robotic manipulatives. By taking an integrated approach that spans two 'cultures', two 'ways of knowing' and two kinds of epistemologies, we can not only support children to develop the skills and ways of thinking needed to solve problems using technology, but also encourage them to think about the cultural needs of society at large.

Acknowledgements

Many people have made this research possible: the students in the DevTech research group and the CEEO (Center for Educational Engineering Outreach) at Tufts University. In particular, I would like to thank Chris Rogers.

References

Alper, J. (1993) The pipe is leaking women all the way along, *Science*, 260: 409–411.

Badra, R. and Palleschi, H. (1993) Partnerships across the disciplines: the humanities, science and technology: making connections. Paper presented at the 73rd Annual National Convention of the American Association of Community Colleges, 'Practicing Community Leadership: Partnerships are the Key to Success', Portland, OR, 28 April–1 May.

Bae, Y. and Smith, T. (1997) *Women in Mathematics and Science: Findings from 'Condition of Education, 1997' No. 11*. Washington, DC: National Center for Education Statistics.

Barab, S. and Squire, K. (2004) Design-based research: putting a stake in the ground, *Journal of the Learning Sciences*, 13(1): 1–14.

Beals, L. and Bers, M. (2006) Robotic technologies: when parents put their learning ahead of their child's, *Journal of Interactive Learning Research*, 17(4): 341–366.

Bers, M. (2004) Parents, children and technology: making robots, exploring cultural heritage and learning together. Presentation to the American Educational Research Association, Los Angeles, April.

Bers, M. (2007) Project InterActions: a multigenerational robotic learning environment, *Journal of Science and Technology Education*, 16(6): 537–552.

Bers, M. (2008a) *Blocks to Robots: Learning with Technology in the Early Childhood Classroom.* New York: Teachers College Press.

Bers, M. (2008b) Engineers and storytellers: using robotic manipulatives to develop technological fluency in early childhood. In O. Saracho and B. Spodek (eds), *Contemporary Perspectives on Science and Technology in Early Childhood Education* (pp. 105–125). Charlotte, NC: Information Age Publishing.

Bers, M. and Cassell, J. (1998) Interactive storytelling systems for children: using technology to explore language and identity, *Journal of Interactive Learning Research*, 9(2): 603–609.

Bers, M. and Urrea, C. (2000) Technological prayers: parents and children working with robotics and values. In A. Druin and J. Hendler (eds), *Robots for Kids: Exploring New Technologies for Learning Experiences* (pp. 194–217). New York: Morgan Kaufman.

Bers, M., Ackermann, E., Cassell, J., Donegan, B., Gonzalez-Heydrich, J., et al. (1998) Interactive storytelling environments: coping with cardiac illness at Boston's children's hospital. In *CHI'98 Conference Proceedings* (pp. 603–609). New York: ACM Press.

Bers, M., Ponte, I., Juelich, K., Viera, A. and Schenker, J. (2002) Teachers as designers: integrating robotics into early childhood education, *Information Technology in Childhood Education (ITCE) Annual 2002*, 1: 123–145.

Bers, M., New, B. and Boudreau, L. (2004) Teaching and learning when no one is expert: children and parents explore technology, *Journal of Early Childhood Research and Practice*, 6(2).

Brockman, J. (1996) *The Third Culture.* New York: Simon & Schuster.

Brown, A.L. (1992) Design experiments: theoretical and methodological challenges in creating complex interventions in classroom settings, *Journal of the Learning Sciences*, 2(2): 141–178.

Brown, J.S., Collins A. and Duguid, P. (1989) Situated cognition and the culture of learning, *Educational Researcher*, 18(1): 32–42.

Brown, S.V. and Clewell, B.C. (1998) *Project Talent Flow: The Non-SEM Field Choices of Black and Latino Undergraduates with the Aptitude for Science, Engineering and Mathematics Careers*, Report to the Alfred P. Sloan Foundation. Baltimore, MD: University of Maryland.

Bruner, J. (1986) *Actual Minds, Possible Worlds.* Cambridge: Harvard University Press.

Cobb, P., Confrey, J., diSessa, A., Lehrer, R. and Schauble, L. (2003) Design experiments in educational research, *Educational Researcher*, 32(1): 9–13.

Davis, M. (1998) Making a case for design-based learning, *Arts Education Policy Review*, 100(2): 7–14.

Erinosho, Y. (1999) Gender differences in interest and performance of school science students: a Nigerian example, *Studies in Educational Evaluation*, 25: 163–171.

Fishman, B., Marx, R., Blumenfeld, P., Krajcik, J. and Soloway, E. (2004) Creating a framework for research on systemic technology innovations, *Journal of the Learning Sciences*, 13(1): 43–76.

Frierson, H. (1996) Comparing science and non-Science minority students' perceptions and satisfaction with a short-term research and mentoring program. Paper presented at the Annual Meeting of the American Educational Research Association, New York, 9 April.

Hammrich, P. (1997) Yes, daughter you can, *Science and Children*, 34(4): 21–24.

Holden, C. (1989) Wanted: 675,000 future scientists and engineers, *Science*, 244(4912).

Kolodner, J., Crismond, C., Gray, J., Holbrook, J. and Puntambekar, S. (1998) Learning by design from theory to practice, *Proceedings of the International Conference of the Learning Sciences, Atlanta, December 1998*. Charlottesville, VA: AACE.

Kubanek, A-M.W. and Waller, M. (1995) Women's confidence in science: problematic notions around young women's career and life choices, *Journal of Women and Minorities in Science and Engineering*, 2: 243–253.

Massachusetts Department of Education (2006) *Science and Technology/Engineering Curriculum Framework*. http://www.doe.mass.edu/frameworks/current.html

National Geographic Television (1998) *Mystery Quest: Alien Adventures into Lost Worlds*, written by Michael Gross and Barry Rossrinehart; directed by James McKenna and Michael Gross. National Geographic Kids Video. Washington, DC.

Papert, S. (1980) *Mindstorms: Children, Computers, and Powerful*. New York: Basic Books.

Perkins, D. (1986) *Knowledge as Design*. Hillside, NJ: Lawrence Erlbaum.

Portsmore, M. (1999) ROBOLAB: Intuitive Robotic Programming Software to Support Life Long Learning, *APPLE Learning Technology Review*, Spring/Summer.

Pulis, L. (2000) Construct-a-catapult, *Science by Design Series*. Arlington, VA: NSTA Press.

Resnick, M., Bruckman, A. and Martin, F. (1996a) *Pianos Not Stereos: Creating Computational Construction Kits, Interactions*, 3(6): 41–50.

Resnick, M., Martin, F., Sargent, R. and Silverman, B. (1996b) Programmable bricks: toys to think with, *IBM Systems Journal*, 35(3): 443–452.

Resnick, M. (1998) Technologies for lifelong kindergarten, *Educational Technology Research and Development*, 46(4): 43–55.

Ritchie, R. (1995) *Primary Design and Technology: A Process for Learning*. London: David Fulton Publishers.

Rogers, C.B., Kearns, S.A., Rogers, C.M., Barsosky, J. and Portsmore, M. (2001) Successful methods for introducing engineering into the first grade classroom. *Proceedings of the American Society of Engineering Education Annual Exposition and Conference, New Mexico, June*.

Schleifer, R. (1997) Disciplinarity and collaboration in the sciences and humanities, *College English*, 59(4): 438–452.

Snow, C.P. (1959) *The Two Cultures*. Cambridge: Cambridge University Press.

Swan, J. (1995) Reflections across the divide: written discourse as a structural mirror in teaching science to nonscience students, *Writing on the Edge*, 6(2): 55–73.

Thom, M. (2001) *Balancing the Equation: Where are the Women and Girls in science, Engineering, and Technology?* New York: National Council for Research on Women.

Turkle, S. and Papert, S. (1992) Epistemological pluralism and the revaluation of the concrete, *Journal of Mathematical Behavior*, 11(1): 3–33.

15 The early years research–policy–practice nexus: challenges and opportunities

Christine Stephen

Introduction

This chapter is concerned with the interface between research, policy and practice. It addresses important issues and questions about the ways in which research might inform the decisions of policy makers, influence early years practices and how researchers should locate their work in light of specific policy initiatives. As academics, teachers and researchers we work in contexts that are informed by policy and research findings, yet dialogue with policy makers and practitioners is often both infrequent and ad hoc. In these circumstances, how can we find out what practitioners want to know more about and ensure that our research findings (even those arrived at with the active involvement of practitioners) inform playroom practices? At the same time we may ask if it is the role of research to provide answers to the problems experienced by practitioners as they work to meet the needs of children, conform to the expectations of policy makers or to ensure that children meet particular targets. Do policy makers want to be informed by research, to have the direction of policy shaped by research, or are they concerned largely with evaluating the impact of policy decisions? Should policy stimulate research and evaluation or is there room for research to inform the decisions about provision that government bodies make?

In order to address some of these issues about the agenda for research we (Stephen et al., 2008a) arranged a series of four seminars which brought together researchers from different disciplines, university educators, policy makers and providers and practitioners from the public, private and voluntary sectors across the UK. This chapter discusses the key themes that emerged from those discussions and considers the implications for an agenda for research in early education and care that will have potential to influence policies and practices. We identified three key themes which are at the heart of the challenges that face early years provision in the UK and in other western, developed countries in contemporary times:

- the *rationale* for or *purposes* of the provision of care and education for children in their early years;
- *diversity* and *designing* learning opportunities that have the potential to meet the range of ethnic, cultural, socio-economic and environmental needs characteristic of citizens in contemporary times;
- *pedagogical strategies* and *practices* that can support learning for young children.

In this chapter I use the term 'early years' to refer, in most cases, to children aged from about 3 to 6 years old. Many of the examples are specific to preschool settings but the issues and arguments also apply to the education of children in the early years of primary school and to the care of children from birth to 3 years of age. I will use the term 'practitioners' to include all those who work with young children, whatever their qualifications or training.

The purposes of early years education and child care

The early years provision offered to children and their families (and the experiences children have in those settings) reflects the expectations and concerns of society in general, and practitioners and policy makers in particular, about appropriate outcomes and goals for young children. These aims and expectations are culturally defined and have their origins in socio-political perspectives and ideas about children, childhood and learning.

For some policy makers and economists, early years education is thought of in terms of enhancing human capital. It is expected that investing in early years provision will contribute to society's future economic benefits and reduce social and economic burdens through specific intervention programmes and, more generally, by preparing children for school and preventing later academic failure. In Scotland, the Early Years Framework (Scottish Government, 2008) makes explicit references to improvements in the early years experiences being a 'central element of our strategy for regenerating communities, reducing crime, tackling substance misuse and improving employability.' The policy document continues by pointing to the 'positive economic return from early years investment' that is highlighted in the work of 'Nobel Prize-winning economist James Heckman' (see Heckman and Masterov, 2004).

The Framework represents a considerable shift in the views and focus of those who are responsible for making decisions about the nature and funding of provision for young children and the workforce that supports their care and education. In the decade prior to the release of the document, policy makers had been concerned with establishing the curriculum and ensuring sufficient quality provision was in place to meet the universal entitlement of 3- and 4-year-olds to a free half-day place five days per week. Scottish policy makers now seem confident that the policies and practices in place for early education and care are adequate to ensure good quality provision. They are now concerned instead with interventions targeting vulnerable younger children and their families, in the belief that these will ensure that a broad range of educational, social and health targets for society will be achieved. As a result, policy makers and politicians are increasingly concerned with evidence about the efficacy of initiatives to support families of very young children, pre-pregnancy and during-pregnancy services, and raising the capacity of families and communities.

At the same time as they are focusing on the efficacy of programmes targeting particular policy goals, policymakers in Scotland (and more widely in the UK) have renewed their interest in ways of measuring developmental gains and obtaining quantitative data to monitor the impact of initiatives and ensure that targets for social and economic improvements are met. The search for simple and manageable measures of success is understandable but problematic and involves a step away from concerns with the experiences of individual children to more macro-measurement and analysis. Measuring gains in children's cognitive development or vocabulary scores is not part of the repertoire of preschool practitioners and many are opposed to the use of such tests. Practitioners are not (yet) being asked to adopt standardized testing methods, but the shift in government thinking poses challenges for practitioners and researchers. For researchers, being commissioned to design and carry out projects that specify particular forms of data collection which are not welcomed by practitioners raises immediate barriers. Furthermore, there is frequently a divide between those researchers who adopt quantitative, and those who adopt qualitative, methods of inquiry, and any move to favour one or the other of these will force researchers to re-evaluate what they do, how they do it and the collaborations that will be necessary to satisfy demands for questions to be answered by particular kinds of data.

In the quest for ways of ensuring that policy outcomes are achieved, the link between the professional qualifications of practitioners and the provision of high quality early years provision has a new significance. The question of 'how much of a teacher' will make a difference to children's learning (and therefore how practitioners should be deployed) is currently exercising decision makers in Scotland, but this is a question to which, as yet, research offers no clear answer. Some research evidence suggests that there is a relationship between the quality of care and education, the social, behavioural and cognitive outcomes for children, and the types of professional qualifications held by practitioners. However, the findings are not clear-cut (see, for example, LoCasale-Crouch et al., 2007), and questions remain about the kind of professional qualifications that those who work with young children should have and the type of 'workforce mix' that optimizes children's experiences and progress. It seems clear that studying the relationship between the training and qualifications of practitioners and the quality of children's experiences and outcomes will remain an area for further research.

Policy makers may be confident that their curriculum and pedagogical guidance ensures good quality early years provision, but researchers are less likely to assume that there is no need to pose further questions. Pence and Pacini-Ketchabaw offer a discussion of salient issues about quality elsewhere in this volume. Here I want to draw attention to two other important areas for future research if we are to understand the impact of early years provision and practices. The first area relates to the demands of policy innovation. Fundamental to any policy change or development of guidance for practice is a strategy for implementation. We need to know more about the efficacy of alternative models of continuing professional learning for practitioners who are repeatedly faced with new expectations and ways of working.

The second area for future research about the impact of early years provision is concerned with the relationship between children's learning at home and in educational settings. We know relatively little about the ways in which children learn at home, although Sammons et al. (2004) found that what they measure as the 'home learning environment' made a substantial contribution to later academic success. Tizard and Hughes (1984), Bryce-Heath (1983) and the other writers in the 'new literacies' tradition raised awareness of the influence of family practices on children's developing talk and literacy, and Rogoff (2003) has studied the processes through which different communities support their children's learning. However, we know little about the specific competences, skills or dispositions that children develop at home, how parents and siblings support learning and what kind of learning is valued for young children at home. Understanding the funds of knowledge that children acquire at home (González et al., 2005), the cultural capital they gain there and how this learning can be built upon when children enter early years provision is a task for researchers and practitioners to tackle together.

While the benefits of interventions targeting disadvantage are acknowledged (for example POST, 2000; Currie, 2001), the view that education in the early years is justified on the grounds of preparation for another stage of education or later economic activity is firmly rejected by many practitioners, providers of educational provision and writers on early years (for example James et al., 1998; Bertram and Pascal, 2002; Moss and Petrie, 2002). The efforts that researchers make to give voice to children's perspectives suggest a concern with current experiences, agency and identity rather than future value. However, it is possible that we are less alert to the ways of constructing children that are implied by our research questions and the use that will be made of our findings. In addition, there are unanswered empirical questions about the impact of the way in which providers and practitioners construe the services they offer and the children who attend their settings. For example, what difference does it make to children's experiences if practitioners see the provision in which they work as a public service, a voluntary agency with an independent remit or a private sector trade competing in the market? Priorities in the private sector may not encourage spending money on staff development, and we need research to explore the implications of different budgets for children's experiences and playroom practices. Developing resilience, well-being and emotional literacy are important goals for some voluntary sector providers (and may take priority over activities designed to support cognitive development or the attainment of particular competences), but these concepts are under-researched in the early years context.

In this section we have reviewed the ways in which the goals of policy makers influence decisions about provision and practice, the kinds of research questions posed and the evidence welcomed. For researchers, this raises two issues. The first relates to the kinds of methods and data with which educational researchers are most familiar and comfortable: the qualitative methods and case study approaches most often adopted do not necessarily meet the expectations of policy makers and politicians. The second concern is that researchers do not always share the same agenda, starting points and assumptions as those who commission research or are the audience for research findings. A tension between the unanswered questions of interest to researchers and the quest of policy makers and practitioners for clear answers to complex and contingent issues is likely to be an enduring feature of the research/policy/practice relationship.

Meeting diverse needs and expectations

The second theme identified as challenging early years is catering for diversity. This policy drive (and associated practices) is unlikely to be criticized by anyone who is interested in creating an equitable society and ensuring a positive developmental trajectory for all young children. Yet, it is apparent that policies designed to bring this about will be less effective if they focus on global solutions or goals and fail to take account of the localized lived experiences of diverse family expectations, values and practices.

Ang (forthcoming) has pointed to the fluidity of young children's cultural identity, shaped by changing contexts and power relations and inequalities in social structures and institutions. However, her analysis of practice guidance for the foundation stage in England makes it clear that these issues are not taken into account in the current curriculum documentation. The rhetoric of 'providing for cultural difference' masks structural inequalities and fails to consider how to provide for a notion of diversity that may be little understood by practitioners and contested by the contradictory expectations of different groups of parents.

There is a role here for researchers to participate in discussions, to problematize goals such as, 'providing for cultural difference', and to consider what we need to understand if such goals are to be achieved. Researchers and policy makers will want to explore the efficacy of professional development programmes and examine how 'cultural clashes' between the expectations held by parents, practitioners and the managers of provision about educational goals and learning processes may be overcome, or at least be managed in ways that are positive for children.

There is a danger that thinking about cultural and ethnic diversity can become focused on the adult concerns of parents and practitioners to the exclusion of the perspective of the children whose care and education is at the centre of those concerns. Children from minority communities can become seasoned 'border crossers', moving between two or more cultures each day. Exploring the development of hybrid and fluid cultural identities is a task for early years researchers that should not be overlooked in the struggle to achieve policy goals about providing for diversity and addressing the concerns of adults. Brooker (2008) has called for researchers (and practitioners) to take children seriously. She argues that 'listening to children' has become an orthodoxy in early years that does not always lead to hearing what children are telling us and that listening should not be presumed to imply understanding. If we construe listening as 'taking common cause', Brooker suggests that researchers and practitioners will approach their engagement with children differently, shifting the focus to understanding the child's experience of cultural reproduction and change (Corsaro, 1997).

Cultural and ethnic diversity is not the only dimension on which children and their families differ. Vincent et al. (2008) have described the way in which choices about which early years services to use and the characteristics of provision important to families vary across social class divides. Feinstein (2003) has demonstrated the influence of early poverty and disadvantage on the education trajectories of children. Using longitudinal, UK cohort data he has demonstrated that the significant differences found in the cognitive development of children from different socio-economic groups at age 22 months continue to shape their educational attainment at age 26 years. 'Narrowing the gap' is a goal of government initiatives in the UK and elsewhere (for example, the Government of Western Australia (2009) has launched the second phase of a strategy to improve literacy and numeracy for all children), but is one which research suggests is difficult to achieve. Experience in the UK suggests that although some interventions have raised the attainment level of children with the lowest levels of performance, the gap remains as those who were already doing well also improved their attainment (see, for example, Fraser et al., 2001).

These initiatives to narrow the gap by supporting the development of vulnerable children and families are often characterized by a normalizing agenda that encourages 'good parenting', support for traditional literacy development and the kinds of interactions with children that Rogoff et al. (2003) have described as typical of the middle-class, western family. But Brooker (2002) has demonstrated that these activities are not part of the cultural practices of some groups in society and they are always going to be challenging for families coping with adversity and stress. Problematizing the issues and recognizing that alternative practices may offer effective support for learning should stimulate research into the influence of varying family activities and contexts on children's emotional, physical, cognitive and social development. In this way we might come to better understand the multiplicity of ways in which families can support their young children's development.

Further stimulus for research around issues of diversity comes from two recent studies that have presented findings about the excluding behaviour of children. Using survey methods, Connolly (2008) has demonstrated how children as young as 3–4 years old in Northern Ireland are beginning to adopt the cultural habits and attitudes of their differing communities. In a study of children of a similar age, but using very different methods, Kutnick and Brighi (2007) found that in 'free play' periods children chose to be part of small, exclusive groups formed by children alike in age and gender and who were considered to be friends. This behaviour is contrary to the practitioners' expressed desire for their playrooms to be inclusive environments. However, they appeared to have little knowledge about how to promote more socially inclusive behaviour in peer-selected groups. These studies suggest that it is not enough to value inclusivity and to expect young children to adopt these values too. Specific interventions to support inclusive behaviour, whether in pedagogical or in social contexts, and evaluating the impact of these interventions, is an area of research that needs to be added to the agenda, with the expectation that both large-scale surveys and the observation techniques of social psychology can contribute to the knowledge base.

The rhetoric of inclusivity and respect for social, linguistic and cultural diversity is strong in early years but challenging to achieve. This is an area where research can contribute ideas to both practice and policy. To do this we need to understand more about the diverse expectations and preferences of families and the effectiveness of the attempts of providers and practitioners to meet their varying needs. In this section we have reviewed evidence which suggests that, although children's behaviour is influenced by community and family values, their perspectives and experiences can be different from those of the adults at home or in early years settings. With this in mind it is important that researchers find ways of articulating the views of children or observing their lived experiences of social and cultural variation, as well as attending to the perspectives of adults. Research has demonstrated the impact of variation in home circumstances on children's later educational attainment. However, our understanding of how and what children learn at home is currently underdeveloped.

Pedagogical strategies and practices that support learning

Perhaps the most ubiquitous pedagogical concept in academic and professional writing is that of scaffolding (Wood et al., 1976). The mediating role of the adult is a central concept in socio-cultural accounts of learning, beginning with the work of Vygotsky (1978) and developed by others such as Wertsch (1985) and Tharp and Gallimore (1991). Those who write about learning in the cultural psychological tradition seek to understand how a child is thinking and how thinking might be transformed with regard to the tools they use and the forms of assistance (working in the zone of proximal development in Vygotskian terms). The research questions that arise from this way of conceptualizing learning focus on how we can know about children's thinking and on the interactions between adults and children that move the child's use of the cognitive and language tools of their society to a more mature level. From this perspective the pedagogical and research challenge is around developing skills of analysis or diagnosis to ensure that the actions of adults meet the children's starting point. In the alternative strand of socio-cultural theory that Edwards (2005) calls 'learning through participation' the focus is on how the social and cultural environment shapes what individuals learn and how they think and act. Looked at in this way the important pedagogical questions are about what leaning is valued in particular contexts, how the environment shapes learning and the ways in which learning situations can be structured to allow individuals to acquire knowledge through legitimate participation.

Rogoff draws attention to the ways in which guided participation (the way in which she conceptualizes the pedagogical process through which learning is supported) differs between communities (Rogoff, 2003; Rogoff et al., 2003). She suggests that the two key forms of guided participation (mutual bridging of meanings and mutual structuring of opportunities) are enacted in culturally specific and appropriate ways. Central to both of these processes is mutuality. While the work of Rommetveit (2003) and Trevarthen (1998) alerts us to the importance of intersubjectivity, this is an area of understanding that is underdeveloped from the perspective of early years pedagogy.

Traditionally, the expectation is that children will learn through observation and participation in tasks that are part of everyday life, yet the playrooms of the western developed world are spaces set aside for children only and employ resources designed specifically to support their learning. In these circumstances we need to research the pedagogical practices that can build mutuality and offer children the kind of authentic and personally meaningful activities that engage young learners. We might ask if there are more effective ways to help children to learn through observation. Or ask what we can learn from work on communities of practice that might help children moving between the home and preschool learning cultures. The questions previously raised about the home learning environment are relevant here too. There is a need for research to extend our understandings about the ways in which children 'pick things up' at home (Plowman et al., 2008), how parents and siblings support and shape learning at home and the ways in which different home learning experiences 'prime' children to learn in particular ways (Brooker, 2002).

Understanding the influence of the ways in which practitioners think about their own role is another relevant task for the research agenda. For example, evidence (see Penn, 1997; Stephen and Brown, 2004) suggests that, in the UK, practitioners construct the child as in need of care from an individual nurturing practitioner – an approach Singer (1993) has characterized as attachment pedagogy. A consequence of this perspective is that practitioners can think of the preschool setting as a substitute home – a view that influences the way provision is managed and staff deployed. If, as Brooker (2008) suggests, practitioners regard children as individuals who play, whose appropriate environment is a playroom and whose disposition is to be playful, this will influence the opportunities the youngsters are offered and the behaviour expected of them. Play as the means by which children learn is firmly entrenched in early years policy and practice in the UK and in developmentally appropriate practice (DAP). Yet the value of play is more often asserted than evidenced (BERA, 2003). There are clear theoretical arguments for the value of play for learning in the work of Vygotsky but, as Bodrova (2008) has pointed out, this is not just any kind of play but play that meets specific criteria. There is a compelling case for placing play on the agenda for further research. We need to know more about the specific contribution that play makes to children's learning, what children do when they play, how practitioners engage in pedagogical interactions when children are playing and what learning outcomes are characteristic of different forms of play.

Alexander (2004) has asked why, despite considerable progress in pedagogical research and the accumulation of evidence about how children learn and about teaching, the development of the UK government strategy for primary education did not reflect knowledge about pedagogy. The same question can be asked of early years educators. Some years ago, Siraj-Blatchford (1999) talked of practitioners 'recoiling' at the term 'pedagogy', which they associated with 'teaching'. Policy makers, managers of early years provision and practitioners have become comfortable with and familiar with written curricula, yet asking about pedagogy still disturbs some practitioners and few can articulate readily why they do the things they do in the playroom. Stengel (2000) argues that part of the difficulty with talking about pedagogy is that we have not yet developed a language for teaching that combines the 'language of technique' (what is effective) with the 'language of manner' (what is ethical, moral or caring). There is clearly an area for further exploration around why there should be this reluctance or hesitation around questions of pedagogy, about the language which practitioners are comfortable using to articulate their role and everyday practices and the implications of their practices for children's experiences and learning.

Stephen and Brown (2004) encountered two 'languages', or forms of discourse, about the role of practitioners which were held in tension. First, there was an espoused notion of pedagogical practice and interaction which we called the 'outsider perspective'. It was largely independent of context and assumed a well ordered and structured reality in which, by adopting certain roles (as planners and providers, as learning facilitators and observers and assessors), practitioners could enable children to achieve the outcomes planned for in the preschool curriculum. However, there was a second discourse present – one which we categorized as the 'insider perspective'. This language of practice was very context dependent, situated and dynamic. What practitioners did depended on the varying outcomes they hoped to promote, the activities they saw as normal and desirable in preschool playrooms, the everyday fluctuating conditions they encountered and their repertoires of actions. Children's experiences are influenced by both outsider expectations and insider understandings. There is a need for research to make explicit the pedagogies that children experience, to compare their experiences with policy prescriptions and explore the relative influence of these alternative forms of discourse and of moral and relational understandings.

New technologies are an integral part of contemporary life for young children, yet research about their use in educational contexts, especially in the early years, has not specifically addressed the ways in which they might be embedded in practice and used for meaning making. Stephen and Plowman (2008) studied young children's encounters with technologies in the playroom and explored the kind of support from adults (conceptualized as guided interaction) that was necessary to enhance engagement and overcome failed or truncated attempts to use the technology. We identified the need for both distal and proximal guided interaction in multiple modes to meet the cognitive, social and emotional needs of young learners. Although practitioners could be found engaging in guided interaction, the practice often lacked the systematic application necessary for effective support for all learners and it was largely implicit and undervalued by staff. This study suggests that there is more research needed to explore the ways in which practitioners think about their interactions with children and the multiple modes in which those interactions need to be enacted if encounters with learning resources in the playroom are to be enhanced.

Yelland et al. (2008) argue that growing up in the twenty-first century demands new forms of learning that go beyond the individually focused cognitive, social and emotional learning traditionally valued. They suggest that early years education should enable children to learn how to use new technologies, to problem solve collaboratively, to know how to learn, to communicate and to access expertise. These goals demand a shift in practice so that the focus is on encouraging communication, group working and shared thinking. And new educational goals pose questions about the pedagogical actions that can most effectively support learning in contemporary times.

In this look at the questions about pedagogical strategies and practices that should be part of the agenda for further research we have drawn attention to the influence of creating a learning environment that builds on mutual understandings and mutual structuring of actions between children and adults and can sustain the features of real world, authentic activities in playrooms and classrooms. Additionally, we might ask what early years practice can learn from studying how children learn at home. The relationship between play and learning, the influence of alternative perspectives on the role of the adult in early years settings and the pedagogical implications of introducing new technologies into the learning environment are all pertinent areas ready for further research which will have implications for policy and practice.

Considering the research process

Regardless of the topic under study, aspects of the research process and the ways in which practitioners and policy makers engage with research findings are ready for review. Researchers and the users of research need to be clear about what is possible when adopting particular paradigms. For example, psychological research can tell us about the kinds of interactions between dyads in specified circumstances which can aid learning or thinking (Doherty-Sneddon and Phelps, 2007), but it requires further steps to explore the ways in which this understanding can be put into practice in busy early years playrooms and classrooms. Large-scale, longitudinal, educational effectiveness studies such as Effective Provision of Preschool Education (Sammons et al., 2004) can demonstrate the added value that attending early years settings contributes to later educational attainment. However, outcome studies such as this cannot explain the learning process (for example the role of interactions and relationships), outcomes that are not easily measured (for instance curiosity) or individual trajectories (Sylva, 2008).

Policy makers and commissioners of research may sometimes have unrealistic expectations of the research process. They are often looking for clear or generalizable recommendations in circumstances that are complex and highly contingent. A particular challenge occurs with case study research. This approach is popular with educational researchers because of its power to represent naturalistic settings and the interactivity and contingency that is typical of issues being investigated in early years. Case study evidence is engaging and makes sense to researchers and the users of research but it does not offer the ability to generalize that policy makers yearn for. Researchers can find themselves caught between using case studies merely as rich illustrations or looking across cases in ways that can turn a portfolio of cases into a less heuristically valuable small sample. But both case studies and large-sample research have contributions to make to productive social science (Flyvbjerg, 2001). Large samples offer breadth but lack depth whereas the case study approach lacks breadth but offers rich narratives that can lead the reader to an awareness of the issues that cannot be drawn from summary tables or theoretical formulations. However, as Connelly (2008) points out, despite the rhetoric in favour of mixed methods,

> there is still very little evidence on the ground of methodological approaches that can move with ease between, and meaningfully draw together, in-depth qualitative and ethnographic research with large scale surveys making use of advanced, mulitivariate and multilevel statistical analyses.
>
> (Connelly, 2008: 20)

The nature of the relationship between research users and researchers can pose challenges and enhance or reduce the value of dissemination activity. Sylva et al. (2007) point out that linear research relationships, in which knowledge is passed from researchers to policy makers, rarely impact on practice. Instead, they advocate knowledge exchange partnerships where researchers and those who commission research 'work together in shaping, implementing and disseminating the research' (ibid.). If early years providers and practitioners are to use research-based evidence to inform their practice, then it is necessary to ensure that the questions addressed and the findings shared are relevant to them, and that all stakeholders acknowledge and respect the varying priorities of the research partners (Carwood-Edwards, 2008).

There is one further area of research practices that should be considered when we are thinking about what needs to be done differently in the future. Understanding young children as competent and active agents has led researchers to find ways to articulate the perspectives of children (see, for example, Christensen, 2004; Clark et al., 2005), but more needs to be achieved in this respect. Researchers should continue to develop methods that are responsive to and reflective of the ways of expressing opinions, preferences and values that are typical of the child's behavioural repertoire (Stephen et al., 2008b) and cover the range of ways of interacting with their social and emotional world that children deploy (Flewitt, 2006). Uprichard (2009) goes further; she argues that the conceptualization of children as active, agentic and knowledgeable implies that researchers and the users of research should go beyond understanding children's experiences of childhood to involve children in research as 'potential informants' about the wider world.

Conclusions

This chapter has explored the research–policy–practice challenges and gaps in understanding that were identified when academic researchers, practitioner educators, policy makers and early years providers and practitioners looked critically at current understandings about early years provision. Three major themes emerged in these discussions: the rationale or purposes for early years provision; diversity and designing provision to meet the range of ethnic, cultural, socio-economic and environmental needs of contemporary families; and the pedagogical strategies and practices that support learning in the early years. These issues and the research questions to which they give rise have been considered in this chapter, along with a look at the research processes necessary to address the questions identified.

The interrogation of research-based understandings about early years provision has produced a substantial list of unexplored areas, unanswered questions and topics that warrant further exploration and a more critical examination. Synergies between research, policy and practice can make an important contribution towards achieving 'quality' early childhood services, but the different perspectives and priorities held by the research partners can make for a challenging relationship. To harness the synergies it is necessary to acknowledge differences, open up opportunities for dialogue and recognize the need to problematize taken-for-granted or consensual perspectives on provision and practices. A fundamental feature of the research process has to be ensuring that among the questions there is one that asks 'what does this mean for young children?'

Acknowledgements

This chapter is based on discussions at a series of seminars ('Critical Issues for Preschool Education: Towards a Research Agenda') funded by the UK Economic and Social Research Council. I am grateful for the stimulating presentations by the invited speakers and the vibrant discussion generated by all who attended. In particular I wish to record the contribution made by Lynn Ang (University of East London) and Liz Brooker (Institute of Education, London), co-convenors of the seminars and valued colleagues.

References

Alexander, R. (2004) Still no pedagogy? Principle, pragmatism and compliance in primary education, *Cambridge Journal of Education*, 34(1): 7–33.

Ang, L. (forthcoming) Critical perspectives on cultural diversity in early childhood: building an inclusive curriculum and provision. *Early Years*.

BERA (British Educational Research Association Early Years Special Interest Group) (2003) *Early Years Research: Pedagogy, Curriculum and Adult Roles, Training and Professionalism.* http://www.bera.ac.uk/files/2008/09/beraearlyyearsreview31may03.pdf (accessed 30 April 2009).

Bertram, T. and Pascal, C. (2002) *Early Years Education: An International Perspective.* London: Qualifications and Curriculum Authority. http://www.inca.org.uk/pdf/early_years.pdf (accessed 11 May 2009).

Bodrova, E. (2008) Make-believe play versus academic skills: a Vygotskian approach to today's dilemma of early childhood education, *European Early Childhood Educational Research Journal*, 16(3): 357–369.

Brooker, L. (2002) *Starting School: Young Children Learning Cultures.* Buckingham: Open University Press.

Brooker, L. (2008) *Taking children seriously: reflections on research and practice.* http://www.ltscotland.org.uk/earlyyears/professionaldevelopment/events/esrc/seminar2/lizbrooker.asp (accessed 15 May 2009).

Bryce-Heath, S. (1983) *Ways with Words: Language, Life and Work in Communities and Classrooms.* New York: McGraw-Hill.

Carwood-Edwards, J. (2008) *Research, Policy and Practice: A Sleeping Giant?* http://www.ltscotland.org.uk/earlyyears/professionaldevelopment/events/esrc/seminar4/jeancarwoodedwards.asp (accessed 15 May 2009).

Christensen, P.H. (2004) Children's participation in ethnographic research: issues of power and representation, *Children and Society*, 18: 165–176.

Clark, A., Kjørholt, A.T. and Moss, P. (2005) *Beyond Listening: Children's Perspectives on Early Childhood Services.* Bristol: The Policy Press.

Connolly, P. (2008) Preschool Children's Awareness of and Attitudes toward Difference: A Study of 3- and 4-year-old Children in Northern Ireland. Paper presented at American Educational Research Association Annual Meeting, New York, March.

Corsaro, W.A. (1997) *The Sociology of Childhood.* Thousand Oaks, CA.: Pine Forge Press.

Currie, J. (2001) Early childhood education programs, *Journal of Economic Perspectives*, 15(2): 213–238.

Doherty-Sneddon, G. and Phelps, F. (2007) Teachers' responses to children's gaze aversion, *Journal of Educational Psychology*, 27: 91–107.

Edwards, A. (2005) Let's get beyond community and practice: the many meanings of learning by participation, *The Curriculum Journal*, 16(1): 53–69.

Feinstein, L. (2003) Inequality in the early cognitive development of British children in the 1970 cohort, *Economica*, 70: 73–97.

Flewitt, R. (2006) Using video to investigate preschool classroom interaction: education research assumptions and methodological practices, *Visual Communication*, 5(1): 25–50.

Flyvbjerg, B. (2001) *Making Social Science Matter*. Cambridge: Cambridge University Press.

Fraser, H., MacDougall, A., Pirrie, A. and Croxford, L. (2001) *Early Intervention in Literacy and Numeracy: Key Issues from the National Evaluation of the Programme*. http://www.scotland.gov.uk/library3/education/ic71-00.asp (accessed 11 May 2009).

González, N., Moll, L. and Amanti, C. (2005) Introduction: Theorizing practices. In N. González, L. Moll and C. Amanti (eds), *Funds of Knowledge: Theorizing Practices in Households, Communities, and Classrooms* (pp. 1–46). Mahwah, NJ: Lawrence Erlbaum Associates.

Government of Western Australia (2009) Early intervention to improve literacy and numeracy levels. http://www.mediastatements.wa.gov.au/Pages/WACabinet MinistersSearch.aspx?ItemId=131238&minister=Constable&admin=Barnett (accessed 11 May 2009).

Heckman, J.J. and Masterov, D.V. (2004) *The Allander Series: Skill Policies for Scotland*. http://www.strath.ac.uk/media/departments/economics/fairse/media_140851_en.pdf (accessed 15 May 2009).

James, A., Jenks, C. and Prout, A. (1998) *Theorizing Childhood*. Cambridge: Polity Press.

Kutnick, P. and Brighi, A. (with others) (2007) The role and practice of interpersonal relationships in European early childhood settings: sites for enhancing social inclusion, personal growth and learning? *European Early Childhood Education Research Journal*, 15(3): 379–406.

LoCasale-Crouch, J., Konold, T., Pianta, R., Howes, C., Burchinal, M., et al. (2007) Observed classroom quality in state-funded pre-kindergarten programs and associations with teacher, program, and classroom characteristics, *Early Childhood Research Quarterly*, 22: 3–17.

Moss, P. and Petrie, P. (2002) *From Children's Services to Children's Spaces*. London: RoutledgeFalmer.

Penn, H. (1997) *Comparing Nurseries*. London: Paul Chapman.

Plowman, L., McPake, J. and Stephen, C. (2008) Just picking it up? Young children learning with technology at home, *Cambridge Journal of Education*, 38(3): 303–319.

POST (Parliamentary Office of Science and Technology) (2000) *Early Years Learning*, POST Report 140. London: POST. www.parliament.uk/post/pn140.pdf

Rogoff, B. (2003) *The Cultural Nature of Human Development*. New York: Oxford University Press.

Rogoff, B., Paradise, R., Arauz, R.M., Correa-Chávez, M. and Angelillo, C. (2003) Firsthand learning through intent participation, *Annual Review of Psychology*, 54: 175–203.

Rommetveit, R. (2003) On the role of 'a psychology of the second person' in studies of meaning, language and mind, *Mind, Culture and Activity*, 10(3): 205–218.

Sammons, P., Elliott, K., Sylva, K., Melhuish, E., Siraj-Blatchford, I. and Taggart, B.

(2004) The impact of pre-school on young children's cognitive attainments at entry to reception, *British Educational Research Journal*, 30(5): 691–712.

Scottish Government (2009) *The Early Years Framework.* http://www.scotland.gov.uk/Publications/2009/01/13095148/2 (accessed 11 May 2009).

Singer, E. (1993) Shared care for children, *Theory and Psychology*, 3(4): 429–449.

Siraj-Blatchford, I. (1999) Early childhood pedagogy: practice, principles and research. In P. Mortimer (ed.), *Understanding Pedagogy and its Impact on Learning* (pp. 20–45). London: Paul Chapman.

Stengel, B. (2000) Pedagogical Response-ability. Paper presented at the American Association of Colleges of Teacher Education Annual Meeting, Chicago, Illinois, February.

Stephen, C. and Brown, S. (2004) The culture of practice in pre-school provision: outsider and insider perspectives, *Research Papers in Education*, 19(3): 323–344.

Stephen, C. and Plowman, L. (2008) Enhancing learning with information and communication technologies in pre-school, *Early Child Development and Care*, 178(6): 637–654.

Stephen, C., Ang, L. and Brooker, L. (2008a) Critical issues for pre-school education: towards a research agenda. http://www.ltscotland.org.uk/earlyyears/professionaldevelopment/events/esrc/index.asp (accessed 11 May 2009).

Stephen, C., McPake, J., Plowman, L. and Berch-Heyman, S. (2008b) Learning from the children: exploring preschool children's encounters with ICT at home, *Journal of Early Childhood Research*, 6(2): 99–117.

Sylva, K. (2008) *How Pre-school and Family Shape Children's Development: Why 'Outcome' Studies?* http://www.ltscotland.org.uk/earlyyears/professionaldevelopment/events/esrc/sinar3/kathysylva.asp (accessed 11 May 2009).

Sylva, K., Taggart, B., Melhuish, E., Sammons, P. and Siraj-Blatchford, I. (2007) Changing models of research to inform educational policy, *Research Papers in Education*, 22(2): 155–168.

Tharp, R. and Gallimore, R. (1991) A theory of teaching as assisted performance. In P. Light, S. Sheldon and M. Woodhead (eds), *Learning to Think* (pp. 42–66). London: Routledge.

Tizard, B. and Hughes, M. (1984) *Young Children Learning*. London: Fontana.

Trevarthen, C. (1998) The concept and foundations of infant intersubjectivity. In S. Bråten (ed.), *Intersubjective Communication and Emotion in Early Ontogeny* (pp. 15–46). Cambridge: Cambridge University Press.

Uprichard, E. (2009) Questioning research with children: discrepancy between theory and practice, *Children and Society* (Early View). http://www3.interscience.wiley.com/cgi-bin/fulltext/121633996/pdfstart (accessed 11 May 2009).

Vincent, C., Braun, A. and Ball, S.J. (2008) Childcare, choice and social class: caring for young children in the UK, *Critical Social Policy*, 28(1): 5–26.

Vytgotsky, L. (1978) *Mind in Society: The Development of Higher Psychological*

Processes, ed. M. Cole, V. John-Steiner, S. Scribner and E. Souberman. Cambridge, MA: Harvard University Press.

Wertsch, J.V. (1985) *Vygotsky and the Social Formation of Mind*. Cambridge, MA: Harvard University Press.

Wood, D., Bruner, J. and Ross, G. (1976) The role of tutoring in problem solving, *Journal of Child Psychology and Psychiatry*, 17: 89–100.

Yelland, N., Lee, L., O'Rouke, M. and Harrison, C. (2008) *Rethinking Learning in Early Childhood Education*. Maidenhead: Open University Press.

Index